The Politics of Historical Memory and Commemoration in Africa

The Politics of Historical Memory and Commemoration in Africa

Essays in Honour of Jan-Georg Deutsch

Edited by Cassandra Mark-Thiesen,
Moritz A. Mihatsch and Michelle M. Sikes

The open access publication of this book has been published with the support of the Swiss National Science Foundation.

SCHWEIZERISCHER NATIONALFONDS
ZUR FÖRDERUNG DER WISSENSCHAFTLICHEN FORSCHUNG

ISBN 978-3-11-135327-2
e-ISBN (PDF) 978-3-11-065531-5
e-ISBN (EPUB) 978-3-11-065549-0
DOI https://doi.org/10.1515/9783110655315

This work is licensed under the Creative Commons Attribution-NonCommercial-NoDerivatives 4.0 International License. For details go to https://creativecommons.org/licenses/by-nc-nd/4.0/.

Library of Congress Control Number: 2021945429

Bibliographic information published by the Deutsche Nationalbibliothek
The Deutsche Nationalbibliothek lists this publication in the Deutsche Nationalbibliografie; detailed bibliographic data are available on the Internet at http://dnb.dnb.de.

© 2023 with the authors, editing © 2022 Cassandra Mark-Thiesen, Moritz Mihatsch, Michelle Sikes; published by Walter de Gruyter GmbH, Berlin/Boston.
This volume is text- and page-identical with the hardback published in 2022.
The book is published with open access at www.degruyter.com.

Cover image: © Desmond R. Bowles, Photograph of the UCT Cecile Rhodes' statue removal (2015) Printing and binding: CPI books GmbH, Leck

www.degruyter.com

Table of Contents

Acknowledgements —— VII

Michelle M. Sikes, Cassandra Mark-Thiesen and Moritz A. Mihatsch
Public Memorialisation and the Politics of Historical Memory in Africa —— 1

I Struggles with Heritage & Historicity

Natacha Filippi
Oral history, Closed Settings and the Formation of Narratives: A South African Example —— 23

Casper Andersen
A "Quest for Relevance": The Memory Politics of UNESCO's General History of Africa —— 47

II Political Commemoration & Memory

Edward Goodman
Remembering Mzee: The Making and Re-making of "Kenyatta Day," 1958–2010 —— 77

Mohamed Haji Ingiriis
Southern Somalia's "Glorious Days Are Our Nightmare": The Performance of Political Memory and Contestations of Commemoration in Northern Somalia (Somaliland) —— 107

III Nostalgia – between Social Connection & Social Ordering

Rouven Kunstmann and Cassandra Mark-Thiesen
The Memory Process in the Commemorations of the Dead in West African Newspapers —— 143

Nina S. Studer
Remembrance of Drinks Past: Wine and Absinthe in Nineteenth-century French Algeria —— 169

Epilogue

Ruramisai Charumbira
The Historian as Memory Practitioner —— 195

Figures —— 217

List of Contributors —— 219

Index of names —— 221

Index of places —— 223

Acknowledgements

The editors would like to express their gratitude to the Swiss National Science Foundation. With its generous support, we were able to bring our contributors together in January 2018 for a lively intellectual exchange at a workshop in Basel, Switzerland in honour of Dr. Jan-Georg Deutsch. The foundation also provided substantial funding for the publication of this volume, in an open access format no less.

The editors would like to thank all those connected with the preparation of this volume, including the anonymous peer reviewers and the editors at the Walter De Gruyter press, especially Rabea Rittgerodt and her team, who were most amiable to work with.

Finally, we are deeply grateful to those who supported us during the earliest stages of the project. Thank you to the faculty of the Oxford University African Studies Centre, the History Faculty, and the fellows of St. Cross College. Special appreciation goes to Heike Schmidt, whose engagement and scholarly input considerably strengthened the volume.

Michelle M. Sikes, Cassandra Mark-Thiesen and Moritz A. Mihatsch
Public Memorialisation and the Politics of Historical Memory in Africa

In 2020, a global wave of anti-racism movements contributed to widespread reconsideration of previously honoured people. From Bristol's slave trader Edward Colston, to confederate generals across the American South, to King Leopold II of Belgium, statues now seen as symbols of white supremacy have fallen.[1] Campaigns in Africa challenged state-endorsed memorialisations, thus contributing to the recent groundswell of alternative interpretations of the past. In the Ethiopian town of Harar, Oromo groups toppled a monument to Haile Selassie's father, Ras Makonnen, seeing both father and son as imperialist oppressors.[2] In Cape Town, a statue of white supremacist Cecil Rhodes at Rhodes Memorial on the slopes of Table Mountain was decapitated.[3] In 2015, protests over another statue of Rhodes located at the University of Cape Town (UCT) channelled memories of past injustices into widespread mobilisation for change, a movement known as #RhodesMustFall (RMF).[4]

---

[1] For the removal Confederate memorials: "George Floyd Protests Reignite Debate Over Confederate Statues," *New York Times*, 3 June 2020, accessed 7 December 2020, https://www.nytimes.com/2020/06/03/us/confederate-statues-george-floyd.html?action=click&module=RelatedLinks&pgtype=Article. For Leopold II, see Monika Pronczuk and Mikir Zaveri, "Statue of Leopold II, Belgian King Who Brutalized Congo, Is Removed in Antwerp," *New York Times*, 9 June 2020, accessed 6 December 2020, https://www.nytimes.com/2020/06/09/world/europe/king-leopold-statue-antwerp.html. For Colston, see "Edward Colston Statue: Protesters Tear Down Slave Trader Monument," *BBC News*, 7 June 2020, accessed 7 December 2020, https://www.bbc.com/news/uk-52954305.
[2] "Ethiopian Opposition Politician held as Protests Continue," *France24*, 7 July 2020, accessed 8 December 2020, https://www.france24.com/en/20200701-ethiopian-opposition-politician-held-as-protests-continue.
[3] "Cecil Rhodes Statue in Cape Town has Head Removed," *BBC News*, 15 July 2020, accessed 6 December 2020, https://www.bbc.com/news/world-africa-53420403.
[4] In March 2015, Chumani Maxwele, a student at the University of Cape Town (UCT), threw human excrement at a statue of Cecil John Rhodes, prompting calls to remove the statue and sparking a movement to reckon with racist pasts and decolonise higher education. These actions have been the focus of a growing body of scholarly work, including: Anton Van Vollenhoven, "Dealing with Statues, Monuments and Memorials in South Africa: A Heritage Based Response to Current Controversies," *South African Journal of Cultural History* 29, no. 1 (2015): 7–21; Shanade Barnabas, "Engagement with Colonial and Apartheid Narratives in Contemporary South Africa: A Monumental Debate," *Journal of Literary Studies* 32, no. 3 (2016): 109–128; and Sabine

OpenAccess. © 2022 Michelle M. Sikes, Cassandra Mark-Thiesen and Moritz A. Mihatsch, published by De Gruyter. This work is licensed under the Creative Commons Attribution 4.0 International License. https://doi.org/10.1515/9783110655315-002

Protests of colonial-era markers and what they represented reverberated across South Africa and beyond. The push to remove the statue of Rhodes in 2015 spread from UCT to universities across the country and to Rhodes' alma mater Oriel College in Oxford, where students marched to remove a memorial of Rhodes overlooking Oxford's High Street.[5] Officials at UCT bowed to pressure and removed the statue of Rhodes. After previously rejecting the demand, Oriel College stated its intention to take down their statue.[6] The demonstrations following the killing of Eric Garner, George Floyd and others in the United States fuelled widespread anger, while in Oxford, RMF campaigns surged, drawing thousands.[7] These campaigns not only took aim at colonial era memorials, monuments, and even street and building names, they also sparked extensive public debate over colonial and apartheid history. Student protesters appealed for change at institutions of higher education and proposed to "decolonise" the academy, insisting on the transformation of institutional practices, personnel, and reading lists, among other concerns.[8]

Discontent with monuments honouring Colston, Rhodes, Robert E. Lee and others was hardly new. However, in the words of historian Robert Gildea, many communities had not yet "gained a voice to demand the symbolic righting of wrongs."[9] Buoyed by what French historian Pierre Nora calls the "democratization of history" as well as global shifts in power, people now question the pres-

---

Marschall, "Targeting Statues: Monument 'Vandalism' as an Expression of Sociopolitical Protest in South Africa," *African Studies Review* 60, no. 3 (2017): 203–219.
5 Britta Knudsen and Casper Andersen, "Affective Politics and Colonial Heritage, '#Rhodes Must Fall' at UCT and Oxford," *International Journal of Heritage Studies* 25, no. 3 (2019): 239–258.
6 Aamna Mohdin, Richard Adams and Ben Quinn, "Oxford College Backs Removal of Cecil Rhodes Statue," *The Guardian*, 17 June 2020, accessed 5 December 2020, https://www.theguardian.com/education/2020/jun/17/end-of-the-rhodes-cecil-oxford-college-ditches-controversial-statue.
7 Estelle Shirbon, "Oxford College Says It Wants to Remove Statue of Colonialist Rhodes," *Reuters*, 17 June 2020, accessed 7 December 2020, https://uk.reuters.com/article/uk-britain-statues-rhodes/oxford-college-says-it-wants-to-remove-statue-of-colonialist-rhodes-idUKKBN23O3B1.
8 Anye Nyamnjoh, "The Phenomenology of Rhodes Must Fall: Student Activism and the Experience of Alienation at the University of Cape Town," *Strategic Review for Southern Africa* 39, no. 1 (2017): 256–277; Gurminder K. Bhambra, Dalia Gebrial, and Kerem Nişancıoğlu, eds., *Decolonising the University: Understanding and Transforming the Universities' Colonial Foundations* (London: Pluto Press, 2018); and Robbie Shilliam, "Behind the Rhodes Statue: Black Competency and the Imperial Academy," *History of the Human Sciences* 32, no. 5 (2019): 3–27.
9 Robert Gildea, *Empires of the Mind: The Colonial Past and the Politics of the Present* (Cambridge: Cambridge University Press, 2019), 12.

ervation of historic tributes to discredited individuals.[10] Public activism contributed to a transformative agenda and altered the cultural landscape, while public appetite for reconsidering the past expanded, animated by these trends as well as demand for racial redress.

As Albert Wirz and Jan-Georg Deutsch observe, "History always involves a reflection on the present. Those who write history – or study history – can therefore never circumvent the question of when, how, why, by whom and for whom a certain kind of historical knowledge was produced and written down."[11] Inspired by the life of Jan-Georg Deutsch, who mentored the authors of this book, and by recent public interest in commemoration and the politics of historical memory, this volume contributes to a growing body of work that examines the monuments, tributes, and cultural objects that evoke colonial history in Africa.[12] It also augments existing work on the politics of historical memory with new studies from across the continent.[13]

The chapters of this volume, dedicated to Deutsch, relate the past to the present through a critical examination of the politics of historical memory and its commemoration in particular African contexts. This introductory chapter examines issues that mediate between the past and the present and show how both have been framed in different contexts in Africa and beyond the continent. Subsequent chapters offer a selection of cases from colonial Nigeria, Algeria, Kenya, a transitioning South Africa, postcolonial Somalia, and Liberia, all examining events in each country and how they were remembered and memorialised.

---

10 Pierre Nora, "Reasons for the Current Upsurge in Memory," *Eurozine*, 9 April 2002, 2. See also Pierre Nora, *Realms of Memory: Rethinking the French Past*, ed. Lawrence D. Kritzman, trans. Arthur Goldhammer, 3 vols (New York: Columbia University Press, 1996–98).
11 Albert Wirz and Jan-Georg Deutsch, "Geschichte in Afrika: Einleitung und Problemaufriß," in *Geschichte in Afrika: Einführung in Probleme und Debatten*, eds. Jan-Georg Deutsch and Albert Wirz (Berlin: Verlag Das Arabische Buch, 1997), 6. Quote translated by the authors.
12 Liz Stanley, *Mourning Becomes...: Post/memory and Commemoration of the Concentration Camps of the South African War 1899–1902* (Manchester: Manchester University Press, 2006); Ifi Amadiume and Abdullah An-Na'im, eds., *The Politics of Memory: Truth, Healing and Social Justice* (London: Zed Books, 2000); and Dominik Geppert and Frank Muller, eds., *Sites of Imperial Memory: Commemorating Colonial Rule in the Nineteenth and Twentieth Centuries* (Manchester: Manchester University Press, 2015).
13 A growing literature at the intersection of knowledge production, politics, and memory in Africa informs this work, including: Derek R. Peterson and Giacomo Macola, eds., *Recasting the Past: History Writing and Political Work in Modern Africa* (Athens, OH: Ohio University Press, 2009); Elisabeth Mudimbe-Boyi, ed., *Remembering Africa* (Portsmouth, NH: Heinmenn, 2002); and Derek R. Peterson, Kodzo Gavua and Ciraj Rassool, eds., *The Politics of Heritage in Africa: Economies, Histories, and Infrastructures* (Cambridge and London: Cambridge University Press and the International African Institute, 2015).

The final chapter considers how collective memory of shared experiences shapes historical writing. Symbols of the past in Africa – including memorials and monuments as well as parades, postage stamps, obituaries, and even alcoholic beverages – are tied to understanding political realities of the continent. These understandings of the past played out not only in the decisions of national leaders of African states but also in everyday discussions and actions.

Of Memory, Commemoration, and Monuments

Though past events are immutable, their significance and interpretation by subsequent generations are not. Re-evaluation can devalue revered figures and commemorative monuments can become focal points. "Historical representations – be they books, commercial exhibits or public commemorations – cannot be conceived only as vehicles for the transmission of knowledge," declared Michel-Rolph Trouillot in *Silencing the Past*, his seminal 1995 interrogation of power and the making of history.[14] He further asserts that historical narratives must respond to present injustices in order to establish an authentic relation to that knowledge.

Collective memory joins the past with the present. In *Commemorating and Forgetting: Challenges for the New South Africa*, Martin Murray defines collective memory as "a shared understanding that belongs to social groups and collectivities of all kinds" and that in general this understanding rests not on a firm foundation of shared values but rather on contested perspectives.[15] Collective memory is derived by way of a wide range of commemorative forms which carry political meaning, including monuments, statues, official holidays, landmarks, rituals, images, symbols, and so forth. Murray adds, "Commemorative practices have always been deeply invested in the shaping of political and national identities."[16]

Trouillot describes memory-history as a particular storage vessel of the past developed by a collective. He critiques this vessel to emphasise that the consequences of a historical event may not correlate to the space allotted to it in pop-

---

[14] Michel-Rolph Trouillot, *Silencing the Past: Power and the Production of History* (Boston, MA: Beacon Press Books, 1995), 149. For work on the impact of *Silencing the Past*, see Alyssa Goldstein Sepinwall, "Still Unthinkable? The Haitian Revolution and the Reception of Michel-Rolph Trouillot's *Silencing the Past*," *The Journal of Haitian Studies* 19, no. 2 (2013): 75–103.
[15] Martin Murray, *Commemorating and Forgetting: Challenges for the New South Africa* (Minneapolis: University of Minnesota Press, 2013), 4.
[16] Murray, *Commemorating and Forgetting*, 7.

ular as well as official recollections of the past. As evidence of this disparity, he notes that the Haitian Revolution played a key role in the ultimate eradication of a global slavery system, yet it endured longstanding omission from history textbooks in France and elsewhere. Confronting the dissonance between events and scholarly analysis of them, Trouillot underscores the silences that pervade the historical record. His concern is with power and selection in the landscape of knowledge production because "the ways in which what happened and that which is said to have happened are and are not the same may itself be historical."[17] Affirming Trouillot's observations, Derek Peterson and Giacomo Macola spurred an awareness of power, politics and ethics in knowledge production about African history in *Recasting the Past: History Writing and Political Work in Modern Africa*.[18]

Momentous events punctuated by the "The Year of Africa" in 1960 when 17 countries declared independence generated continent-wide opportunities for investigating the political uses of memory. Many African leaders removed, reworked or substituted colonial-era memorials with fresh symbols.[19] Streets, buildings, and even countries were renamed, as new national historiographies were crafted.[20] As Derek Peterson observes in his introduction to *The Politics of Heritage in Africa*, "the lifeways of the past were made into capital, a store of authentic knowledge on which contemporary political actors could draw."[21] Yet memorialisation in these new independent states also proved particularly fractious. A statue of independent Ghana's first president Kwame Nkrumah in Accra erected in 1958 was attacked for the first time in 1961 and then decapitated and toppled after a coup in 1966. In 1992, a government that approved of Nkrumah's rule created a replica. Fifteen years later, a new government with a different view of Nkrumah resurrected and displayed the original beheaded statue alongside the replica.[22] This dual commemoration of Nkrumah, while satisfying neither side, nonetheless communicates a more nuanced commemoration of

---

17 Trouillot, *Silencing the Past*, 22.
18 Peterson and Macola, *Recasting the Past*.
19 Heike Becker, "Commemorating Heroes in Windhoek and Eenhana: Memory, Culture and Nationalism in Namibia, 1990–2010," *Africa* 81, no. 4 (2011): 519–543.
20 Carola Lentz and Dave Lowe, *Remembering Independence* (New York: Routledge, 2018); Ruramisai Charumbira, *Imagining a Nation: History and Memory in Making Zimbabwe* (Charlottesville: University of Virginia Press, 2015); and Felicitas Becker, "Remembering Nyerere: Political Rhetoric and Dissent in Contemporary Tanzania," *African Affairs* 112, no. 447 (2013): 238–261.
21 Derek R. Peterson, "Introduction: Heritage Management in Colonial and Contemporary Africa," in Peterson, Gavua, and Rassool, *The Politics of Heritage in Africa*, 2.
22 Carola Lentz, "'Ghanaian 'Monument Wars': The Contested History of the Nkrumah Statues," *Cahiers D' Études Africaines* 52, no. 3 (2017): 551–582.

him, both as father of the nation and as an authoritarian leader who suppressed opposition.

In North Africa, the potency of monuments as well as their removal has a long tradition. Historian Emily Teeter observes that for ancient Egyptians, figurative representation served more than a decorative function and that "portraying an individual ensured that person's existence as long as the image itself was preserved [...]. Conversely, if the image of an individual was effaced, the existence of that person was effectively erased."[23] As Christianity spread in Egypt, many depictions fell victim to iconoclasts who rejected the ideas of previous generations of Egyptians, yet recognised the power of their visual representations.[24] Converts effaced sculptures in temples and at graves, often removing the eyes from stone figures in a symbolic act intended to deny their power to instruct.

Studies of public memorialisation and memory in post-apartheid South Africa are numerous.[25] Memory studies scholar Sabine Marschall considers how people and events are represented in that country's monuments, which she defines as structures that are "commemorative" and "intentionally construct-

---

[23] Emily Teeter, "Religion and Ritual," in Melinda Hartwig, ed. *A Companion to Ancient Egyptian Art* (Chichester: John Wiley & Sons Ltd., 2015), 328.

[24] For discussion of Christian iconoclasm in Egypt, see David Frankfurter, "Iconoclasm and Christianization in Late Antique Egypt: Christian Treatments of Space and Image," in *From Temple to Church: Destruction and Renewal of Local Cultic Topography in Late Antiquity*, eds. Johannes Hahn, Stephen Emmel, and Ulrich Gotter (Boston, MA: Brill, 2008), 135–160.

[25] See, for instance: Sarah Nuttall and Carli Coetzee, eds. *Negotiating the Past: The Making of Memory in South Africa* (Cape Town: Oxford University Press, 1998); Ciraj Rassool, "The Rise of Heritage and the Reconstitution of History in South Africa," *Kronos* 26 (2000): 1–21; Sabine Marschall, *Landscape of Memory: Commemorative Monuments, Memorials, and Public Statuary in Post-apartheid South Africa* (Leiden: Brill, 2010); Lynn Meskell, *The Nature of Heritage: The New South Africa* (Oxford: Wiley-Blackwell, 2012); Daniel Herwitz, *Heritage, Culture, and Politics in the Postcolony* (New York: Columbia University Press, 2012); and Murray, *Commemorating and Forgetting*. For museums commemorating communities fractured during apartheid, see Ciraj Rassool and Sandra Prosalendis, eds. *Recalling Community in Cape Town: Creating and Curating the District Six Museum* (Cape Town: District Six Museum Foundation, 2001); and Sean Field, "Imagining Communities: Memory, Loss, and Resilience in Post-Apartheid Cape Town," in *Oral History and Public Memories*, eds. Paula Hamilton and Linda Shopes (Philadelphia, PA: Temple University Press, 2008), 107–124. For work on the public memorialisation of South African sport, see Peter Alegi, "The Football Heritage Complex: History, Tourism and Development in South Africa," *Africa Spectrum* 41, no. 3 (2006): 415–426; Ciraj Rassool and Virgil Slade, "'Fields of Play': The District Six Museum and the History of Football in Cape Town," *Soccer and Society* 13, no. 2 (2012): 188–206; and Marizanne Grundlingh, "Showcasing the Springboks: The Commercialization of South African Rugby Heritage," *South African Review of Sociology* 46, no. 1 (2015): 106–128.

ed."²⁶ Focusing on issues of style, design and form, rather than on who or what is being commemorated, she notes that Western traditions have long influenced South African monuments and that this trend continued after apartheid through the "filling of old forms with new content."²⁷ In her 2003 work on *Visual Culture and Public Memory in a Democratic South Africa*, Annie Coombes asserts that the significance of a monument is always renewed in conversation with the past.²⁸ New sites such as the Robben Island Museum, Apartheid Museum, Constitution Hill complex, Nelson Mandela Heritage complex, Ncome/Blood River Museum, Luthuli Museum and Freedom Park did not displace older colonial monuments and were often deliberately juxtaposed with existing monuments.²⁹ Almost a decade before the #RhodesMustFall movement, Marschall noted that commemorative monuments reflect post-apartheid South Africa's "delicate balancing act."³⁰ Memorials that preserved the country's fractured history permitted discussion of contested interpretations of the past. Disagreements over the symbolic realm, which includes official monuments such as statues of high-profile individuals and important events, could "inflame powerful emotions and even lead to violence," testing efforts to reconcile and build a post-apartheid state.³¹

The statuary of Cecil Rhodes served as one such focus of controversy. As RMF gained momentum, some approved of public displays of the British imperialist. Others condemned his continued memorialisation. Political scientist Anthony Lemon contends that Cecil Rhodes must "be assessed in terms of the values of his day" and Robert Gildea summarises this view, stating, "Rhodes was a man of his time and that was that."³² Dissenters emphasise that opposition to Rhodes existed during his lifetime. In an article titled "Why Rhodes Must Fall," historian John Newsinger argues that reverence for Rhodes rested on the fortune he amassed as one of the founders of De Beers Consolidated Mines, which was built on the exploitation of Black labourers, as well as the leading

---

26 Sabine Marschall, "Transforming the Landscape of Memory," *South African Historical Journal* 55 (2006): 166.
27 Marschall, "Transforming the Landscape," 178; Murray, *Commemorating and Forgetting*, 4.
28 Annie Coombes, *History After Apartheid: Visual Culture and Public Memory in a Democratic South Africa* (Durham and London: Duke University Press, 2003), 12.
29 Coombes, *History After Apartheid*. See also Rassool, "The Rise of Heritage"; Marschall, "Transforming the Landscape of Memory"; and Sabine Marschall, "The Long Shadow of Apartheid: A Critical Assessment of Heritage Transformation in South Africa 25 years on," *International Journal of Heritage Studies* 25, no. 10 (2019): 1088–1102.
30 Marschall, "Transforming the Landscape," 184.
31 Marschall, *Landscape of Memory*.
32 Anthony Lemon, "'Rhodes Must Fall': The Dangers of Re-Writing History," *The Round Table* 105, no. 2 (2016): 217–219; Gildea, *Empires of the Mind*, 12.

role he played in British colonisation in southern Africa, which included the colony of Rhodesia named after him.[33] Cultural historian Yuliya Komska emphasises that the ultimate significance of protests over memorials stems not from their demolition or preservation but from the intensified scrutiny that these representations engendered. In her words, "The removal of the relics of a hateful social order is not in itself cause for celebration. It is the aftermath that matters."[34]

Cultural productions of historical memory and the campaigns they incite become elemental components of contemporary politics. In European nations, where descendants of previously colonised peoples have become citizens, long-standing monuments honouring imperialists have sparked wider discussion about which people and events are worthy of collective celebration. In Ernest Renan's 1882 classic "What is a Nation?" he observed that a nation is partially constructed around a collective narrative of the past and that the creation of a nation depends on "forgetting" and "historical error."[35] If the demographic composition of the nation changes to include descendants of those victimised by that nation's imperialism, that collective narrative and its public representation become negotiable. For Gildea, battles over the memory of empire do not "remain simply as memory."[36] They continue to shape politics and public commentary.

Some suggest that tangible cultural markers inherited from a previous order should be preserved and that nations should retain commemorations of previous leaders, however reprehensible, as valuable reminders of slavery, colonialism, and racism. Scholars of memory Cynthia Mills and Pamela Simpson observe that public memorials can serve as spaces in which layers of history can accumulate, noting that "the old message is not erased, but new language is written over it or beside it."[37] A memorial to World War Two leader Erwin Rommel in his hometown of Heidenheim in Germany is one example.[38] Rather than remove a massive stone monument to Rommel, city officials added a silhouette of a man who has lost one leg to a land mine. The starkness of his impairment in

---

33 John Newsinger, "Why Rhodes Must Fall," *Race and Class* 58, no. 2 (2016): 70–78.
34 "What to do with Confederate Monuments: Seven Lessons from Germany," *Washington Post*, 17 August 2017, accessed 5 December 2020, https://www.washingtonpost.com/news/made-by-history/wp/2017/08/17/what-to-do-with-confederate-monuments-seven-lessons-from-germany/. See also Barnabas, "Engagement with Colonial and Apartheid Narratives."
35 Ernest Renan, "What is a Nation?" in *Nation and Narration*, ed. Homi K. Bhabha (London: Routledge, 1990), 11.
36 Gildea, *Empires of the Mind*, 11.
37 Cynthia Mills and Pamela H. Simpson, eds., *Monuments to the Lost Cause: Women, Art, and the Landscapes of Southern Memory* (Knoxville: The University of Tennessee Press, 2003), xxv.
38 Marschall has termed these types of adjustments "strategic juxtaposition." See: Marschall, *Landscape of Memory*, 298.

front of the original monument alters it in a way that emphasises the fact that under the German general's command, untold numbers of mines were buried in northeast Africa to devastating effect for allied soldiers and local populations.[39] Heidenheim Mayor Bernhard Ilg declared, "A statue does not proclaim a truth, but encourages people to seek it."[40]

Struggles over controversial statues go beyond altering their original meaning. In his study of monuments of the civil rights movement in the American South, historian of architecture and material culture Dell Upton argues that many who oppose removing monuments believe that these memorials represent a historic reality.[41] He observes that people often draw distinctions between memory and history in an effort to understand the past and that for monument preservationists, to damage or alter a public memorial is to erase history. From this perspective, the removal of a statue constitutes an insupportable deprivation for future generations of the instruction that these creations impart. In contrast, in his book #RhodesMustFall, inspired by the movement to topple Cecil Rhodes' statue at UCT, social anthropologist Francis B. Nyamnjoh observes that removing that statue was only an erasure of history to those who had veiled Rhodes' past in order to forget fraught aspects of this life.[42] "Invariably," argues Nyamnjoh, "such a stance would entail an enforcement of a disconnect with history, an inducement of amnesia, so as to mask a fundamental truth of history together with its enduring legacy of violence."[43]

Many descendants of enslaved people in West Africa continue to experience marginalisation based on their heritage. Yet governments and local communities struggle to address this injustice in a public forum. Harvard historian Emmanuel Akyeampong has outlined the challenge as follows:

---

39 One South African example of the "juxtaposition model" can be seen in Freedom Park, an anti-apartheid struggle memorial built opposite the Voortrekker Monument (VTM), which commemorates the Great Trek. See: Marschall, *Landscape of Memory*, and Mia Swart, "Name Change as Symbolic Reparation after Transition: The Example of Germany and South Africa," *German Law Journal* 9, no. 2 (2008): 105–121. For a study of the VTM, see Robyn Autry, "The Monumental Reconstruction of Memory in South Africa: The Voortrekker Monument," *Theory, Culture & Society* 29, no. 6 (2012): 146–164.
40 Darko Janjevic, "Germany: Amputee Statue Added to Erwin Rommel Monument in His Hometown," *Deutsche Welle*, 12 July 2020, accessed 8 December 2020, https://www.dw.com/en/germany-amputee-statue-added-to-erwin-rommel-monument-in-his-hometown/a-54300881.
41 Dell Upton, *What Can and Can't be Said: Race, Uplift and Monument Building in the Contemporary South* (New Haven: Yale University Press, 2015).
42 Francis B. Nyamnjoh, *#RhodesMustFall: Nibbling at Resilient Colonialism in South Africa* (Mankon, Bamenda: Langaa Research & Publishing CIG, 2016).
43 Nyamnjoh, *#RhodesMustFall*, 277.

Perhaps, because those of slave descent constitute significant proportions of local populations in various parts of West Africa, to bring slavery and its legacy within the realm of public discussion threatens national integration in recently independent countries. Even in precolonial times, the powerful state of Asante acknowledged the large incorporation of peoples of unfree origins into its polity by enshrining a prohibition in its national laws against highlighting anyone's slave origins.[44]

The memory of indigenous slavery has proven to be persistent if not ineradicable. Its legacy taints social and political life and coming to terms with that legacy presents many challenges. University of Ghana professor Victoria Ellen Smith explains how in the Akan region of Ghana, the *Ntam Kɛse* oath forbids any mention of ancestral slavery.[45] However, the very need for an oath of silence emphasises the persistence of the inequities spawned by indigenous slavery. Oaths of silence do not necessarily improve the lives of individuals whose ancestors were enslaved. They and others advocate for a more truthful representation of ancestral slavery. These efforts, in addition to new memorials chronicling that history, are necessary for those threatened by dominant narratives of the past. As Akyeampong contends, "memory is simultaneously political and moral, and 'preserved' memory can serve political and/or moral agendas."[46]

Reassessment of slavery continues worldwide. Scholars at the University of Glasgow, Brown University and other institutions have engaged in a public reappraisal of their university's ties to and benefits from slavery. In 2019 officials at the University of Glasgow and The University of the West Indies struck an unprecedented agreement to develop a Glasgow-Caribbean Centre for Development Research to raise public awareness, both in Scotland and in the Caribbean, about the history and impact of the Trans-Atlantic slave trade.[47] Glasgow University's "reparative justice" laid the groundwork for future discussions of reparations for past wrong-doings of exploited peoples and territories.

Academics, institutions and governments in recent years have sought to address the imbalanced landscape of memorialisation across the African diaspora. Christina Sharpe, scholar of English literature and Black Studies, addresses the

---

[44] Emmanuel Akyeampong, "History, Memory, Slave-Trade and Slavery in Anlo (Ghana)," *Slavery and Abolition* 22, no. 3 (2001): 1.

[45] Victoria Ellen Smith, "Secrets of West African Slave Ancestry: Fante Strategies of Silence and the Didactic Narrative in Ghanaian Literature," *Journal of West African History* 2, no. 2 (2016): 109–131.

[46] Akyeampong, "History, Memory, Slave-Trade and Slavery," 2.

[47] "Historic Agreement Sealed Between Glasgow and West Indies Universities," University News, University of Glasgow, 23 August 2019, accessed 7 December 2020, https://www.gla.ac.uk/news/headline_667960_en.html.

topics of monuments, memory and reparations in her work *In the Wake: On Blackness and Being* wherein she examines the construction of new public memorials and museums that attempt to undo past narratives by creating new discourses about the Trans-Atlantic slave trade. She draws attention to "Mémorial ACTe" in Guadeloupe, which is dedicated to the memory and history of slavery and slave trade in the Caribbean archipelago and the Ark of Return located at the African Burial Ground in New York City. These memorials have played a role in inspiring people to address the question of reparations. Sharpe asks, "But what is a moral debt? How is it paid? Is it that Black people can only be the objects of transaction and not the beneficiaries of one, historical or not?"[48]

Unresolved questions over memory, commemorations, and the legacy of slavery and colonialism occupy current discussions. From Cape Town to Charlottesville, societies are grappling with historical consciousness and the evolution of public memory. Officials entrusted with maintaining national commemorative landscapes are increasingly held accountable for holistic representations of the past. How and why communities remember and forget, what should serve as symbols of collective memory, and whether there exists space for multiple memory cultures are topics of on-going debate. These discussions present challenges to national commemorative landscapes and interpretations of the past.

Chapter overviews

Philosopher and sociologist Maurice Halbwachs drew a distinction between various groups' collective memories and the official interpretation of national history.[49] Shared memories are part of a group's identity, and ordinary citizens can preserve a collective consciousness of the past in ways that oppose the official remembrances of elites. In his ethnographic work on political terror and memory in South Africa, cultural anthropologist Allen Feldman affirms the potency of collective memory in sustaining an understanding of the past that the state intended to erase.[50] In Chapter Two of this volume, Natacha Filippi observes these dynamics in a Cape Town prison and in a psychiatric hospital. Apart-

---

[48] Christina Sharpe, *In the Wake: On Blackness and Being* (Durham and London, Duke University Press, 2016), 60.
[49] Maurice Halbwachs, *La Mémoire Collective* (Paris: Albin Michel, 1997 [1950 posthumous]). See also Nicolas Russell, "Collective Memory Before and After Halbwachs," *The French Review* 79, no. 4 (2006): 792–804.
[50] Allen Feldman, "Political Terror and the Technologies of Memory: Excuse, Sacrifice, Commodification, and Actuarial Moralities," *Radical History Review* 85 (2003): 58–73.

heid-era prisons had been incubators for subversive activity, where radical politics were harboured and where severe injustices had occurred. In post-apartheid South Africa, some prisons, most notably Robben Island, became museums for the memorialisation of the horrors of the apartheid era. However, at other prisons, incarcerated South Africans' collective memories differed from governmental proclamations of reform. Filippi shares the challenges she encountered in these controlled institutions that limited her ability to interact with the subjects of her study. She observes that remembrance consists of more than the written or spoken word and that architecture, objects, and even tattoos can transfer memories.

In Chapter Three, Casper Andersen discusses contributions that academics and international organisations made to the politics of African memory formation during the early decades of the independence era. In 1964 the United Nations Educational, Scientific and Cultural Organisation (UNESCO) initiated the *General History of Africa*, an ambitious multi-volume book project comprising 30 years of collaborative work among more than 230 historians who sought to reconstruct the entirety of the continent's past. The eight-volume collection addressed racial biases and the general lack of knowledge of African history. Andersen's work takes up Frederick Cooper's call to examine how the politics of historical knowledge production were involved in supporting or discrediting power.[51] Andersen highlights the exuberant hope for liberal democracy that African scholars involved with the project held but their optimistic anticipation for democratic state-building faced the harsh realities confronted by these nascent states. Applying Ngũgĩ wa Thiong'o's concept of the "quest for relevance," Andersen explains the ambitions of these authors who saw political independence and decolonised, African-centred histories as inextricable.

With the onset of independence, people across the continent wrestled with how to reconcile conflicting legacies of colonial rule. The names that post-colonial governments attached to national days of remembrance carried important symbolism and political weight. At independence in 1963, the government of Kenya declared October 20th Kenyatta Day, a national holiday dedicated to the new nation's first Prime Minister. In Chapter Four, Ed Goodman traces the history of Kenyatta Day, the rituals that marked it, the stories people told about it and the demands that emerged from the mid-1990s to recast the day as "Heroes Day." In the early postcolonial years, Jomo Kenyatta was revered as an adherent of Kenyan nationhood. People hoped that respect for him would transcend long-

---

[51] Frederick Cooper, "Conflict and Connection: Rethinking African History," *American Historical Review* 99, no. 5 (1994): 1516–1545.

standing ethnic divisions in the country. By the 1990s, as opposition to the government of president Daniel arap Moi smouldered, critics recast the day's meaning, claiming that post-colonial governments had forgotten the nation's true heroes. With commemorative days dedicated first to Kenyatta and then to Moi, critics protested these deliberate ploys by authoritarian governments to symbolically reinforce their autocratic regimes. Many argued that Moi and Kenyatta Days should be replaced by a more inclusive Heroes' Day, as promulgated in the 2010 constitution. Kenyanist historiography on memory principally concerns the Mau Mau rebellion of the 1950s, which many scholars have described as "state sanctioned amnesia" about that conflict.[52] Goodman's chapter breaks new ground with his analysis of what the state *did* remember.

In Chapter Five, Mohamed Haji Ingiriis addresses the challenges faced by post-civil war Somalis in their efforts to build an independent nation. Grievances stemming from that conflict deepened divisions not only between Somaliland and southern Somalia but also between and within clan and sub-clan groups. Ingiriis demonstrates that injustices meant to legitimise an independent Somaliland simultaneously inhibited the emergence of a broad "Somalilander" identity. From interviews with a broad range of interlocutors, he demonstrates that memories of violence of the civil war as well as specific events such as the "Hargeisa Holocaust" evolved as a new generation sought to make sense of that past. Applying Ernest Renan's theory of nationhood, Ingiriis' work affirms the link between nationalist narratives and memories of violence and loss. Though not specific to Africa such connections comprise the core of nation building. Ingiriis demonstrates that recognition of the horrors people endured during that conflict offer a collective catharsis and can lead to social change.

Obituaries are another form of memory production. In Chapter Six, Rouven Kunstmann and Cassandra Mark-Thiesen examine West African obituaries and in-memoriams from the 1940s to the 1960s. Regarding the Asante people of Ghana, historian Tom McCaskie observes, "Death was and is a social event, conceived of and observed as something that happens to an individual person, but only within the contexts of family (ancestry and posterity as well as the living)

---

52 See, for instance: Annie E. Coombes, Lottie Hughes and Karega-Munene, eds., *Managing Heritage, Making Peace: History, Identity and Memory in Contemporary Kenya* (London: I.B Tauris, 2014); Marshall S. Clough, *Mau Mau Memoirs: History, Memory, and Politics* (Boulder: Lynne Rienner Publishers, 1998); and Julie MacArthur, ed., *Dedan Kimathi on Trial: Colonial Justice and Popular Memory in Kenya's Mau Mau Rebellion* (Athens, OH: Ohio University Press, 2017).

and community."[53] In Nigerian and Liberian newspapers, death notices were similarly seen as rituals with social and political implications. Extensive text-only obituaries of the elite published by the state are analysed next to succinct in-memoriams, usually featuring a photograph of the deceased, placed in newspapers by private citizens. Kunstmann and Mark-Thiesen demonstrate that obituaries have as much to do with the future of the mourners as they do with the memorialisation of the deceased.

In Chapter Seven, Nina Studer looks at interactions between local populations and French colonists in colonial Algeria. Observing the significance of alcohol and particularly wine in French self-image, she examines what people thought about the drinking habits of the French settlers and the political meanings that they attributed to its consumption. Nostalgia for the early years of colonial conquest often coalesced with reference to alcohol in accounts of that period, or what Studer calls "Frenchness in a bottle." Ironically the French feared that immoderation by both colonised and coloniser threatened their oversight of Algeria.

In the final chapter, historian of memory Ruramisai Charumbira stresses the importance of indigenous languages in historical writing and reflects on the dissonances that arise when historians attempt to erase themselves and their worldviews from their writings. In contrast, what she calls "embodied writing practices" create space for indigenous theories of knowledge because these practices highlight "the importance of bodies *and* places to accessing the past and maintaining history."[54] Her work complements Ross Gibson's claim in his 2015 *Memoryscopes* that "memory-work" is "lodged in human bodies, but also in places [and] in landscapes."[55] Charumbira focuses on three scholars who employ this practice: Kenyan activist and Nobel Prize winner Wangari Maathai, Professor of Indigenous Education Linda Tuhiwai Smith of the University of Waikato in New Zealand, and State University of New York Professor of Environmental and Forest Biology Robin Wall Kimmerer, a member of the Potawatomi Nation. Each has devised ways to connect academic work with personal and cultural his-

---

[53] Tom McCaskie, "Writing, Reading, and Printing Death: Obituaries and Commemoration in Asante," in *Africa's Hidden Histories: Everyday Literacy and Making the Self*, ed. Karin Barber (Bloomington, IN: Indiana University Press, 2006), 342.
[54] Jodie Stewart, "History by Doing: Reclaiming Indigenous Women's Sovereignty through Embodied History," *Lilith: A Feminist History Journal* 25 (2019): 95. Emphasis added.
[55] Ross Gibson, *Memoryscopes: Remnants, Forensics, Aesthetics* (Crawley: University of Western Australian Publishing, 2015), 7. See also Deborah Bird Rose, "Writing Place," in *Writing Histories: Imagination and Narration*, eds. Ann Curthoys and Ann McGrath (Melbourne: Monash University Publishing, 2000), 64–74.

tories that centre the natural world, what Charumbira calls "indigenous ways of knowing and being."

The Politics of Historical Memory and Commemoration in Africa: A final note in honour of Jan-Georg Deutsch

This *Gedenkschrift* is a communal effort honouring Jan-Georg Deutsch. By publishing this volume, we honour his life and legacy and the appreciation we share for his range of interests and the influence that he has had on our lives. To our knowledge, this volume is unique in connecting the theme of memorialisation with the concept of a *Gedenkschrift* – a memorial publication commemorating a respected scholar, developed posthumously – to honour a historian whose work was itself focused on historical memory. Except for the final essay by Ruramisai Charumbira, his doctoral students wrote and edited all chapters in this volume. In early 2017, we first discussed the possibility of a commemorative volume, and in January 2018, exactly one year after his funeral, we met in Basel, Switzerland to discuss the content of this work. We are grateful for all we learnt from Jan-Georg Deutsch, for the laughs we shared, and for the inspiration we gained from him. In the spirit of Georg's graduate seminars, we suggest that you enjoy a packet of biscuits or chocolate while reading the chapters of this volume.

Jan-Georg Deutsch was born 1956 in the small German town of Marburg and grew up close to Hannover, where he attended university. He went to London to write his doctorate at the School of Oriental and African Studies. Under the supervision of Richard Rathbone, he completed his dissertation in 1990, titled "Educating the Middlemen: A Political and Economic History of Statutory Cocoa Marketing in Nigeria, 1936–1947."[56] Deutsch eventually returned to Germany, where he first affiliated with the University of Düsseldorf, followed by the Zentrum Moderner Orient (ZMO) in Berlin in 1996. Among other publications, he co-edited with Albert Wirz *Geschichte in Afrika: Einführung in Probleme und Debatten*, a volume on problems and debates in African history.[57] He completed his

---

[56] Jan-Georg Deutsch, *Educating the Middlemen: A Political and Economic History of Statutory Cocoa Marketing in Nigeria, 1936–1947*, Studien (Förderungsgesellschaft Wissenschaftliche Neuvorhaben. Forschungsschwerpunkt Moderner Orient); Nr. 3 (Berlin: Verlag das Arabische Buch, 1995).

[57] Deutsch and Wirz, eds. *Geschichte in Afrika: Einführung in Probleme und Debatten.*

Habilitation in 2000 on "Slavery under German Colonial Rule in East Africa, c. 1860–1914" at Humboldt University.[58] In 2002 he became a fellow at St. Cross College, Oxford University where he remained until his untimely death in December 2016. One of his final research projects, which remains unpublished, was a comparative examination of memory sites, including South Africa's Robben Island, Gorée island off the coast of Senegal, Elmina Castle in Ghana, and the Slave Market Memorial in Zanzibar. He leaves behind a meaningful academic imprint on the history of social, economic and political life on the African continent and in research areas ranging from slavery to colonial law and order, and economic relations across the continent of Africa.

Bibliography

Akyeampong, Emmanuel. "History, Memory, Slave-Trade and Slavery in Anlo (Ghana)." *Slavery and Abolition* 22, no. 3 (2001): 1–24.

Alegi, Peter. "The Football Heritage Complex: History, Tourism and Development in South Africa." *Africa Spectrum* 41, no. 3 (2006): 415–426.

Amadiume, Ifi, and Abdullah An-Na'im, eds. *The Politics of Memory: Truth, Healing and Social Justice*. London: Zed Books, 2000.

Autry, Robyn. "The Monumental Reconstruction of Memory in South Africa: The Voortrekker Monument." *Theory, Culture & Society* 29, no. 6 (2012): 146–164.

Barnabas, Shanade. "Engagement with Colonial and Apartheid Narratives in Contemporary South Africa: A Monumental Debate." *Journal of Literary Studies* 32, no. 3 (2016): 109–128.

Becker, Felicitas. "Remembering Nyerere: Political Rhetoric and Dissent in Contemporary Tanzania." *African Affairs* 112, no. 447 (2013): 238–261.

Becker, Heike. "Commemorating Heroes in Windhoek and Eenhana: Memory, Culture and Nationalism in Namibia, 1990–2010." *Africa* 81, no. 4 (2011): 519–543.

Bhambra, Gurminder K., Dalia Gebrial, and Kerem Nişancıoğlu, eds. *Decolonising the University: Understanding and Transforming the Universities' Colonial Foundations*. London: Pluto Press, 2018.

"Cecil Rhodes Statue in Cape Town has Head Removed," *BBC News*, 15 July 2020, accessed 6 December 2020, https://www.bbc.com/news/world-africa-53420403.

Charumbira, Ruramisai. *Imagining a Nation: History and Memory in Making Zimbabwe*. Charlottesville: University of Virginia Press, 2015.

Clough, Marshall S. *Mau Mau Memoirs: History, Memory, and Politics*. Boulder: Lynne Rienner Publishers, 1998.

Coombes, Annie. *History After Apartheid: Visual Culture and Public Memory in a Democratic South Africa*. Durham and London: Duke University Press, 2003.

---

58 His habilitation became the basis of a monograph: Jan-Georg Deutsch, *Emancipation without Abolition in German East Africa, c.1884–1914* (Oxford: James Currey, 2006).

Coombes, Annie, Lottie Hughes, and Karega-Munene, eds. *Managing Heritage, Making Peace: History, Identity and Memory in Contemporary Kenya*. London: Bloomsbury, I.B Tauris, 2014.

Cooper, Frederick. "Conflict and Connection: Rethinking African History." *American Historical Review* 99, no. 5 (1994): 1516–1545.

Deutsch, Jan-Georg. *Educating the Middlemen: A Political and Economic History of Statutory Cocoa Marketing in Nigeria, 1936–1947* Studien (Förderungsgesellschaft Wissenschaftliche Neuvorhaben. Forschungsschwerpunkt Moderner Orient); Nr. 3. Berlin: Verlag das Arabische Buch, 1995.

Deutsch, Jan-Georg. *Emancipation without Abolition in German East Africa, c.1884–1914*. Oxford: James Currey, 2006.

Deutsch, Jan-Georg, and Albert Wirz, eds. *Geschichte in Afrika: Einführung in Probleme und Debatten*. Berlin: Verlag Das Arabische Buch, 1997.

"Edward Colston Statue: Protesters Tear Down Slave Trader Monument," *BBC News*, 7 June 2020, accessed 7 December 2020, https://www.bbc.com/news/uk-52954305.

"Ethiopian Opposition Politician held as Protests Continue," *France24*, 7 July 2020, accessed 8 December 2020, https://www.france24.com/en/20200701-ethiopian-opposition-politician-held-as-protests-continue.

Feldman, Allen. "Political Terror and the Technologies of Memory: Excuse, Sacrifice, Commodification, and Actuarial Moralities." *Radical History Review* 85 (2003): 58–73.

Field, Sean. "Imagining Communities: Memory, Loss, and Resilience in Post-Apartheid Cape Town." In *Oral History and Public Memories*, edited by Hamilton Paula and Shopes Linda, 107–124. Philadelphia, PA: Temple University Press, 2008.

Frankfurter, David. "Iconoclasm and Christianization in Late Antique Egypt: Christian Treatments of Space and Image." In *From Temple to Church: Destruction and Renewal of Local Cultic Topography in Late Antiquity*, edited by Johannes Hahn, Stephen Emmel, and Ulrich Gotter, 135–160. Boston: Brill, 2008.

"George Floyd Protests Reignite Debate Over Confederate Statues," *New York Times*, 3 June 2020, accessed 7 December 2020, https://www.nytimes.com/2020/06/03/us/confederate-statues-george-floyd.html?action=click&module=RelatedLinks&pgtype=Article.

Geppert, Dominik, and Frank Muller, eds. *Sites of Imperial Memory: Commemorating Colonial Rule in the Nineteenth and Twentieth Centuries*. Manchester, UK: Manchester University Press, 2015.

Gibson, Ross. *Memoryscopes: Remnants Forensics Aesthetics*. Crawley, Australia: University of Western Australia Publishing, 2015.

Gildea, Robert. *Empires of the Mind: The Colonial Past and the Politics of the Present*. Cambridge: Cambridge University Press, 2019.

Grundlingh, Marizanne. "Showcasing the Springboks: The Commercialization of South African Rugby Heritage." *South African Review of Sociology* 46, no. 1 (2015): 106–128.

Halbwachs, Maurice. *La Mémoire Collective* (Paris: Albin Michel, 1997 [1950 posthumous]).

Herwitz, Daniel. *Heritage, Culture, and Politics in the Postcolony*. New York: Columbia University Press, 2012.

"Historic Agreement Sealed Between Glasgow and West Indies Universities," University of Glasgow, *University News*, 23 August 2019, accessed 7 December 2020, https://www.gla.ac.uk/news/headline_667960_en.html.

Janjevic, Darko. "Germany: Amputee Statue Added to Erwin Rommel Monument in His Hometown," *Deutsche Welle*, 23 July 2020, accessed 8 December 2020, https://www.dw.com/en/germany-amputee-statue-added-to-erwin-rommel-monument-in-his-hometown/a-54300881.

Knudsen, Britta and Casper Andersen. "Affective Politics and Colonial Heritage, '#Rhodes Must Fall' at UCT and Oxford." *International Journal of Heritage Studies* 25, no. 3 (2019): 239–258.

Lemon, Anthony. "'Rhodes Must Fall': The Dangers of Re-Writing History." *The Round Table* 105, no. 2 (2016): 217–219.

Lentz, Carola. "Ghanaian 'Monument Wars': The Contested History of the Nkrumah Statues." *Cahiers D' Études Africaines* 52, no. 3 (2017): 551–582.

MacArthur, Julie ed. *Dedan Kimathi on Trial: Colonial Justice and Popular Memory in Kenya's Mau Mau Rebellion*. Athens, OH: Ohio University Press, 2017.

Marschall, Sabine. "Transforming the Landscape of Memory." *South African Historical Journal* 55 (2006): 165–185.

Marschall, Sabine. *Landscape of Memory: Commemorative Monuments, Memorials and Public Statuary in Post-apartheid South Africa*. Leiden: Brill, 2010.

Marschall, Sabine. "Targeting Statues: Monument 'Vandalism' as an Expression of Sociopolitical Protest in South Africa." *African Studies Review* 60, no. 3 (2017): 203–219.

Marschall, Sabine. "The Long Shadow of Apartheid: A Critical Assessment of Heritage Transformation in South Africa 25 Years On." *International Journal of Heritage Studies* 25, no. 10 (2019): 1088–1102.

McCaskie, Tom. "Writing, Reading, and Printing Death: Obituaries and Commemoration in Asante." In *Africa's Hidden Histories: Everyday Literacy and Making the Self*, edited by Karin Barber, 341–384. Bloomington, IN: Indiana University Press, 2006.

Meskell, Lynn. *The Nature of Heritage: The New South Africa*. Oxford: Wiley-Blackwell, 2012.

Mills, Cynthia, and Pamela H. Simpson, eds. *Monuments to the Lost Cause: Women, Art, and the Landscapes of Southern Memory*. Knoxville: The University of Tennessee Press, 2003.

Mohdin, Aamna, Richard Adams, and Ben Quinn. "Oxford College Backs Removal of Cecil Rhodes Statue," *The Guardian*, 17 June 2020, accessed 5 December 2020, https://www.theguardian.com/education/2020/jun/17/end-of-the-rhodes-cecil-oxford-college-ditches-controversial-statue.

Mudimbe-Boyi, Elisabeth, ed. *Remembering Africa*. Portsmouth, NH: Heinemann, 2002.

Murray, Martin J. *Commemorating and Forgetting: Challenges for the New South Africa*. Minneapolis: University of Minnesota Press, 2013.

Newsinger, John. "Why Rhodes Must Fall." *Race and Class* 58, no. 2 (2016): 70–78.

Nuttall, Sarah, and Carli Coetzee, eds. *Negotiating the Past: The Making of Memory in South Africa*. Cape Town: Oxford University Press, 1998.

Nyamnjoh, Anye. "The Phenomenology of Rhodes Must Fall: Student Activism and the Experience of Alienation at the University of Cape Town." *Strategic Review for Southern Africa* 39, no. 1 (2017): 256–277.

Nyamnjoh, Francis B. *#RhodesMustFall: Nibbling at Resilient Colonialism in South Africa*. Mankon, Bamenda: Langaa Research & Publishing CIG, 2016.

Nora, Pierre. *Realms of Memory: Rethinking the French Past*. Translated by Lawrence D. Kritzman, edited by Arthur Goldhammer, 3 vols. New York: Columbia University Press, 1996–98.

Nora, Pierre. "Reasons for the Current Upsurge in Memory." *Eurozine*, April 9, 2002, 2.

Peterson, Derek R. "Introduction: Heritage Management in Colonial and Contemporary Africa." In *The Politics of Heritage in Africa: Economies, Histories, and Infrastructures*, edited by Derek R. Peterson, Kodzo Gavua and Ciraj Rassool, 1–36. Cambridge and London: Cambridge University Press and the International African Institute, 2015.

Peterson, Derek R., and Giacomo Macola, eds. *Recasting the Past: History Writing and Political Work in Modern Africa*. Athens, OH: Ohio University Press, 2009.

Peterson, Derek R., Kodzo Gavua and Ciraj Rassool, eds. *The Politics of Heritage in Africa: Economies, Histories, and Infrastructures*. Cambridge and London: Cambridge University Press and the International African Institute, 2015.

Pronczuk, Monika, and Mikir Zaveri. "Statue of Leopold II, Belgian King Who Brutalized Congo, Is Removed in Antwerp," *New York Times*, 9 June 2020, accessed 6 December 2020, https://www.nytimes.com/2020/06/09/world/europe/king-leopold-statue-antwerp.html.

Rassool, Ciraj. "The Rise of Heritage and the Reconstitution of History in South Africa." *Kronos* 26 (2000): 1–21.

Rassool, Ciraj, and Sandra Prosalendis, eds. *Recalling Community in Cape Town: Creating and Curating the District Six Museum*. Cape Town: District Six Museum Foundation, 2001.

Rassool, Ciraj, and Virgil Slade. "Fields of Play": The District Six Museum and the History of Football in Cape Town." *Soccer and Society* 13, no. 2 (2012): 188–206.

Renan, Ernest. "What is a Nation?" In *Nation and Narration*, edited by Homi K. Bhabha, 8–22. London: Routledge, 1990.

Rose, Deborah Bird. "Writing Place." In *Writing Histories: Imagination and Narration*, edited by Ann Curthoys and Ann McGrath, 64–74. Melbourne: Monash University Publishing, 2000.

Russell, Nicolas. "Collective Memory Before and After Halbwachs." *The French Review* 79, no. 4 (2006): 792–804.

Sepinwall, Alyssa Goldstein. "Still Unthinkable? The Haitian Revolution and the Reception of Michel Rolph Trouillot's *Silencing the Past*." *The Journal of Haitian Studies* 19, no. 2 (2013): 75–103.

Sharpe, Christina. *In the Wake: On Blackness and Being*. Durham: Duke University Press, 2016.

Shilliam, Robbie. "Behind the Rhodes Statue: Black Competency and the Imperial Academy." *History of the Human Sciences* 32, no. 5 (2019): 3–27.

Shirbon, Estelle. "Oxford College Says It Wants to Remove Statue of Colonialist Rhodes," *Reuters*, 17 June 2020, accessed 7 December 2020, https://uk.reuters.com/article/uk-britain-statues-rhodes/oxford-college-says-it-wants-to-remove-statue-of-colonialist-rhodes-idUKKBN23O3B1.

"Should Looted Colonial Art be Returned?" *The Art Newspaper*, 14 December 2018, accessed 7 December 2020, https://www.theartnewspaper.com/podcast/should-looted-african-art-be-returned.

Smith, Victoria Ellen. "Secrets of West African Slave Ancestry: Fante Strategies of Silence and the Didactic Narrative in Ghanaian Literature." *Journal of West African History* 2, no. 2 (2016): 109–131.

Stanley, Liz. *Mourning Becomes…: Post/memory and Commemoration of the Concentration Camps of the South African War 1899–1902*. Manchester: Manchester University Press, 2006.

Stewart, Jodie. "History by Doing: Reclaiming Indigenous Women's Sovereignty through Embodied History." *Lilith: A Feminist History Journal* 25 (2019): 93–106.

Swart, Mia. "Name Change as Symbolic Reparation after Transition: The Example of Germany and South Africa." *German Law Journal* 9, no. 2 (2008): 105–121.

Teeter, Emily. "Religion and Ritual." In *A Companion to Ancient Egyptian Art*, edited by Melinda Hartwig, 328–343. Chichester, UK: John Wiley & Sons Ltd., 2015.

Trouillot, Michel-Rolph. *Silencing the Past: Power and the Production of History*. Boston, MA: Beacon Press Books, 1995.

Upton, Dell. *What Can and Can't be Said: Race, Uplift and Monument Building in the Contemporary South*. New Haven, CT: Yale University Press, 2015.

Van Vollenhoven, Anton. "Dealing with Statues, Monuments and Memorials in South Africa: A Heritage Based Response to Current Controversies." *South African Journal of Cultural History* 29, no. 1 (2015): 7–21.

"What to do with Confederate Monuments: Seven Lessons from Germany," *Washington Post*, 17 August 2017, accessed 5 December 2020, https://www.washingtonpost.com/news/made-by-history/wp/2017/08/17/what-to-do-with-confederate-monuments-seven-lessons-from-germany/.

Wirz, Albert and Jan-Georg Deutsch. "Geschichte in Afrika: Einleitung und Problemaufriß." In *Geschichte in Afrika: Einführung in Probleme und Debatten*, edited by Jan-Georg Deutsch and Albert Wirz, 5–16. Berlin: Verlag Das Arabische Buch, 1997.

I | **Struggles with Heritage & Historicity**

Natacha Filippi
Oral history, Closed Settings and the Formation of Narratives: A South African Example

Abstract: Leading interviews in prison, in a post-colonial and post-authoritarian democracy, raises many questions as to the problematic definition of consent, the power dynamics at play and the shortcomings of oral history. Focusing on two South African closed settings, this chapter investigates the extent to which oral history methodology, when completed with the study of other sources such as rumours, silence and the body, can still prove useful. This is especially true when one wishes to analyse the role of violence in the formation of past and present narrative. A brief comparative study of prisons transformed into heritage sites worldwide helps understand the gap between prisoners' collective memory and the official memory of post-authoritarian democracies, and how they tend to return prisoners' voices to the silenced margins of society.

When I first began to visit Pollsmoor Prison in 2005, I was taken aback by the intensity of a collective memory, at the time unknown to me, that seemed to flow from the walls, echo in the corridors and was passed down by even the youngest inmates. Pollsmoor Prison is located some 13 miles southwest of Cape Town, in the South African Cape Peninsula. As I came to learn from research in this setting that I conducted over several years, the very location and architecture of the prison represented a point of intersection between official history and collective memory, between silenced voices and deafening rumours, and between violence, legitimacy and the construction of narratives. In 2010, Jan-Georg Deutsch, who supervised my doctoral thesis, came to Cape Town. We first went to stand outside the Maximum Security Section of Valkenberg Psychiatric Hospital. We then drove to Pollsmoor Prison. Jan-Georg Deutsch was one of Oxford's fiercest advocates for the use of oral history in the study of post-colonial African settings. As we stood outside the prison, we could hear shouts and sounds coming from the buildings whose entrance board read: "Welcome to Pollsmoor Correctional Services – 'a Place of New Beginnings.'"

Now that my memory of Jan-Georg Deutsch has joined the blurred space between grief and commemoration, I write these lines keeping in mind his conversations and comments, and how they shaped my understanding of the usefulness and shortcomings of oral history in any realm of inquiry.[1] The debate over the use of oral history and its link to the construction of social memory has remained very much alive since the publication of Maurice Halbwachs's pathbreaking *Les cadres sociaux de la mémoire* in 1925.[2] Since its emergence, oral history has militated against the idea of presenting a linear and uniform historical narrative. Paul Thompson's call for a "complex and multi-voiced chronicle" led historians to search for the voices of the many absentees: first the working-class, then, through the development of feminist and subaltern studies, women and colonial subjects.[3] It soon became clear, however, that behind the quest to retrieve the experience of subjects "hidden from history" lay a series of illusions and paradoxes that threatened the validity of narratives based on oral history techniques.[4]

In the 2000s, new studies advanced the notion that in order to reframe the field of oral history, historians should analyse and reflect on how oral testimonies meshed with the construction of collective memory. Works like Jennifer Cole's *Forget Colonialism? Sacrifice and the Art of Memory in Madagascar* highlighted the importance of studying silence in order to understand the definition of social identities.[5] Her study of a Madagascan village is frequently mentioned as an excellent example of memories as "palimpsests" constituted of different layers, surfacing at specific moments, and otherwise remaining unarticulated.[6] Analysing the silences in memory does not mean, however, that colonial practices of domination and resistance are necessarily inscribed in postcolonial memories and are merely awaiting their "rediscovery" by anthropologists and historians. Ann Laura Stoler and Karen Strassler observe that this idea assumes the

---

1 On the blurred frontier between private and public forms of mourning, between grief and commemoration, see Francis Baker, *The Culture of Violence: Essays on Tragedy and History* (Chicago: University of Chicago Press, 1993).
2 Maurice Halbwachs, *Les Cadres Sociaux de la Mémoire* (Paris: Alcan, 1925).
3 Paul Thompson, "The Voice of the Past: Oral History," extracted from Paul Thompson, *The Voice of the Past: Oral History* (Oxford: Oxford University Press, 1988), in *The Oral History Reader*, ed. Robert Perks and Alistair Thomson (London: Routledge, 1998), 25–31; Gayatri Spivak, "Can the Subaltern Speak?" in *Marxism and the Interpretation of Culture*, ed. Lawrence Grossberg and Cary Nelson (Urbana: University of Illinois Press, 1988), 217–313.
4 See Rowbotham's history of women's social condition: Sheila Rowbotham, *Hidden from History* (London: Pluto Press, 1977).
5 Jennifer Cole, *Forget Colonialism? Sacrifice and the Art of Memory in Madagascar* (Berkeley: University of California Press, 2001).
6 Ibid, 17.

necessary "production of a narrative and the prevalence of telling."[7] Silences do not equate to forgetting but reveal the limitations of orality. This perspective challenges oral history projects when restricted to the collection of testimonies through interviews, even when they attempt to understand the reasons for this wordlessness.

In addition, other sources persist, beyond written archives or formal oral testimonies. Architecture, objects, rumours, gossip and bodily practices can be indicative of colonial memories. In a setting like Pollsmoor Prison, silence, as well as rumours, tattoos, the organisation of space, and changing logos form the landscapes on which memory is inscribed and conveyed. It is particularly relevant to bear this idea in mind when studying contexts wherein historical actors have remained voiceless and where violence has constituted a main feature of individual action, collective mobilisation and social memory.[8]

The investigation of violent events as part of an oral history project raises several ethical questions and methodological issues.[9] When one visits an archive, reading manuscripts alongside other people undertaking historical investigation, it might be easier to forget the distance that separates the researcher from his/her subject of research. In contrast, the gap between the social background of the interviewer and her interviewee is often far more striking. The results of my research cannot be understood without taking into account that I conducted interviews as a white, young, female and foreign researcher while most of my interviewees were black or coloured inmates, over forty years old and with limited literacy. As Daphne Patai points out, it is not enough for the historian to prove this self-reflexivity by engaging "in merely rhetorical manoeuvres that are rapidly acquiring the status of incantations" by adopting the popular strategy of "'situating' oneself by prior announcement."[10] In a prison setting, the heavy presence of violence, silence and trauma in the construction of

---

[7] Ann L. Stoler, with Karen Strassler, "Memory Work in Java. A Cautionary Tale," in *Carnal Knowledge and Imperial Power: Race and the Intimate in Colonial Rule*, ed. Ann L. Stoler (Berkeley: University of California Press, 2002), 283–309.
[8] The term 'subjectivity' that I use in this chapter refers to the process of political subjectivation necessary to the existence of 'politics', as developed by Jacques Rancière. See Jacques Rancière, *La Mésentente. Politique et Philosophie* (Paris: Galilée, 1995).
[9] I began to explore this theme in Natacha Filippi, "Institutional Violence and the Law in South Africa," *Journal of Colonialism and Colonial History* 17, 3 (2016), accessed 18 December 2020, doi:10.1353/cch.2016.0038.
[10] Daphne Patai, "U.S. Academics and Third World Women: Is Ethical Research Possible?" in *Women's Words: the Feminist Practice of Oral History*, ed. Sherna B. Gluck and Daphne Patai (New York: Routledge, 1991), 137–153.

autobiographies and collective memories reinforces these issues. They also offer a starting point to question the role of violence in the formation of past and present narratives.[11]

In this study, I investigate the interaction between violence, silence, forgetting and legitimacy at two different levels. On one hand, the construction of social memory inside Pollsmoor Prison highlights the role that violence played, especially in its collective manifestations. On the other hand, after the South African democratic transition from 1990 to 1994, the history of prisons at a national level was fashioned to facilitate the emergence of an official historical discourse that made no mention of certain aspects of the collective memory that persisted within each site of confinement. Both the specificities of the South African context and the extent to which a comparison with other contexts marked by either the experience of an authoritarian regime or by colonialism will be taken into account.

This work concentrates on two settings: Pollsmoor prison and the maximum-security section of a psychiatric hospital in South Africa. It focuses on the period from the second half of apartheid to the democratic transition, but also draws conclusions from research I am leading on the links between memory and prison in the context of other democratic transitions. Written sources include a variety of documents such as letters smuggled out by prisoners, letters sent to organisations of support, commissions of inquiry, trials, department circulars, newspaper clippings, Amnesty International reports and government statistics.[12] In order to contrast with and expand beyond these written sources, I led more than 40 interviews with prisoners, former inmates (both common-law and political), judges, lawyers, psychologists and psychiatrists. Disparate sources such as body marks and tattoos, symbols and architecture complement these oral and written materials.

This chapter first focuses on the ambivalence of oral history as a methodology that wavers between building bridges that connect different realities and temporalities on one side and the illusionary quest for authentic and repressed voices on the other. The analysis then moves to the micro-historical level of Pollsmoor Prison, exploring the specificities of this context in relation to oral history and the construction of social memory. The last section will consider how official historical discourses developed from the South African democratic transition on-

---

11 For a gripping testimony on the impact of violence on the formation of memory, see Pumla Gobodo-Madikizela, *A Human Being Died that Night: A South African Women Confronts the Legacy of Apartheid* (New York: Mariner Books, 2004).
12 For a deconstruction of commissions of inquiry and government reports, see Anne L. Stoler, "Colonial Archives and the Arts of Governance," *Archival Science* 2 (2002): 87–109.

wards elevated the prison institution as an ideal symbol of a new human rights–based democracy supposedly reflective of a sharp break with a repressive past.

Oral History in Closed Settings: Issues of Consent and Authenticity

The desire to overcome the bias of written sources and access the authentic, original voices of Africa was particularly prominent in the oral tradition school led by Jan Vansina. In *Oral Tradition as History*, he developed a methodology that aimed to recover the tradition of precolonial Africa through the precise analysis of collected oral narratives.[13] His techniques, taken up by many scholars, assumed the possibility of overriding the impact of the colonial and postcolonial periods on "African voices." Vansina's school can be appreciated for its consideration of multiple oral ways to convey memory, in particular gossip, tales, proverbs and poems. However, its attempts to reach the "true" oral tradition through interviews paradoxically tended to reinforce the myth of "discovering" Africa and the illusionary objectivity of the historian's sources, whether written or oral.[14]

Oral tradition exemplifies how the mere fact of contesting the supremacy of written primary material may not challenge dominant historiographical trends per se. As recent studies have observed, one of the most important drawbacks of oral history can be the quest for genuine African, or women, or subaltern voices.[15] This quest can be explained by the necessity to break with the idea of oral sources as "a spontaneous uncontrollable mass of fluid, amorphous material," and to reassert the authority of the historical knowledge produced in the academic realm.[16] The tendency to romanticise these "original" voices has led to two trends, one establishing a new essentialism denying the influence of any hegemonic mechanisms on the emergence of these voices, the other reinforcing the

---

[13] Jan Vansina, *Oral Tradition as History* (Madison: University of Wisconsin Press, 1985).
[14] David W. Cohen, Stephan F. Miescher, and Luise White, "Introduction: Voices, Words, and African History," *African Words, African Voices, Critical Practices in Oral History* (Bloomington: Indiana University Press, 2001), 14; Abdullahi A. Ibrahim, "The Birth of the Interview: The Thin and the Fat of It," in Cohen, Miescher and White, *African Words, African Voices*, 103–124.
[15] For an extensive critical review of the limitations of oral history projects, see Cohen, Miescher and White, *African Words, African Voices*.
[16] Alessandro Portelli, "What Makes Oral History Different?" in Perks and Thomson, *The Oral History Reader*, 33.

illusion according to which power dynamics can be overcome by the methods of oral history.[17]

While feminist historians played a crucial role in the emergence of oral history as a new field of research, they also contributed to its constitution as a "privileged" way to retrieve African voices. The myth of universal sisterhood was used as a tool to legitimise the erasure of any notion of difference between the female narrator and the female researcher.[18] Confronted by the reality of leading interviews and by a range of harsh criticisms originating in different disciplines and opinions, this argument was, however, rapidly discarded. Many feminist researchers decided to abandon easy dichotomies and shift the attention to contested "grey areas."[19] By focusing on the fine balance between the necessity to challenge binarisms and the tendency to reify the "Other," they moved on to other controversies, including the power relationships inherent to oral history.

Despite these cautions, oral history can provide a bridge between different spaces, temporalities, and realities. According to Alessandro Portelli, "oral history is a work of relationships; in the first place, a relationship between the past and the present; then, a relationship between the interviewer and the interviewee, and between the oral form of the narrative and the written or audiovisual form of the historian's product." Even more interesting is how he describes the emergence of memory in oral history methodology: "In oral history, in fact, we do not simply reconstruct the history of an event but also the history of its memory, the ways in which it grows, changes, and operated in the time between then and now."[20]

It is exactly in the ways that memory is constructed and constantly redefined that oral history projects in prisons prove to be useful. Prisoners' voices only emerge at occasional moments in the written archives of a prison. If archives can be considered as "a set of discursive rules," the power relations inscribed in Pollsmoor Prison did not act in favour of the representation of prisoners' sub-

---

[17] Jeffrey K. Olick and Joyce Robbins, "Social Memory Studies: From 'Collective Memory' to the Historical Sociology of Mnemonic Practices," *Annual Review of Sociology* 24 (1998): 105–140; Megan Vaughan, "Reported Speech and Other Kinds of Testimony," in Cohen, Miescher and White, *African Words, African Voices*, 65; Alison Baker, *Voices of Resistance, an Oral History of Moroccan Women* (Albany: State University of New York Press, 1998).
[18] Sylvie Vandecasteele-Schweitzer and Danièle Voldman, "The Oral Sources for Women's History," in *Writing Women's History*, ed. Michelle Perrot (Oxford: Blackwell Publishers, 1992), 41–50.
[19] Michelle Perrot, "Introduction," *Writing Women's History*, 7.
[20] Alessandro Portelli, "What Makes Oral History Different," in *Oral History, Oral Culture, and Italian Americans*, ed. Luisa Giudice (New York: Palgrave Macmillan, 2009), 21–30.

jectivity.[21] The only instances when their voices do appear is under the form of a written complaint against the administration or a fellow inmate addressed to senior officers or to the commissioner, or under the form of an affidavit related to an offence committed on the prison grounds. While working on these archives, it soon became evident that prisoners who did not know how to write asked the help of a fellow prisoner or a social worker in order to put his/her requests on paper. This implied two translations: a first rephrasing of one's thoughts forced by the necessary adaptation to the rules set forth by the prison administration, and a second translation by the person actually writing the letter. In the Pollsmoor archives, the invisibility of female prisoners was even more striking, and could not merely be explained by the small percentage of women in the prison population. In 1989, just before the beginning of the democratic transition, female prisoners represented a mere 3.5 percent of the prison population, though the rate had reached 6.55 percent in 1977.[22] Most archive files related to Pollsmoor Women's Prison were practically empty.

Non-censored prisoners' letters can be found in the records of organisations of support such as the Black Sash, the South African Prisoners' Organisation for Human Rights, the Detention Resource Centre Archive or the Cape Town Legal Resources Centre. These letters, smuggled out throughout the apartheid period, are now scattered throughout different South African archives and represent a rich addition to the letters conserved in the Pollsmoor archives. Interviews inside and outside prison during late apartheid and the democratic transition produced a narrative that came to fill a great number of gaps left by the written sources.

If the interviews I conducted outside the prison with former prisoners, psychiatrists, psychologists, lawyers and judges related to the general ethical problem of leading interviews in a post-colonial country, conducting them on prison grounds raised different issues. At Pollsmoor, language was definitely an issue, as the interviews were conducted in English, which was not the mother tongue of most black and coloured inmates. Gaining their consent to interview raised other concerns. A small number of studies, mostly from a criminology perspective, have tackled the specific problem of consent in oral history projects taking place in closed settings.[23] Despite the information they provide on the legal

---

21 Stoler, "Colonial Archives."
22 Government Publications, University of Cape Town (GP, UCT), Annual Reports of the Commissioner of Prisons, 1976–1977 & 1989–1990.
23 See, for instance, Jennifer A. Schlosser, "Issues in Interviewing Inmates. Navigating the Methodological Landmines of Prison Research," *Qualitative Inquiry* 14, no. 8 (2008): 1500– 1525; James B. Waldram, "Anthropology in Prison: Negotiating Consent and Accountability with a 'Captured Population,'" *Human Organization* 57, no. 2 (1998): 238–244.

framework of these interviews and the difficulties encountered in closed settings across the world, these studies often fail to provide a meaningful explanation of the dynamics between consent, silence, the damage left by the experience of violence – as either victim or perpetrator – and the definition of historical subjectivity.

This specific configuration would have been ever more striking in the context of Valkenberg Psychiatric Hospital. One of the shortcomings of the research I undertook in South Africa was my inability to interview current and former psychiatric patients. In the first case, Valkenberg psychiatrists dismissed the very idea of such a possibility. In the second case, the memory of this experience of confinement seems to have been too painful and stigmatising to permit conversation about it. Even if I had been allowed to conduct interviews within Valkenberg, the impossibility of agreement on what constituted "official consent" in this medicalised context would have constrained the research. Indeed, the few archived letters by Valkenberg patients highlight the annihilation of subjectivity that took place on the hospital grounds. Once individuals entered the hospital and became patients, whether voluntarily or not, the on-going medical diagnosis deprived their voice of legitimacy. Their status as a Valkenberg convalescent reduced each phrase, each request, and each complaint to a mere symptom of mental illness. The letters that patients sent to police commissioners or judges and that passed through the authorities' censorship often bore comments in the margins from the head psychiatrist.[24] The only legitimate voice in the highly hierarchical Valkenberg was, indeed, that of the psychiatrist.[25] Not even the nurses or the psychologists who worked there were entitled to elaborate a discourse based on "truth" and "reason." The collective memory that perpetuated itself within the psychiatric hospital's walls was characterised by overwhelming acts of silencing: silencing of patients' subjectivity, of the violence and mistreatment to which they were subjected, of the margins of manoeuvre and small acts of resistance or collaboration they manage to create, and of the possible collective mobilisations that took place in the hospital.[26]

Returning to the issue of consent in prison settings, the general idea of a "contract" tying together the interviewer and the interviewee, including clauses on anonymity and confidentiality, raises several problems. Students and re-

---

[24] Cape Town Archive Repository (CTAR), HVG, 2/1/1. Secretary for the Interior to Valkenberg, 7 November 1932.
[25] Michel Foucault, *Histoire de la folie à l'âge classique* (Paris: Gallimard, 1972), 616 & 623.
[26] While newspaper clippings attest the existence of such mobilisations in rare occasions, there is no trace of these events in the archives. *Cape Times*, 18 February 1992; Interview, Mr. Colman, forensic psychiatrist at Valkenberg, Cape Town, 10 December 2010.

searchers who engage in oral history projects are often provided with or construct for themselves an interview consent form. Once signed, this document is intended to prove the interviewee's willingness to participate in the project. Consent forms are variable, depending on the nature of the information collected and on its future use. The idea of a contract at the core of the definition of consent in oral history assumes that the two parties are "competent," i.e. able to act autonomously.[27] Although the problematic of informed consent and the power relationships it covers underly most oral history projects, in closed institutions this problematic becomes exacerbated. Prisons, reformatories or asylums all create circumstances where the oral historian will struggle to analyse how genuine her interlocutors' consent can be. This is reinforced when one considers the difficulty of speaking about "consent" when non-reciprocity characterises the relationship between the two parties.[28]

Hence, in addition to potentially sensitive, stigmatising and dangerous elements communicated to the researcher, often causing uneasiness, the confined interviewee is in a position where both the researcher and his/her custodians may summon the individual to speak.[29] Although the interviewee might find in the oral history project a freer space to speak and an opportunity to break with the silence that otherwise encloses his/her situation, a fine line divides the will to speak from the obligation, imposed by his/her social surroundings, to engage the researcher.

Within Pollsmoor Prison, I undertook interviews at different moments during my doctoral fieldwork, speaking with long-term prisoners and repeat offenders who had been incarcerated during the late apartheid period or the democratic transition. I began research in the Medium B Prison, then moved to the Maximum Security Section, and finally worked in the Women's Prison. Indeed Pollsmoor, like many other South African prisons, includes a female wing in its buildings. In none of these prisons did I have the chance to speak directly to a collective of prisoners first in order to explain my research project and ask who would be willing to join. I could only describe my project to the head of the particular prison. That person would then assign to a warder the specific task of recruiting inmates for the interviews. I waited in a small room in the area of the senior staff's offices while the warder surveyed the section. The room was

---

27 Joseph Rommey, "Legal Considerations in Oral History," *The Oral History Review* 1 (1973): 69.
28 Patai, "U.S. Academics," 141.
29 Boschma, Yonge and Mychajlunow have extensively described the strain endured by nurses recalling their experiences in mental hospitals. See Geertje Boschma, Olive Yonge and Lorraine Mychajlunow, "Consent in Oral History Interviews: Unique Challenges," *Qualitative Health Research* 13, no. 1 (2003): 129–135.

furnished with a table and two chairs. Each time the warder arrived with an inmate, I explained to the latter the goal of the interview and asked if he/she would indeed consent to speak about his/her past experiences in the prison. Congruent with the idea that interviews within prisons represent at least a small break, a digression in the monotony of everyday life, at that point the inmate invariably agreed to participate. In only one instance, the interview lasted a mere 15 minutes, as the female prisoner who remained standing in front of me had obviously no desire to answer my questions. Warders in general seemed little interested in being interviewed, though some did speak expressively. While conducting oral history in Pollsmoor, I was therefore unable to appraise the degree of consent given by the warders and prisoners I interviewed or whether any potential participants were denied the right to speak. Each interview revealed the difficulty of determining where exactly agency lay in a prison environment, while reinforcing John Lonsdale's argument of the close links between agency, oral history, and memory, particularly in the context of African history projects.[30]

Establishing trust in this environment was an arduous, if not impossible, task. I attempted to make the most of every small margin for manoeuvre. One of the most effective actions was to close the door before beginning the interview. Prison administrators advised against this but it was essential to converse meaningfully in a closed environment otherwise filled with the sounds of gates, keys, metallic noises and shouts. What ethical position should the historian adopt in such circumstances? Most researchers are confronted with a dilemma as soon as they enter a prison, between complying with the prevailing rules – once they have understood their implicit and changing character – and conducting research regulated by the prison authorities, or attempting to skirt the rules, with the danger of disrupting the social setting and having to end the project prematurely. In her work on collaborative oral history in the context of Brown Creek Correctional Institution in the United States, Alicia Rouverol explains how she managed to find an intermediate solution by respecting certain directives while altering others according to what she gauged would best facilitate her research.[31]

Reciprocity in such contexts presents another intricate issue. The oral historian, attempting to "recover" the voices of the marginalised, might raise narrators' expectations in the form of recognition of their personal historical signifi-

---

[30] John Lonsdale, "Agency in Tight Corners: Narrative and Initiative in African History," *Journal of African Cultural Studies*, 13, no. 1 (2000): 5–16.
[31] Alicia J. Rouverol, "Collaborative Oral History in a Correctional Setting: Promise and Pitfalls," *Oral History Review* 30, no. 1 (2003): 61–85.

cance or improvement in their conditions of prison life.[32] The illusion of reciprocity thus created might increase narrators' motivation to participate in the project and will most likely end in deception. These difficulties should not, however, be interpreted as an incitement to silence these marginalised voices. The interpretation of sources, from written documents and oral testimonies to inscriptions on prison architecture and the body, enables the interviewer to retrace narratives where violence, silence, resistance and subjectivity are intertwined. These narratives are the basis of a collective memory that is conveyed, generation after generation, in Pollsmoor Prison.

A Confined Collective Memory

One of the ethical issues that arises when undertaking interviews with prisoners, warders, policemen, freedom fighters and other individuals who have been victim of violence or have perpetrated violence is how to approach the often still traumatic event. Even if the researcher is careful not to ask any direct question about her interlocutor's personal experience of violence, when the latter does emerge in an interview, it is essential to let the conversation flow, leaving the interviewee to reconstruct their personal narrative. Sometimes the interviewee chooses to avoid the event at the last moment. At other times, the narrator decides to describe the event, inducing a potentially intense remembrance. During the interviews that I conducted with inmates in Pollsmoor, interviewees who described situations of physical violence mainly referred to police and warders' acts of brutality, solitary confinement, inmate fights and sexual assaults. Evocations of structural and psychological violence generally dotted the narratives in more diffuse ways.

The interviewee's circumspections are subsequently reflected in and reinforced by the historian's narrative choices. How can one describe and analyse other people's personal memories of violence without reproducing this very violence?[33] To which extent is it possible to explore the dynamics of silence and amnesia in the construction of individual and collective memory? In *El Vano Ayer*, Isaac Rosa questions the possibility of writing a novel about the Francoist dictatorship without using a series of stereotypically narrative tricks common to most

---

32 Belinda Bozzoli, "Interviewing the Women of Phokeng," extracted from Belinda Lozzoli, with Mmantho Nkotsoe, *Women of Phokeng, Life Strategy and Migrancy in South Africa, 1900–1983* (London: Heinemann, 1991) in Perks and Thomson, *The Oral History Reader*, 159.
33 Susan Sontag, *Regarding the Pain of Others* (London: Penguin, 2004).

Spanish texts on the period.[34] He devotes several chapters to the phenomenon of torture. Describing imaginary cases of torture in the Madrid headquarters of the security police (*Dirección General de Seguridad*), Rosa shifts between narrating voices – a male student, a female student, an anarchist, and a handbook of torture addressed to policemen – and styles, from allusive accounts to extremely detailed description to ironic representation as staged pain and repression. One of his characters, in the midst of having his fingers broken one after the next by the Francoist police of the late 1960s, asserts that it is useless to attempt to convey the experience of pain. Only in-depth research on the historical practice of torture can make up for this impossibility:

> Because speaking of torture using generalities is like saying nothing; when one says that under Francoism people were tortured, it is fundamental to describe the ways people were tortured, the patterns, the methods, the intensity; because not doing so means disregarding the real suffering; it is not possible to dismiss the question with general assertions like "torture was a common practice" or "thousands of men and women were tortured"; this amounts to saying nothing, to awarding impunities; it is imperative to collect testimonies, to specify the methods of torture, so that it will not have been in vain.[35]

The role of the historian might consist in rescuing the most detailed accounts of violence, as different actors involved in the maintenance or undermining of authoritarian regimes perpetuated it. However, as contexts like South Africa and Spain show in different ways, to *forget* traumatic events is an essential feature of collective memory. Forgetting is often linked to the muffling of voices that threaten the coherence of official historical discourses, yet sometimes it can be a necessary means to deal with the memory of trauma and loss.[36] There is, indeed, a fine line between a silence that is imposed from outside and a silence that is crucial for one's own reconstruction and mental health. These considerations often confront oral history projects that relate to violence, requiring the historian to carefully navigate between them. The main idea is to avoid both the re-enactment of violence and the reproduction of the official silencing of marginalised voices.

During my interviews at Pollsmoor Prison, I witnessed different ways of dealing with the memory of violence. Each of these approaches was a telling ex-

---

34 Isaac Rosa, *El Vano Ayer* (Barcelona: Seix Barral, 2012).
35 Ibid, 156. Author's translation.
36 Dario Paez, Nekane Basabe and Jose Luis Gonzalez, "Social Processes and Collective Memory: A Cross-Cultural Approach to Remembering Political Events," *Collective Memory of Political Events: Social Psychological Perspectives*, ed. James W. Pennebaker, Diario Paez and Bernard Rim (Mahwah, NJ: Lawrence Erlbaum Associates, 1997), 147–174.

ample as to the difficulties of coping with the memory of illegal, unsettling and disruptive life events. Generally, some slight differences emerged between the accounts of violence presented by male and female prisoners to a female researcher. Both male and female inmates talked quite openly about everyday assaults by warders as well as more exceptional tactics of repression, sometimes headed by the emergency task force, that took place during the second half of apartheid and during the democratic transition. Many men spoke about the way they became involved in violence against warders and fellow inmates. Sexual assaults were alluded to but not described, and certainly not as a first-person account. Women, in contrast, suggested the possibility of inmate fights but could, at times, give precise details about intimate relationships, gender performances and sexual abuses. In one case, a female prisoner narrated how she was raped on her first day of confinement, an event that still remains a vivid memory for her: "This is a day that I will never really forget. It was the most scary day of my life. I think it was the first time reality really came down on me. [...] You know this was a long time ago! And I never really talked about it because I never wanted to relive that evening."[37] Despite this assertion she seems to have felt the need to break her silence around the traumatic event. Indeed, the precise account of abuse was the answer she offered to the standard question on her first day in prison.

Interviews with warders also shed light on distinct ways of remembering – and accepting – the use of repressive violence. Some warders framed past measures as legitimate, pondered and measured actions. They saw it not as repression but principled discipline. The disappearance of "law and order" measures explained the chaos they thought prevailed in present-day prisons. Other warders, representing a new post-apartheid generation, criticised the former methods but still legitimised them through an "other era – hierarchical orders" argument. One of the most disturbing themes for warders seems to have been the memory of the Police and Prisons Civil Rights Union (POPCRU). Each time I broached the subject of POPCRU at Pollsmoor Prison and the affiliation of warders to the trade union, the warders expressed embarrassment or fear. Only a few declared themselves to have been directly and proudly involved in the union, which was illegally funded in 1989 and formally authorised in 1994. Warders alluded to the authorities' violence in vague terms. They spoke more freely about inmate violence, such as the staff member who recalled how he used to collect "dead inmates that were murdered, during the night maybe."[38]

---

37 Interview, Mrs. Tillis, Pollsmoor Women Prison, 30 March 2011
38 Interview, Mr. Hillier, head of section, Pollsmoor Medium B Prison, 26 February 2008.

In this context, one interview stood out. One of the youngest warders I interviewed began work at Pollsmoor in 1993, the year before widespread inmate revolts shook South African prisons. He narrated the pacification of a unit in the Maximum Security Section, the D2 Unit, in the following terms:

> After this incident, in D2 unit, nobody wanted to work there, because the inmates were stressed out, they were ready to fight anything, they were just doing the opposite they had to do. And of the whole total of 400 members working there, no one wanted to work there. Big or strong, small or weak, black, white, nobody wanted to go there. I can promise you, I can remember that, the 22nd of September, I was so sick of that, watching every morning the head of prison must beg for people to go and work in that unit, to open the unit, to give the people food, and nobody wanted to go. He was begging everyone. No sir, no sir, it's dangerous, I'm not going to put my life in danger. You know, that morning, I said no man, we are warders, inmates can't control our prison, I said that to myself. And I go to the head of prison and say listen, if you give me 5 minutes, to talk to guys I knew, if those guys say yes I'm going with you to that unit, your problem is solved. I talked to three of my friends, telling them I want to go to D2, and I want to take that unit back from the inmates. Are you willing to go with me. And all three said : Mr. ..., with you I'll go to war. [...] We opened up that unit that morning, and for a month we worked. Every morning everything was bloody when you came in. It was just a matter of: it's you or me. The inmates are rude, they were trying to stab us, they were trying to kill us, but we beat them, we beat them in every way, because we were committed. If one goes in, everybody goes in. Same in every cell. Six months later, you didn't even hear about D2. There was discipline. Before no members wanted to walk through the section, even when the doors were locked. Now everybody, even the head of prison is walking through the unit.[39]

Although this warder did not describe in detail the way he "disciplined" the inmates, he clearly portrayed the intensity of the violence used during this conflict. This uncommon testimony ended with yet another surprising comment for an interview that took place on prison grounds:

> Today I am sick of the prison. We live like with a split personality. If I come home in the afternoon, I wash my face, I wash my hands. It takes 5 minutes to realise: you're at home now. You're not at the prison. You must be a father now, you must be a husband, you must chill now. This place really makes you sick.[40]

Speaking with male and female prisoners and with warders of different generations revealed the existence of multiple approaches to the memory of violence. While interviews with former prisoners and warders conducted outside Pollsmoor retraced such memories with a distant gaze, interviews that took place

---

[39] Interview, Mr. Jacobs, warder, Pollsmoor Medium B Prison, 25 February 2008.
[40] Ibid.

within the prison walls evoked violence as a continued phenomenon that marked the past as much as the present. The inscription of memory on the prisoners' bodies and other "social surfaces and cultural landscapes" also reinforced the blurring between past and present brutality.[41]

Analysing different manifestations of collective memory – on the body as well as on the uniforms and the buildings – provides crucial elements to overcome the shortcomings of this kind of oral history project. The existence, within Pollsmoor and every South African prison, of powerful gangs, some of them dating back to the end of the nineteenth century, has helped to maintain alternative historical narratives of resistance and political agency. Though some gangs, like the Big Fives, based their actions on a systematic collaboration with the administration, the majority of gangs were formed to resist the anomie and brutality of prison life.[42] The Number, formed by three "brother" gangs, the 26's, 27's and 28's, was particularly leading during apartheid and up to the democratic transition. As studied by Charles Von Onselen, the gang first emerged in the 1980s in the Rand region as a group of bandits who refused to work in the mines.[43] After their leader was incarcerated, the gangs only survived in prison, where they strove and developed emblems, tattoos and symbols that permitted the visualisation of their structure. They linked these symbols to determined military ranks and completed this visual language with a spoken one, called *sabela*.

This organisation, based on a *mimicry*[44] of the late nineteenth-century colonial army and penal system, based its internal discipline on a violent judicial system. The gang shared many features with other structures whose illegality and use of violence placed them on the blurred frontier between "criminal" and "freedom fighter." In his investigation of the Irish Republican paramilitary organisations, Allen Feldman portrays how "the vernacular depiction of history and the mobilization of popular memory inform and structure political agency" and how "violent acts on the body," especially as a consequence of an internal

---

41 Allen Feldman, "Political Terror and the Technologies of Memory: Excuse, Sacrifice, Commodification, and Actuarial Moralities," *Radical History Review* 85 (2003): 62.
42 History Papers, Witwatersrand (HPW), AG3012. "Prison Gangs, Western Cape," Confidential report by the Intelligence Coordination, 1991; Jonny Steinberg, *The Number. One Man's Search for Identity in the Cape Underworld and Prison Gangs* (Cape Town: Jonathan Ball, 2004).
43 Charles Van Onselen, *The Small Matter of a Horse: The Life of "Nongoloza" Mathebula, 1867–1948* (Johannesburg: Ravan Press, 1984).
44 Homi Bhabha, "Of Mimicry and Man: The Ambivalence of Colonial Discourse," *October* 28 (1984), reprinted in Homi Bhabha, *The Location of Culture* (New York: Routledge, 1994, 85–92.

disciplinary code, "constituted a material vehicle for constructing memory and embedding the self in social and institutional memory."[45]

In Pollsmoor, tattoos constituted a visible part of a mythological organisation based on diverse symbols, including flags and military ranks. Tattoos of specific images such as sabres, dice, crowns and poison reflected one's belonging to a specific gang, while other elements, like stars and glasses, indicated the member's rank. The practice was gendered, in that tattoos were not as widespread in the Women's Prison. In the male sections, memory, subjectivity and identity were tied together on the decorated bodies of the prisoners. Tattoos reflected a memory practice and offered a proof of agency, an ultimate power that resided in the ability to hide or exhibit one's personal and collective history.[46] In a closed environment characterised by anomie and the near impossibility of self-determination, modifying one's body was a way to regain some control. Beyond this, tattoos, alongside the rehearsed history of and rumours about the machinations of the Number, enabled the materialisation of a collective memory otherwise silenced by an official historical discourse that featured a supposedly strict rupture between prisons during the apartheid regime and their new purpose under a democracy.

Prisons, Heritage Sites and Official Memory

During the first years of the South African democratic transition, prisons across the country witnessed an increasing number of protests, individual and collective hunger strikes, work strikes and refusals to return to the cells. Prisoners clamoured for amnesty, remissions of sentences and improved conditions inside the prison. Tension escalated in 1994 ahead of the first democratic elections of the country when the right to vote was restricted to very select categories of prisoners.[47] A first wave of revolts shook the country's prisons in March and April of 1994. Prisoners set fire to their cells, risking their lives to catch the attention of those beyond their prisons' walls. Inmates tore down buildings, coordinated a series of collective strikes, wrote letters to a series of organisations explaining their point of view, and fought against warders and fellow inmates to create "shocking news" that would reach the newspapers. Eventually, on 25 April,

---

45 Feldman, "Political Terror," 60.
46 I wish to thank Heike Schmidt for her precious comments on the links between tattoos, agency and memory.
47 HPW, A2084. Department of Correctional Services to the Independent Electoral Commission, 1 February 1994.

the Independent Electoral Commission and the political parties involved in the transition negotiations extended the franchise to the majority of categories of prisoner and allowed these inmates to vote on 26 April, one day before the rest of society.[48]

Protest movements continued, emboldened by the initial success. When the new Government of National Unity, presided by African National Congress (ANC) leader Nelson Mandela, did not grant a general amnesty, these movements became large-scale revolts in June 1994. Deaths, injuries and damage to buildings increased. The newly-elected post-apartheid government answered the protests with fierce repression.[49] A task force restored law and order in prisons by all means available, and the government granted a general six-month reduction of sentence to all prisoners. The democratic transition was complete. Prisons were expected to return to the silenced margins of society while an official historical discourse portrayed prisons as necessary 'correctional centers' that could be reformed and could constitute the basis of a liberal South African constitutionalism. Meanwhile, the former repressive regime was assimilated to a specific type of confinement, deriving from the specific racial laws and social inequalities prevailing at the time. In this movement, whole sections of prisoners' collective memory were obliterated, such as the broad basis of resistance movements against the apartheid system, before being arrested, and the relevance of prison resistance, which culminated during the years 1991 to 1994.

The 1994 prison revolts to some extent made public the claims of common-law prisoners. Most political prisoners, with the exception of some members of the Pan Africanist Congress (PAC) involved in attacks during the democratic transition, were released through the amnesty procedures of 1990 and 1991. Common-law prisoners, however, considered that the political parties involved in the transition negotiations failed to take their fights and struggles into account. These inmates claimed that their contribution to the construction of the new South African democracy was crucial and asked for acknowledgement of their specific political participation. Although they were not affiliated to an official anti-apartheid struggle organisation, they asserted that they, too, had suffered from and fought against the apartheid regime.[50]

---

48 Pollsmoor Archives (PA), 1/4/5/14. Department of Correctional Services to all Regional Commissioners, 25 April 1994.
49 Johann Kriegler, *Unrest in Prisons: Final Report of the Commission of Inquiry into Unrest in Prisons Appointed by the President on 27 June 1994* (Pretoria, 1995).
50 South African Historical Archives (SAHA), AL2604. Constitution's proposal by SAPOHR, 1994.

Their argument was three-fold. First, common-law prisoners maintained that they were victims of the apartheid economy and racist laws, which had forced them to turn to illegal activities to survive. Most lacked education, their schooling interrupted by the political events of the late 1970s and 1980s, when the police regularly invaded school grounds and students spearheaded a number of national protest movements.[51] Second, these inmates fought against and endured the abuse, segregation, humiliation and repression enforced by the prison administration on a daily basis. If life in prison could be considered as an exacerbated extension of apartheid, then inmate organisation via gang involvement and conflict with staff members conferred certain legitimacy on them as "freedom fighters."[52] In Pollsmoor, this idea of a legitimate struggle was reinforced by the fact that renowned political prisoners like Nelson Mandela and Walter Sisulu were transferred to an isolated section of the prison during the 1980s. Contact with other political prisoners, held in more accessible cells, induced a transmission of political vocabulary, values and modes of action that influenced common-law prisoners.[53] Third, the protest movements that inmates managed to organise, first from within the prison with the help of the Number and then, during the democratic transition, from beyond its walls with assistance from the South African Prisoners' Organisation for Human Rights (SAPOHR), constituted definitive proof of their shared political relevance.

As with other democratic transitions, common-law prisoners' claim to be considered as *bandiets* – freedom fighters or social prisoners – reached the public sphere, thanks notably to the intensity of the violence employed during the prison revolts and to the fact that outside organisations of support relayed the prisoners' declarations.[54] Yet even though common-law prisoners convinced specific sectors of society of the legitimacy of their claims, this recognition was never sufficiently widespread or lasting to achieve their objectives on a wide scale. In contrast with prisoners who were officially recognised as "political," common-law prisoners' assertion of self and historical trajectory rarely – if ever – became incorporated within official national memory. Soon after the prison revolts ended, the voices of these prisoners lapsed back into silence. For most new democratic regimes, the prison is a place of reform, not of radical question-

---

51 Interview, Mr. Hendricks, prisoner, Pollsmoor Medium B Prison, 28 February 2008.
52 Interview, Mr. Stevens, prisoner, Pollsmoor Medium B Prison, 28 February 2008.
53 Interview, Mr. Khumalo, former PAC prisoner held in Pollsmoor in 1965, Cape Town, 5 April 2011; Letlapa Mphahlele, *Child of this Soil: My Life as a Freedom Fighter* (Cape Town: Kwela Books, 2002).
54 César Lorenzo Rubio, *Cárceles en llamas. El movimiento de presos sociales en la transición* (Barcelona: Virus Editorial, 2013).

ing. In South Africa, there was very little staff renewal in the prison or police services. More generally, the judicial and penal system slowly adapted to the new post-apartheid law. Few were the judges, lawyers and other members of these services who decided, or were forced, to resign.

As Guy Podoler stated in his analysis of a "prison turned memorial site in Seoul," post-colonial or post-dictatorship prison life enters the official historical discourse as a former "facility of colonial oppression" and a new "correctional facility" for the current regime. Typically, Podoler adds, "[t]he thousands of Korean political prisoners incarcerated at Sŏdaemun by post-liberation authoritarian governments have been 'forgotten.'"[55] Take, for instance, the boat trip to the reproduced cells of Robben Island (South Africa), the first guided visits to the now empty Modelo Prison (Spain), the voyeuristic museification of torture at Sŏdaemun (Korea), the tourist cruise to Alcatraz Federal Prison (United States) and the museum Malvinas e Islas del Atlántico Sur built on land pertaining to the former detention centre ESMA (*Escuela de Suboficiales de Mecánica de la Armada*) (Argentina). Despite the significant differences existing between these historical contexts, in all these cases, the transformation of a specific prison into a heritage site speaks more about the construction of an official national memory, rarely benevolent to those considered as "criminal" members of a former regime, than about what really happened behind the walls of these places of confinement. Edward Goodman, in his chapter on the making and re-making of Kenyatta Day, gives an example of "state sanctioned amnesia" contrasting with these museification processes. He retraces how the date when Jomo Kenyatta was imprisoned in 1952 subsequently became a national "Heroes Day" in post-colonial Kenya, unveiling yet another way to build an official prison history to fit a national agenda.[56]

For the case of South Africa, Kelly Gillespie has analysed the transformation of Robben Island into a museum. She studies in particular the discourse on prisons evinced by the new democratic regime. Referring to the years that immediately followed the democratic transition and the work realised by the Truth and Reconciliation Commission (TRC), she outlines that:

> The reconciliatory gestures of this period, while admirable in their attempt to reach beyond legal precedent towards a new national life, cut short serious social and structural engage-

---

[55] Guy Podoler, "The Effect of Japanese Colonial Brutality on Shaping Korean Identity: An Analysis of a Prison Turned Memorial Site in Seoul," in *War and Militarism in Modern Japan. Issues of History and Identity*, ed. Guy Podoler (Kent: Global Oriental Ltd., 2009), 204–205.
[56] See Edward Goodman in this volume.

ment with reconciliation, and in so doing, created a national climate in which criminality could become purified as the marker of a simple brutality, pathology, even barbarism.[57]

One of the official aims of the TRC, established in 1995, was to consider amnesty applications from prisoners. However, by choosing not to take into account the blurred features of many violent actions of protest and accepting only 24 percent of these applications, the TRC lengthened the chasm between political and common-law prisoners.[58] The selection criteria reinforced the discrimination against common-law prisoners, as they rarely had access to the legal help necessary to complete the amnesty application forms. The South African prison revolts of 1994 represented an exceptional moment both in terms of intensity and scale and in terms of visibility for common-law prisoners' assertion of self. During the following years, the combination of state repression, TRC work, transformation of Robben Island into a museum and heavy changes to prison gang hierarchies all conspired once again to silence prisoners' voices.

Conclusion

Oral history projects confront issues of identity, memory and representation. From the early 1920s to the moment when I discovered the debates around this methodology during a workshop on the topic organised by Jan-Georg Deutsch, the growth and development of oral history and memory studies as an approach to historical research continues to present important concerns for Africanist historians. The quest for "authentic" and "marginalised" voices raised questions about essentialism and the reliability of sources, oral and written. The emergence of oral history as a methodology also had repercussions for the controversy over how power shapes a research field, especially in post-colonial countries. It soon became clear that oral testimonies were not any more reliable than government commissions of inquiry and that all sources should be approached critically. Oral history projects could furthermore reinforce the exploitative nature of some interpretations of past events, in some cases because of the radical gap that separated the researcher from her "object" of study. In addition, classic oral history investigations emphasised spoken narratives and had failed

---

57 Kelly Gillespie, "Criminal Abstractions and the Post-Apartheid Prison," (PhD Diss., University of Chicago, 2007).
58 Leigh A. Payne, *Unsettling Accounts: Neither Truth nor Reconciliation in Confessions of State Violence* (Durham and London: Duke University Press, 2008).

to recognise the importance of silence, rumours, bodily inscriptions and other cultural landscapes in the constellation of collective memory.

With these shortcomings in mind, it became possible to address issues specific to research conducted within a closed institution in a country whose history included colonialism and authoritarian forms of governance. In addition to issues stemming from race, age, class and gender categories, consent constituted a significant stumbling block. It proved difficult, if not impossible, in my research to gain valid consent from prisoners. Consent bases itself on free will, and where there is no institutional freedom as in a prison like Pollsmoor, a number of inescapable outcomes hamper effective research. The problematic re-emergence of traumatic life events, predominantly characterised by violence, is yet another characteristic of undertaking an oral history project within a prison. The choice of the questions formulated during semi-directed interviews, the ability to let stories unfold and the subsequent selection of narrative techniques are crucial elements that demand reflection while conducting this kind of research. Interviews with inmates and warders revealed the existence of multiple approaches to dealing with traumatic or discomforting recollections.

In addition, the case study of the Number gangs, with their enduring mythological structure, gives hints as to the existence of a specific collective memory within the walls of Pollsmoor. The inside history of South African gangs cannot be found in documents. It is passed down to new generations of members through the spoken rehearsal of the group's mythology and through inscription on members' bodies. Indeed, the history and internal structure of the Numbers is re-enacted through corporal punishment whenever a disciplinary measure is taken. The marked body of the punished member acts as a collective reminder of the Number' set of rules. Simultaneously, the use of codified tattoos reflects a materialisation of an otherwise invisible mythology and also enables the inmate to regain some control over his own body. The practice of tattooing in Pollsmoor Women's Prison was far more limited in the case of female inmates, and the links between identity, self-assertion and memory in that setting should be investigated more thoroughly.

The widespread South African prison revolts of 1994 represented a sudden upsurge of common-law prisoners' political claims within the public sphere. Inmates asked for a deeper questioning of the blurred frontier between political and common-law prisoners, requesting the government to grant them general amnesty and the right to vote during the first democratic elections of April 1994. State reaction to the protest movements revealed the sharp contrast between the prisoners' collective memory, based on the assertion of a historical political subjectivity, and the official discourse on national memory elaborated at the time. Specific prisons, like Robben Island, were transformed into heritage sites that aimed to engender a sharp rupture between an authoritarian past and a new democratic society whose prisons allegedly played a radically distinct role. These museums, in their reiteration of the non-political character of common-law confinement, constitute one of the most efficient ways to return prisoners' voices to the silenced margins of society.

Oral history projects present a means through which to confront the muffling of the historical experiences of common-law prisoners. Such projects, despite the various shortcomings entailed by the prison context, can contribute to the broader narration and articulation of their confined collective memory. By historicising the experiences of actors that official discourse on political memory have rendered illegitimate, it is possible to make these experiences accessible to a society as a "cultural resource."[59] The post-transition South Africa, characterised, among others, by the disappearance of ANC political hegemony, has unveiled the political stakes hidden by the silencing of histories of struggle and the importance of recovering them in order to understand contemporary protest movements.

Bibliography

Baker, Alison. *Voices of Resistance, an Oral History of Moroccan Women*. Albany: State University of New York Press, 1998.

Baker, Francis. *The Culture of Violence: Essays on Tragedy and History*. Chicago: University of Chicago Press, 1993.

Bhabha, Homi. "Of Mimicry and Man: The Ambivalence of Colonial Discourse." *October* 28 (1984), reprinted in Bhabha, Homi. *The Location of Culture*, 85–92. New York: Routledge, 1994.

Boschma, Geertje, Olive Yonge, and Lorraine Mychajlunow. "Consent in Oral History Interviews: Unique Challenges." *Qualitative Health Research* 13, no. 1 (2003): 129–135.

Bozzoli, Belinda. "Interviewing the Women of Phokeng." Extracted from Bozzoli, Belinda and Nkotsoe, Mmantho. *Women of Phokeng, Life Strategy and Migrancy in South Africa, 1900–1983*. London: James Currey, 1991. In *The Oral History Reader*, edited by Robert Perks and Alistair Thomson, 155–165. London: Routledge, 1998.

Cohen, David W., Stephan F. Miescher, and Luise White. "Introduction: Voices, Words, and African History." In *African Words, African Voices, Critical Practices in Oral History*, 1–27. Bloomington: Indiana University Press, 2001.

Cole, Jennifer. *Forget Colonialism? Sacrifice and the Art of Memory in Madagascar*. Berkeley: University of California Press, 2001.

Feldman, Allen. "Political Terror and the Technologies of Memory: Excuse, Sacrifice, Commodification, and Actuarial Moralities." *Radical History Review* 85 (2003): 58–73.

---

59 Feldman, "Political Terror," 60.

Filippi, Natacha. "Institutional Violence and the Law in South Africa." *Journal of Colonialism and Colonial History* 17, no. 3 (2016), accessed 18 December 2020, doi:10.1353/cch.2016.0038.

Foucault, Michel. *Histoire de la folie à l'âge classique*. Paris: Gallimard, 1972.

Gillespie, Kelly. "Criminal Abstractions and the Post-Apartheid Prison." PhD Diss., University of Chicago, 2007.

Gobodo-Madikizela, Pumla. *A Human Being Died that Night: A South African Women Confronts the Legacy of Apartheid*. New York: Mariner Books, 2004.

Halbwachs, Maurice. *Les Cadres Sociaux de la Mémoire*. Paris: Alcan, 1925.

Ibrahim, Abdullahi A. "The Birth of the Interview: The Thin and the Fat of It." In *African Words, African Voices, Critical Practices in Oral History*, edited by David W. Cohen, Stephan F. Miescher, and Luise White, 103–124. Bloomington: Indiana University Press, 2001.

Kriegler, Johann. *Unrest in Prisons: Final Report of the Commission of Inquiry into Unrest in Prisons Appointed by the President on 27 June 1994*. Pretoria, 1995.

Lonsdale, John. "Agency in Tight Corners: Narrative and Initiative in African history." *Journal of African Cultural Studies*, 13, no. 1 (2000): 5–16.

Mphahlele, Letlapa. *Child of this Soil: My Life as a Freedom Fighter*. Cape Town: Kwela Books, 2002.

Olick, Jeffrey K., and Joyce Robbins. "Social Memory Studies: From 'Collective Memory' to the Historical Sociology of Mnemonic Practices." *Annual Review of Sociology* 24 (1998): 105–140.

Paez, Dario, Nekane Basabe, and Jose Luis Gonzalez. "Social Processes and Collective Memory: A Cross-Cultural Approach to Remembering Political Events." In *Collective Memory of Political Events: Social Psychological Perspectives*, edited by James W. Pennebaker, Diario Paez and Bernard Rim, 147–174. Mahwah, New Jersey: Lawrence Erlbaum Associates, 1997.

Patai, Daphne. "U.S. Academics and Third Word Women: Is Ethical Research Possible?" In *Women's Words: The Feminist Practice of Oral History*, edited by Sherna B. Gluck, and Daphne Patai, 137–153. New York: Routledge, 1991.

Payne, Leigh. A. *Unsettling Accounts. Neither Truth nor Reconciliation in Confessions of State Violence*. Durham and London: Duke University Press, 2008.

Podoler, Guy. "The Effect of Japanese Colonial Brutality on Shaping Korean Identity: An Analysis of a Prison Turned Memorial Site in Seoul." In *War and Militarism in Modern Japan. Issues of History and Identity*, edited by Guy Podoler, 199–214. Kent: Global Oriental Ltd., 2009.

Portelli, Alistair. "What Makes Oral History Different?" In *The Oral History Reader*, edited by Robert Perks and Alistair Thomson, 32–42. London: Routledge, 1998.

Portelli, Alistair. "What Makes Oral History Different." In *Oral History, Oral Culture, and Italian Americans*, edited by Luisa Giudice, 21–30. New York: Palgrave Macmillan, 2009.

Rancière, Jacques. *La Mésentente. Politique et philosophie*. Paris: Galilée, 1995.

Rommey, Joseph. "Legal Considerations in Oral History." *The Oral History Review* 1 (1973): 66–76.

Rosa, Isaac. *El Vano Ayer*. Barcelona: Seix Barral, 2012.

Rouverol, Alicia J. "Collaborative Oral History in a Correctional Setting: Promise and Pitfalls." *Oral History Review* 30, no. 1 (2003): 61–85.

Rowbotham, Sheila. *Hidden from History.* London: Pluto Press, 1977.
Rubio, César Lorenzo. *Cárceles en llamas. El movimiento de presos sociales en la transición.* Barcelona: Virus Editorial, 2013.
Schlosser, Jennifer A. "Issues in Interviewing Inmates. Navigating the Methodological Landmines of Prison Research." *Qualitative Inquiry* 14, no. 8 (2008): 1500–1525.
Sontag, Susan. *Regarding the Pain of Others.* London: Penguin, 2004.
Spivak, Gayatri. "Can the Subaltern Speak?" In *Marxism and the Interpretation of Culture*, edited by Lawrence Grossberg and Cary Nelson, 217–313. Urbana: University of Illinois Press, 1988.
Steinberg, Jonny. *The Number. One Man's Search for Identity in the Cape Underworld and Prison Gangs* (Cape Town: Jonathan Ball, 2004).
Stoler, Ann L. "Colonial Archives and the Arts of Governance." *Archival Science* 2 (2002): 87–109.
Stoler, Ann L., with Strassler, Karen. "Memory Work in Java. A Cautionary Tale." In *Carnal Knowledge and Imperial Power: Race and the Intimate in Colonial Rule*, edited by Ann L. Stoler, 283–309. Berkeley: University of California Press, 2002.
Thompson, Paul. "The Voice of the Past: Oral History," extracted from Paul Thompson, *The Voice of the Past: Oral History,* Oxford: Oxford University Press, 1988. In *The Oral History Reader*, edited by Robert Perks and Alistair Thomson, 25–31. London: Routledge, 1998.
Vandecasteele-Schweitzer, Sylvie, and Danièle Voldman. "The Oral Sources for Women's History." In *Writing Women's History*, edited by Michelle Perrot, 41–50. Oxford: Blackwell, 1992.
Van Onselen, Charles. *The Small Matter of a Horse: The Life of "Nongoloza" Mathebula, 1867–1948.* Johannesburg: Ravan Press, 1984.
Vansina, Jan. *Oral Tradition as History.* Madison: University of Wisconsin Press, 1985.
Vaughan, Megan. "Reported Speech and Other Kinds of Testimony." In *African Words, African Voices, Critical Practices in Oral History*, edited by David W. Cohen, Stephan F. Miescher, and Luise White, 53–77. Bloomington: Indiana University Press, 2001.
Waldram, James. "Anthropology in Prison: Negotiating Consent and Accountability with a 'Captured Population.'" *Human Organization* 57, no. 2 (1998): 238–244.

Casper Andersen

A "Quest for Relevance": The Memory Politics of UNESCO's General History of Africa

Abstract: In 1963, the United Nations Educational, Scientific and Cultural Organization (UNESCO) launched the General History of Africa (GHA) project which ran for over three decades. The stated aim of the project was to produce "a scientific history of African unity and culture from the inside" – a history written by Africans for Africans on the continent and in the diaspora. Those involved in the GHA as contributors, editors and UNESCO officials were motivated by what Ngũgĩ wa Thiong'o has labelled a "quest for relevance" which was felt strongly among African cultural elites during the decades after 1940. This quest for relevance involved contributing to the decolonisation of the mind based on the idea that the ending of formal colonial rule would be incomplete and meaningless without a cultural decolonisation in education, science, and the arts, including history. In this chapter I revisit the chequered history of the GHA and place the project in its historical context of Pan-Africanism and nation building. I unravel the institutional context and argue that the project was shaped by an agenda centred on the politics of historical memory shared by this generation of Africans and by UNESCO.

> Africa scholars put more emphasis on showing that Africans had a history than on asking how Africans' history-making was implicated in establishing or contesting power. (Frederick Cooper, 1994)[1]

In November 2015, UNESCO – the UN special agency for education, science and culture – celebrated its 70th anniversary with proceedings that included a conference on the organisation's history.[2] During the celebrations, former Director-General and Senegalese geographer and diplomat Amadou Mahtar M'Bow explained what UNESCO had achieved during his Director-Generalship from 1974 to 1983.

---

[1] Frederick Cooper, "Conflict and Connection: Rethinking African History," *American Historical Review* 99, no. 5 (1994): 1528.
[2] Mads K. Mogensen and Ivan. L Christensen, "Report on: Making a Difference: Seventy Years of UNESCO Actions UNESCO Anniversary Conference, UNESCO, Paris, 28 – 29 October 2015," *UNESDOC Digital Library*, 2015, accessed 28 November 2019, https://unesdoc.unesco.org/ark:/48223/pf0000244030.

ə OpenAccess. © 2022 Casper Andersen, published by De Gruyter. This work is licensed under the Creative Commons Attribution 4.0 International License. https://doi.org/10.1515/9783110655315-004

M'Bow was the first African to head a UN special agency and when he took the stand at the UNESCO anniversary conference, he was well into his nineties. M'Bow's speech focused on UNESCO's *General History of Africa* project (hereafter the GHA) as the most important undertaking during his tenure. The former Director-General explained how a group of gifted and dedicated African historians had come together under the auspices of UNESCO to rewrite the entire history of a previously marginalised continent "so that teachers in Africa no longer had to teach history using European textbooks in which the children could read that their ancestors were the Gauls."[3] M'Bow pointed out that the GHA marked a watershed not only in the study of African history, but also in the history of UNESCO as the project instigated UNESCO's engagements with African history and heritage which had since grown to include African entries in the *World Heritage List*, *The Slave Route Project* (1994–), and the *UN International Decade for People of African Descent* (2015–2024).

The GHA was launched in 1963 and continued for more than three decades. The undertaking was instigated at the request of the Organization of African Unity and the idea for a new history of the African continent can be traced to the *International Congress of Africanists* held in Accra in 1962 with the support of UNESCO.[4] The tangible outcome of the GHA project was a 6,500-page history of Africa in eight volumes published initially in French, English, and Arabic.[5] In over 200 chapters, the GHA covered the history of Africa from prehistoric times to the 1980s. Distinct volumes and abridged versions were also published in several languages – Chinese, Portuguese, Spanish, Swahili, Hausa, Pular and Fulani among others.[6] Over the course of the project, UNESCO organised 12 conferences devoted to specific issues in African history that required special attention. Substantial proceedings from these meetings were published as *UNESCO General*

---

3 Ibid, 8.
4 Muryatan Santana Barbosa, "The Construction of the African Perspective: A History of the General History of Africa," Revista Brasileira de História 32, no. 64 (2012): 196. Barbosa provides a concise institutional history of the GHA. Another informative overview and discussion is Chloé Maurel, "L'histoire "générale de l'Afrique de l'Unesco: Un projet de coopération intellectuelle transnationale d'esprit afro-centré (1964–1999)," Cahiers d'Études Africaines 54 (2014): 715–37.
5 The volumes are freely available from UNESCOs Digital library UNESDOC, accessed 4 January 2019, https://unesdoc.unesco.org. For a discussion of the archival sources relating to the UNESCO GHA, see Larissa Schulte Nordholt, "From Metropole to Margin in UNESCO's General History of Africa–Documents of Historiographical Decolonization in Paris and Ibadan," History in Africa 46 (2019): 1–10.
6 Maurel, "L'Histoire," 731.

*History of Africa: Studies and Documents.*⁷ A third component of the GHA project consisted of a program to develop and maintain archival and oral history resources in a number of African countries.⁸ The GHA was and remains a major achievement in the development of African history as an academic field.⁹

The GHA was launched in the wake of formal decolonisation at a time when newly independent African countries joined UNESCO. As one of the key members of the GHA organisation, historian Jan Vansina pointed out "the links between pan-African nationalism and this [GHA] project" were close.¹⁰ The main ambition was to write a history with Africans as active subjects rather than passive objects – a history written by Africans for Africans on the continent and in the diaspora. The GHA was a politically committed and self-confident undertaking that aimed to produce "useful pasts" for the needs of its time.¹¹ It was a scholarly undertaking but at the same time was regarded as a frame for the enactment of national and transnational memory political agendas that shifted during the decades the project spanned.

The aim of this chapter is to unravel and analyse these agendas. I will explore what kind of African history was considered relevant by whom and for whom in the GHA project. I am particularly concerned with understanding what the answers to these questions meant for the African historians who grappled with writing about Africa's past in ways they considered useful and necessary for the present and future.

The memory politics of the GHA was profoundly influenced by UNESCO – an organisation that brought its own ideas and agendas into the GHA project. Indeed, UNESCO has played a prominent, but still insufficiently explored, role

---

7 The Studies and Documents publications are available from UNESCOs digital library UNESDOC.
8 UNESCO, *Ten-year plan for the study of African oral traditions and the promotion of African languages* (Paris: UNESCO Publishing 1972).
9 In 2007, a second stage of the project officially commenced, entitled "The Pedagogical Use of the General History of Africa." Its purpose was to extend the use of the GHA in educational sectors, particularly in Africa. Currently, UNESCO is organizing a 9th volume to cover the last three decades of African history. The plan is also to update and revise the first eight volumes in light new research findings and changing terminology. See UNESCO website, accessed 28 November 2019, http://www.unesco.org/new/en/social-and-human-sciences/themes/general-history-of-africa/volume-ix/.
10 Jan Vansina, "Unesco and African Historiography," *History in Africa* 20 (1993): 337. Vansina was a very active member of the scientific commission for the GHA project from 1971 to its completion.
11 Edmund E. Jabobitti, ed., *Composing Useful Pasts: History as Contemporary Politics* (New York: State of New York University Press, 2000).

as a transnational site for African memory politics for more than half a century. In this chapter I flesh out this dimension particularly by comparing the GHA with the *UNESCO History of Mankind* project launched in 1950 and which served as a model for the GHA with respect to organisational set up and structure.[12] Teasing out the UNESCO dimension opens a historiographical path for placing African memory politics in a wider international context.

The GHA engaged with issues concerning the politics and positionalities of knowledge production. These concerns are highly topical in the calls to decolonize African history and academic knowledge production more generally.[13] Among other things decolonizing knowledge means to engage with thinkers, concepts and theories from the global south.[14] The GHA was a collective project that enable us to engage with ideas of a number of significant African intellectuals and historians. Moreover, an equally important aspect of knowledge decolonization is an historical awareness of the context in which scholarly knowledge has been produced. The GHA helps us think through the complexities of this issue at a pivotal juncture in the field of African history.

The Quest for Relevance and Wholeness: Nationalism and Pan-Africanism

Those involved in the GHA as contributors, editors, and UNESCO officials were driven by what Ngũgĩ wa Thiong'o has labelled a "quest for relevance" which was felt strongly among African cultural elites during the first decades after 1945.[15] This quest for relevance involved contributing to the decolonisation of the mind based on the idea that the ending of formal colonial rule would be in-

---

[12] The first of the seven volumes in UNESCO's *History of Mankind* was published in 1964. Poul Duedahl, "Selling Mankind: UNESCO and the Invention of Global History, 1945–76," *Journal of World History* 22, no. 1 (2011): 101–133; Paul Betts, "Humanity's New Heritage: UNESCO and the Rewriting of World History," *Past & Present* 228, no. 1 (2015): 249–85. The history of mankind project was later renamed "History of Humanity."
[13] Sabelo J. Ndlovu-Gatsheni, and Siphamandla Zondi (eds). *Decolonizing the university, knowledge systems and disciplines in Africa.* (Durham North Carolina, Carolina Academic Press 2016); Gurminder Bhambra, Dalia Gebrial, and Kerem Nişancıoğlu *Decolonising the University* (London: Pluto Press, 2018).
[14] Sabelo J. Ndlovu-Gatsheni, "Decoloniality as the future of Africa." *History Compass* 13 no.10 (2015): 485–496; Raewyn Connell, Fran Collyer, João Maia and Robert Morrell *Knowledge and global power. Making new sciences in the south*, (Clayton: Monash University Press 2019).
[15] Ngũgĩ wa Thiong'o, *Decolonizing the Mind: The Politics of Language in African Literature* (London: James Curry, 1986), 87–111.

complete without cultural decolonisation in education, science, the arts and not least approaches to history. In the words of the Kenyan historian Bethwell A. Ogot, who chaired UNESCO's International Expert Commission for the project from 1971 to 1983, "political independence could only have meaning if it was accompanied by historical independence."[16] A notable component in the quest for relevance was a sense of the need to restore African pride that had been compromised by outsiders who had denied Africans their rationality, humanity, and history. As Hannington Ochwada has noted, African scholars and historians were

> faced with the challenges of building institutions to decolonize the minds of their compatriots and the masses by deliberately producing usable past knowledge. They were charged with the responsibility of producing the history of ideas relating to the socio-political and economic realities obtaining in the early years of independence.[17]

Moreover, the sense of urgency among African intellectuals and historians to produce this usable past was fuelled also by the conviction that a dislocation from one's past was morally destructive, particularly for the new African elites coming into power. Without a developed sense of history these elites would remain embarrassed by their African identity and could easily shrug off their obligations towards fellow Africans thus compromising the gains of independence.

In political terms, the quest was connected to ideas and processes of nation-building that among historians developed into what Toyin Falola has labelled "nationalist historiography," that is,

> the use of history in the service of the nation, and a way of writing that makes history valuable in defining the nation and shaping its future. Nationalist historiography is the representation of elite interests in the nation, as the elite uses its knowledge to define its leadership role. It is a counter discourse for attacking European representations of Africa. It is a deliberate attempt to provide credible evidence for the achievement of Africa and the glories of the past in order to indicate possibilities for the future and combat racist views that Africans are incapable of managing themselves [...]. Nationalist historiography is about power: the ability of an intelligentsia to assert itself, to generate knowledge about its own people and continent.[18]

---

16 Bethwell A. Ogot, "Towards a History of Kenya," *Kenya Historical Review* 4, no. 1 (2004): 1.
17 Hannington Ochwada, "Historians, Nationalism and Pan-Africanism: Myths and Realities," in *African Intellectuals: Rethinking Politics, Language, Gender and Development*, ed. Thandika Mkandawire (London: Zed Books, 2005), 194.
18 Toyin Falola, *Nationalism and African Intellectuals* (Rochester: University of Rochester Press, 2004), 225.

Nationalist historiography dominated academic history writing in Africa during the 1950s and 1960s with main centres in Dakar, Legon, Ibadan and Makerere.[19] This form of politically committed "history for self-government" has been subjected to intensive academic discussion. From the outset, nationalist historiography was criticised on political, historiographical and epistemological grounds.[20] However, the influences of nationalist historiography were considerable in the GHA. The Nigerian historian Kenneth O. Dike was the first scientific director of GHA project and listing the directors for the individual volumes reads like a roster of the towering figures in the tradition of African nationalist historiography: Joseph Ki-Zerbo (Vol. 1), B. A. Ogot (Vol. 5), J. F. Ade Ajayi (Vol. 6), Adu Boahen (Vol. 7), and Ali Mazrui (Vol. 8) each directed a volume.[21] With good reason, Ade Ajayi has represented the GHA as the ultimate victory of nationalist history.[22]

If nation-building and the commitment to nationalist historiography constituted one side of the quest for relevance among this generation of historians and intellectuals, then Pan-Africanist ideas and African unity constituted the other.[23] As Ngũgĩ has specified more recently, the quest for relevance was also "a quest for wholeness," which he regards as the core of African political and intellectual struggle since the era of the transatlantic slave trade – a dismembering process that stifled African development but at the same time provided the foundation for an African Renaissance.[24] In connecting the quest for wholeness to the history of Pan-Africanism, Ngũgĩ underscores the importance of memory and re-membering:

> Creative imagination is one of the greatest re-membering practices. The relationship of writers to their social memory is central to their quest and mission. Memory is the link between past and present, between space and time, and it is the base of our dreams. Writers and

---

19 Bogumil Jewsiewicki and David Newbury, eds., *African Historiographies: What History for Which Africa?* (Beverly Hills: Sage, 1986); Falola, *Nationalism and African Intellectuals*, 223–260.
20 See, for example, Donald Denoon and Adam Kuper, "Nationalist Historians in Search of a Nation: The 'New Historiography' in Dar-es-Salaam," *African Affairs* 217 (1980): 329–349.
21 The term "Director" was preferred over the term editor as the editorial responsibility ultimately rested on the international commission. See Vansina, "UNESCO and African," 339–340.
22 Falola, *Nationalism and African Intellectuals*, 237.
23 Thandika Mkandawire, "African Intellectuals and Nationalism," in Mkandawire, *African Intellectuals*, 10–55; Toyin Falola and Kwame Essien, *Pan-Africanism and the Politics of African Citizenship and Identity* (Oxford: Routledge, 2014). For a critical discussion of this theme in the GHA see Stephen Howe, *Afrocentrism. Mythical Pasts and Imagined Homes* (London and New York: Verso, 1998), 180–85.
24 Ngũgĩ wa Thiong'o, *Something Torn and Something New: An African Renaissance* (New York: Basic Civitas Books, 2009).

intellectuals in these [Pan-African] movements are aware that without a reconnection with African memory, there is no wholeness.[25]

Pan-Africanism came in many variants during the 1950s and 1960s. In geographical terms, the dominant form of Pan-Africanism expressed in the GHA was what Ali Mazrui, the director of Volume 8, has called "continental Pan-Africanism" which stressed African unity across the Sahara.[26] Chapters analysing connections with the diaspora, particularly in the Americas, supplemented this continental perspective. The basis of African unity differed between volumes. For example, Volume 3 which covered the period from the seventh to the eleventh century saw the basis for African unity in the spread and response to Islam while Volume 7 on the period 1880 to 1935 found African unity in resistance to colonial rule. In Volume 8 on the years since 1935, the basis for African unity was found in the idea of "Africa's triple heritage" of Islam, Eurocentric colonialism/capitalism and indigenous cultural traditions – an idea that had been promoted by Ali Mazrui, who directed this volume.[27]

Pan-Africanism stressed African unity in ways that had to be reconciled with nationalist commitments. Indeed, the birth of new African nations was regarded by many as the triumph of independence, but intellectuals involved in the GHA were keenly aware that the separations of people of African descent created by the slave trade still existed and that colonial borders remained intact after decolonisation. A notable ambivalence towards the nation as the unit for African history and memory therefore fuelled the intellectual endeavour to provide a unifying historical perspective in the GHA.

The UNESCO Context for the GHA

The Pan-African dimension of the GHA received further impetus from the fact that UNESCO – an institution with its own quest for relevance during the de-

---

[25] Ibid, 39.
[26] Ali Mazrui, *Africa's International Relations: The Diplomacy of Dependency and Change* (Chicago: Westview Press, 1977); Ali Mazrui, "Pan-Africanism and the Intellectuals: Rise, Decline, Revival," in Mkandawire, *African Intellectuals*, 56–78; Ali Mazrui, "Pan-Africanism: From Poetry to Power," *A Journal of Opinion* 23, no. 1 (1995): 35–38.
[27] Ali Mazrui, *The Africans: A Triple Heritage* (Boston: Little Brown & Co., 1986). The concept of Africa's triple heritage also formed the conceptual basis of a BBC documentary written by Mazrui.

colonisation era – organised the project.[28] Founded in the immediate aftermath of World War Two as the intellectual branch of the UN system, UNESCO embodied a specific form of idealist internationalism with an explicit aim to create a new foundation for humanity.[29] It was idealist in the sense that UNESCO was based on the conviction that it was in the realm of ideas that a new foundation for peaceful co-existence and progress among the world's nations (and remaining empires) had to be created.[30] The oft-quoted UNESCO preamble written in 1945 stated that, "Since wars begin in the minds of men, it is in the minds of men that the defences of peace must be constructed."[31]

While the stated aim of UNESCO's diverse post-war activities was to create a new peaceful foundation for humanity based on programs in education, science and culture, the organisation was also preoccupied with making the past useful for the present. This involved the preservation of "global patrimony" which from the 1970s evolved into the World Heritage List.[32] From early on, the preoccupation with humanity's "global past" – an idea that came into being through the activities of organisations such as UNESCO – also involved writing history in the form of the UNESCO History of Mankind project.[33] Originating in the 1950s and completed during the 1970s, the *UNESCO History of Mankind* was published in six volumes. The project was born out of the perceived need to restore a sense of common humanity after 1945. The history focused on exchanges and connections between cultures and so-called "civilisations." It prioritised ideas in science, culture and technology over political history, nationalism and wars, and it sought to adopt an explicitly non-Eurocentric view to explain how the world had come to its present state of interconnected *Schicksalsgemeinschaft* (commu-

---

28 Casper Andersen, "Capacity Building, Scientific Independence, and the Establishment of UNESCO's Science and Technology Agenda for Africa," *Canadian Journal of African Studies* 50, no. 3 (2017): 379–393.
29 Fernando Valderrama Martinez, *A History of UNESCO* (Paris: UNESCO Publishing, 1995); Chloé Maurel, *Histoire L'Unesco. Les Trente Premiére Annnées 1945–74* (Paris: L'Harmatten, 2008).
30 Jean-Jacques Renoliet, *L'UNESCO: La Société des Nations et la Coopération Intellectuelle (1919–1946)* (Paris: UNESCO, 1999); Betts, "Humanity's New Heritage," 249–251.
31 UNESCO's constitution was signed November 1945. "UNESCO Constitution," *United Nations Educational, Scientific and Cultural Organiyzation*, 16 November 1945, accessed 4 January 2019, http://portal.unesco.org/en/ev.php-URL_ID=15244&URL_DO=DO_TOPIC&URL_SECTION=201.html.
32 Lynn Meskell, "UNESCO's World Heritage Convention at 40: Challenging the Economic and Political Order of International Heritage Conservation," *Current Anthropology* 54, no. 4 (2013): 483–494.
33 Duedahl, "Selling Mankind."

nity of shared destiny).³⁴ This kind of history reflected the ideas of "one-worldism" and anti-nationalism among the Western scientists and intellectuals whose views dominated UNESCO during the organisation's founding decade.³⁵

The History of Mankind project predated the GHA by a decade and set a precedent in important respects. It was organised and edited by an international committee of experts who oversaw the project on behalf of UNESCO. A similar course was adopted for the GHA. In the case of the History of Mankind, the international committee consisted almost exclusively of Western scholars. Despite the presence of notable non-western scholars and intellectuals, such as Leopold Senghor, the History of Mankind was shaped by the ideas of "one-worldism" and positivist progressivism of Julian Huxley, Joseph Needham and others with whom the idea originated. For the GHA, however, it was established from the outset that at least two-thirds of the members of the organising committee should be Africans representing different parts of the continent. Moreover, the director of each of the eight volumes should be selected from different African countries with a suitable geographical spread across the continent.³⁶ The difference between the History of Mankind and the GHA in this respect is indicative of gradual but notable shift in UNESCO's cultural and educational sector during this period towards an emphasis on Africanization of programmes and structures.³⁷

The international GHA committee was established in 1971 with 39 members. It boasted an impressive list of the foremost African historians, scholars and writers. Notably, there were only two female members of the committee, and they appear to have played only minor roles.³⁸ The international expert committee met every two years until 1985. At UNESCO, a small secretariat headed by Maurice

---

34 Betts, "Humanity's New Heritage."
35 Aant Elzinga, "Unesco and the Politics of Scientific Internationalism," in *Science and Internationalism*, ed. Aant Elzinga and Catharina Landström (London: Taylor Graham, 1996), 89–132; Glenda Sluga, "UNESCO and the (One) World of Julian Huxley," *Journal of World History* 22, no. 3 (2010): 393–418.
36 Maurel, "L'histoire générale."
37 Damiano Matasci, "Assessing needs, fostering development: UNESCO, illiteracy and the global politics of education (1945–1960)," *Comparative Education* 53, no.1 (2017): 35–53; Damiano Matasci, Miguel Bandeira Jerónimo and Hugo Gonçalves Dores, *Education and Development in Colonial and Postcolonial Africa: Policies, Paradigms, and Entanglements, 1890s–1980s.* Springer Nature, 2020: 14–18.
38 Discussions of gender representation did not play a prominent role in the GHA which confirms Amina Mama's assertion that "whether their consciousness was nationalist or Pan-Africanist, however, African intellectuals have continued to display a quite remarkable reticence over questions of gender." Amina Mama, "Gender Studies for Africa's Transformation," in *African Intellectuals: Rethinking Politics, Language, Gender and Development*, ed. Thandika Mkandawire (London: Zed Books, 2005), 105.

Glélé from Benin was in charge of the difficult task of ensuring coherence and progression across all volumes and steering it through internal controversies among editors, expert committees and contributors as well as external concerns arising from volatile geopolitics influenced by Cold War tensions and the decolonisation process, particularly in southern Africa.[39] Internal and external factors caused continuous delays and at certain points the project was in real danger of collapsing completely. According to Jan Vansina, who was a member of the scientific committee for the duration of the project, it was thanks to the work of rarely credited UNESCO officials – and particularly Maurice Glélé – that the project was completed despite continuous delays.[40]

A Scientific History of African Unity and Culture Written from the Inside

In one sentence the intention of the GHA was to produce a scientific history of African unity and culture written from within. The starting point emphasised several times in all the GHA volumes was that the history of Africa had been neglected and marginalised as racial, cultural, and historiographical prejudice largely denied Africans of any history at all. Ki-Zerbo wrote the succinct opening sentence in the GHA that stated simply: "Africa has a History."[41] In the volumes and numerous UNESCO reports about the GHA as well as in articles in UNESCO's widely circulated magazine, *The Courier*, references to assertions by G.W.F. Hegel and Hugh Trevor-Roper that Africa was not part of history were invoked to underscore the need for a new UN-backed history of the continent.[42] The Director-General's preface to the GHA volumes stated that:

> African societies were looked upon as societies that could have no history [...]. In fact, there was a refusal to see Africans as the creators of original cultures which flowered and sur-

---

[39] Andersen, "Capacity Building," 381–383.
[40] Vansina, "Unesco and African Historiography," 341.
[41] Joseph Ki-Zerbo, "General Introduction," in *General History of Africa: Vol 1: Methodology and African Prehistory*, ed. Joseph Ki-Zerbo (London: Heinemann, 1983), 23.
[42] See, for example, Kenneth O. Dike, "The Scientific Study of Africa," *The UNESCO Courier* 20, no. 6 (1967): 8–13; Barbosa, "Constructing the African Perspective," 196–198. The agenda to insist on Africa's place in history had been present in UNESCO prior to the start of the GHA project. In 1959, *The Courier* devoted a thematic issue to "Africa's Lost Past." It emphasised Africa's neglected prehistory – what Basil Davidson in the opening article referred to as "pre-European Africa." Basil Davidson, "The Rediscovery of Africa," *The UNESCO Courier* 12, no. 10 (1959): 5.

vived over the centuries in patterns of their own making and which historians are unable to grasp unless they forgo their prejudices and rethink their approach.[43]

The GHA was to fill this critical gap and provide a new approach. To achieve this, the international expert committee of the GHA adopted four principles at an important project meeting in Addis Ababa in 1970.[44] According to the first principle, the GHA should be a history of the highest scientific standard. This meant that it was not intended to be a dogmatic, exhaustive history of Africa. Rather, it should state the problems and current knowledge in the scientific study of African history with a view on the main trends in research. It should also display a willingness to show divergence of opinion where such existed. This principle was, for example, employed in *Volume II: The Ancient Civilizations of Africa*. A chapter by Cheikh Anta Diop presented his controversial thesis that ancient Egypt had been populated by a homogeneous black African race from the earliest times to the Persian invasion in the sixth century BC. Because the Egyptian civilisation in Diop's interpretation was purely black African in origin, he concluded, "Egyptian antiquity is to African culture what Graeco-Roman antiquity is to Western culture. The building up of a corpus of African humanities should be based on this fact."[45]

Diop aimed to restore the historical consciousness of African peoples as a basis for an African renaissance – a point and agenda he also developed in his widely read and influential books.[46] However, Diop's chapter in the GHA was criticised in the ensuing pages of the volume, which featured a lengthy extract from a UNESCO symposium on "The Peopling of Ancient Egypt" held in Cairo in 1974. At that symposium, Diop had presented his analysis which was criticised severely by other experts who claimed that his interpretation was based on selective evidence. They also noted that Diop's claim of the blackness of ancient Egypt rested on an outdated, essentialist notion of race. The critics

---

[43] Amadou-Mahtar M'Bow "Preface," in Ki-Zerbo, *General History of Africa: Vol 1*, xviii.
[44] UNESCO, *Guide for the Preparation of the General History of Africa* (Paris: UNESCO Publishing, 1971), accessed 4 January 2019, https://unesdoc.unesco.org/ark:/48223/pf0000000408?posInSet=4&queryId=N-EXPLORE-fc2f4f6e-a4a5-4f52-8848-4236e473d574; Barbosa, "Constructing the African Perspective," 200–204; Bethwell A. Ogot, "Description of the Project," in Ki-Zerbo, *General History of Africa: Vol 1*, xxiii–xxvii.
[45] Cheik Anta Diop, "Origin of Ancient Egyptians," in *General History of Africa: Vol 2: The Ancient Civilizations of Africa*, ed. G. Mokhtar (London: Heinemann, 1983), 49.
[46] Cheik Anta Diop, *Nations Nègres et Culture* (Dakar: Présence Africaine, 1955); Cheik Anta Diop, *The African Origins of Civilization: Myth or Reality* (Westport: Laurence Hill, 1974).

thus claimed that Diop's interpretation adhered to a now scientifically discredited racial model that posits three well-defined races of white, black and yellow.[47]

Readers of the GHA were thus presented with two opposing views followed by a passage from the volume director who explained why divergent opinions were to be found therein.[48] This exposed a tension in the GHA. The new scientific history should challenge longstanding assumptions about the inferiority of Africa and African peoples that had been undergirded by appeals to science and history carrying the stamp of academia. Yet, as Ki-Zerbo's general introduction argues,

> [t]he history of Africa needs rewriting, for up till now it has often been masked, faked, distorted, mutilated, by force of circumstance – i.e. through ignorance or self-interest. [...] And this image has been projected and extrapolated indefinitely in time, as a justification of both the present and the future. It is not our purpose to write a history which will be a mere settling of scores, with colonialist history backfiring on its authors, but rather to change the perspective and revive images which have been forgotten or lost. We must turn once more to science in order to create genuine cultural awareness. We must reconstruct the real course of events. And we must find another mode of discourse.[49]

The general introduction insisted on the need to turn *once more* to science in order to accomplish the dual purpose of creating cultural awareness and reconstructing the real course of events. The GHA was based on a belief that the new history could only serve its purpose if it met the highest scientific standards and, when necessary, question entrenched biases and unscientific assumptions within academic disciplines. The idea was thus that false assumptions in science could be eradicated through improved science. To do so required disciplinary boundaries to broaden. In particular, sustained efforts were made in the GHA to develop scientific methods in oral history and include these approaches in the scientific repertoire for writing about Africa's past.[50]

The idea that the biases and prejudices of false or pseudo-science could be dismantled through and by improved science lay at the core of the positivist ide-

---

47 UNESCO, *The Peopling of Ancient Egypt and the Deciphering of Meroitic Script: Proceedings* (Paris: UNESCO publishing, 1978).
48 G. Mokhtar, "Annex to Chapter 1: Deciphering of the Meroitic Script," in Mokhtar, *General History of Africa: Vol 2*, 59–84.
49 Ki Zerbo, "General Introduction," 3.
50 For a discussion of oral history methodology by one of its pioneers, see Jan Vansina, "Oral Tradition and its Methodology," in Ki-Zerbo, *General History of Africa: Vol 1*, 142–166.

alism prominent in UNESCO.⁵¹ The most notable example was the *UNESCO Statements on Race* which were issued during the 1950s. In the wake of World War Two, UNESCO gathered a group of international scientific experts to debunk myths about race and provide an authoritative view on the issue.⁵² In different wordings, the UNESCO statements on race agreed that science demonstrated that the concept of race lacked any foundation in modern biology and that from a scientific standpoint "race was a social myth rather than a biological fact."⁵³

In the context of the GHA, the UNESCO-sanctioned scientific dismissal of the concept of race, however, turned out to be complicated and contested as when critics argued against Diop's race-based interpretation of Egypt as a black civilisation by pointing out that his analysis adhered to a scientifically disproved, essentialist race model.⁵⁴ Diop, however, defended the validity of the idea of distinct black, white and yellow races. In an intervention that hardly left readers any less confused about the scientific status of the concept of race, Maurice Glélé insisted that UNESCO had in fact not abandoned the term "race" in its work and that "the authors of the *General History of Africa* would make use of words to which readers were already accustomed."⁵⁵ Using science to reform science is always a complicated exercise. In the GHA, it involved balancing the highest scientific criteria of its time with the need to provide a basis for African unity.⁵⁶

The principle of highest scientific standard was connected to the interpretation of another foundational principle of the GHA, which stated that the GHA should be a history of Africa "from the inside."⁵⁷ Opinions diverged about what "from the inside" entailed. According to John D. Fage – who contributed

---

51 Casper Andersen, "The Zero Hours of Technology and the Founding of UNESCO," in *Zero Hours: Conceptual Beginnings Vol. 2*, ed. Hagen Schulz Forberg (Oxford: Palgrave Macmillan, 2021 [forthcoming]), Ch. 6.
52 Ashley Montagu, *Statement on Race: An Annotated Elaboration and Exposition of the Four Statements on Race Issued by the United Nations Educational, Scientific, and Cultural Organization* (Paris: UNESCO Publishing, 1972), 54.
53 Michelle Brattain, "Race, Racism, and Antiracism: UNESCO and the Politics of Presenting Science to the Postwar Public," *American Historical Review* 112, no. 5 (2007): 1386–1413; Anthony Q. Hazard, "A Racialized Deconstruction? Ashley Montagu and the 1950 UNESCO Statement on Race," *Transforming Anthropology* 19, no. 2 (2011): 174–186.
54 Vercoutter, "Annex to Chapter 1," 68–69.
55 M. Glélé, "Annex to Chapter 1," 72.
56 Robin Derricourt, *Inventing Africa: History, Archaeology and Ideas* (London: Pluto Press, 2011), 110–115.
57 Ogot, "Description of the Project," xv.

to the GHA and co-edited the *Cambridge History of Africa* published during the same decades – state of the art history of Africa produced at this time was written from the inside in the sense that it studied African societies based on sources and approaches from within the continent. Specific challenges emerged when writing the history of different parts of Africa, not least with respect to available sources, but according to Fage, the study of Africa's past belonged to the same scholarly tradition used to study other parts of the world.[58]

Other contributors understood the meaning of "the inside view" differently. In the words of Ogot, "from the inside" meant that the GHA should be "a faithful reflection of the way in which African authors view their own civilisation. While prepared in an international framework and drawing, to the full, on present stock of scientific knowledge," the history was to offer a particular "conception of human values" associated with African heritage and unity.[59] Again the general introduction is striking in its attempt to balance the opposing views:

> The brand image of Africa has been shaped by so many interested external attitudes, right up to those of present-day films, that it is time to turn a new look on Africa – one from the inside, one of identity, authenticity, awakening [...]. A real Copernican revolution is needed, a revolution which would be semantic in the first place, and which, without denying the demands of universal science, would take up the whole historical flow of Africa and guide it into new moulds.[60]

The search for these new moulds was a central epistemological concern of the GHA. In Ngũgĩ's terms, the quest for relevance involved the search for "a liberating perspective within which to see ourselves clearly in relationship to ourselves and to other selves in the universe."[61] In the context of the GHA this aspect of the quest for relevance was a search for a "third space" – to paraphrase Homi Bhabha – that would connect the demands of science with the perspective from within.[62]

---

[58] John D. Fage, "The Development of African Historiography," in Ki-Zerbo, *General History of Africa: Vol 1*, 25–43.
[59] Ogot, "Description of the Project," xxiii–xiv. For an elaboration of Ogot's view on this matter, see Bethwell A. Ogot, "Rereading the History and Historiography of Epistemic Domination and Resistance in Africa," *African Studies Review* 52, no. 1 (2009): 1–22.
[60] Ki-Zerbo, "General Introduction," 19–20.
[61] Ngũgĩ, *Decolonizing the Mind*, 87.
[62] Homi Bhabha, "Of Mimicry and Man. The Ambivalence of Colonial Discourse," *Discipleship: A Special Issue on Psychoanalysis*, 28 (1984): 125–133.

Unity, Connections and Resistance

Two further foundational principles of the GHA stated that the project should focus on ideas and culture and that it should be a history of African unity within the continent and between all people of African descent. These principles aimed to emphasise Africa's place in the world and its contributions to the development of humankind. Using Ngũgĩ's terms, the "quest for relevance" and "the quest for wholeness" were intimately connected in the memory politics that guided the GHA.[63] Unity meant that the history was to focus more on connections rather than boundaries – be they ecological boundaries (such as the Sahara) or political boundaries. The two GHA volumes covering the period after 1880, for example, did not divide chapters according to colonial or nation-state boundaries but rather adopted a mix of regional and topical divisions.

The focus on unity and connections across continents mirrored the direction adopted by UNESCO in the History of Mankind Project, which presented a history of exchanges and growing interconnectedness among the peoples of the world in explicitly anti-nationalist terms in line with "the one-worldism" of UNESCO. However, the GHA differed from the History of Mankind project with respect to what connections were considered important. The volume on the late nineteenth century emphasised how linkages "between what became the two principal spheres of the black world – Africa and the Americas – were maintained over time through exchanges of personnel, cultural materials, and political ideology."[64] In the preface to the GHA volumes, Director-General M'Bow stated that the GHA was important because it shed "light on the historical unity of Africa and also its relations with other continents, particularly the Americas and the Caribbean" and because it brought out "Africa's relations with southern Asia across the Indian Ocean."[65] UNESCO devoted a GHA conference to this latter topic in 1975.[66] M'Bow did not mention European connections. This was a form of anti-Eurocentrism that differed markedly from the 1959 *UNESCO Courier*'s

---

[63] Ngũgĩ, *Something Torn*, 38.
[64] Richard D. Ralston with sections on Latin America and the Caribbean by Maura Albuquerque, "Africa in the New World" in *General History of Africa: Vol. 7: Africa under Colonial Domination, 1880–1935*, ed. Adu A. Boahen (London: Heinemann, 1985): 780
[65] M'Bow, "Preface," xx.
[66] UNESCO, "Conference: Meeting of Experts on Historical Contacts between East Africa and Madagascar on the One Hand, and South East Asia on the Other, across the Indian Ocean," *GHA Sources and Documents* (Paris: UNESCO Publishing, 1974).

take on "Africa's Lost Past" in which re-assessment of African history maintained a division between pre- and post-European colonial presence in Africa.[67]

The focus on the GHA as "a history of ideas, and civilisations, societies and institutions"[68] also followed UNESCO's previous approaches to history. Like the GHA, the History of Mankind project had also been, primarily, a history of ideas, technology, belief systems and exchanges that prioritised developments in science and culture. In the GHA, the focus on belief systems, ideas and culture was notable in the selection of themes and also with respect to contributors which included several non-professional historians. Vansina hinted that the appointment of Africans who were not professional historians as contributors resulted from a shortage of trained professionals in some parts of the continent.[69] Yet the inclusion of authors and public intellectuals was integral to UNESCO's engagements with Africa's history and heritage at this time.[70] The most prominent example in the context of the GHA was that of the Nobel Laureate Wole Soyinka who contributed a chapter on "The Arts in Africa During the Period of Colonial rule" to Volume 7 which covered the period 1880 to 1935.[71] In his chapter, which surely ranks among the best in all the GHA volumes, Soyinka detailed a wide range of art forms and historical contexts. The chapter discussed the role of the colonial state, connections across the Atlantic and the patronage of black missionaries to exemplify "processes of transposition from traditional to adaptive modes" in African art forms.[72] Soyinka emphasised African agency and how this heritage continued to inspire creative artists in the present. "The reality that we extract from this period," he concluded, "is the resilience and even increased vitality of the forms and values of the authentic cultures of the peoples" in spite of the violent intrusion of the European colonisers.[73] A creative third space had been carved out through the resistance to colonialism. This inter-

---

67 UNESCO, "Africa's Lost Past," 4–9.
68 Ogot, "Description of the Project," xxiii.
69 Vansina, "UNESCO and African Historiography," 47–48.
70 One early example is Chinua Achebe whose first affiliation with UNESCO was in 1961 when he received a UNESCO creative artist travel grant. UNESCO, "1961–1962: Regular Programme. Creative Artists. Albert Achebe. Writer," UNESCO Archives. EDU/TE/26: 2003.35–44. Accessed 6 January 2019, https://atom.archives.unesco.org/uploads/r/5c00 m/5/5/55059/EDV-FE-26_-_1961–62_Regular_Programme_-_Creative_Artists_-_Nigeria_-_Albert_Achebe_-_Writer_com pressed.pdf.
71 Wole Soyinka, "The Arts in Africa During the Period of Colonial Rule," in *General History of Africa: Vol. 7: Africa under Colonial Domination, 1880–1935*, ed. Adu A. Boahen (London: Heinemann, 1985), 539–564.
72 Ibid, 549
73 Ibid, 540

pretation of a past capable of inspiring the present was in line with the memory politics of Volume 7 as a whole.

Adu Boahen and the View from the Inside

In 1985, UNESCO published *Volume VII: Africa under Colonial Domination, 1880– 1935*. The illustration on the volume jacket featured a relief from the walls of the Palace of the Kings of Dahomey. It depicted a white figure pointing a giant loaded firearm at the nose of a black figure carrying a bow (Fig. 1). Judged by the jacket illustration, the message of the volume seems clear: Europeans exploiting their superior military strength to wage merciless warfare against Africans. However, for the director of the volume, the Ghanaian historian Adu Boahen, this was not the primary idea. Rather, he explained that he chose the illustration of "an African armed only with bow and arrow defiantly and squarely facing a European armed with a gun" because it showed "the weight of the odds against them [the Africans] on the one hand and the strength of the determination to resist at any price on the other."[74] It was a message of resistance.

Boahen's influence on volume 7 was profound. He wrote the introduction and the concluding chapter and authored and co-authored several other chapters. His correspondence with contributors and with UNESCO officials shows that he had a firm editorial hand in appointing contributors and revising their contributions particularly to present "the view from the inside" firmly in all chapters.[75] His influence in the GHA was further enhanced in 1983 when he replaced Ogot as chairman of UNESCO's International Expert Committee.

Boahen had obtained a degree in history in Ghana before the country became independent and a doctorate from the School of Oriental and African Studies (SOAS) in London in 1959. He lectured at Legon from that year on and was chairman of the history department for nearly two decades. In 1999, he was awarded the UNESCO Avicenna Silver medal for his contributions to the *General History of Africa* project.[76] As Toyin Falola has stressed in a short intellectual biography, Boahen saw it as his mission to contribute to the Africanisation of history in order to transcend a Eurocentric perspective of the continent, an agenda

---

[74] Albert A Boahen, "Africa and the Colonial Challenge," in Boahen, *General History of Africa: Vol. 7*, 10.
[75] UNESCO Archives, CLT/CS/7.1 Auteurs VOL VII 1973/1982.
[76] For a brief biographical sketch see: "Boahen, A. Adu 1932–2006," *ecylcopedia.com*, 2020, accessed 12 January 2019, https://www.encyclopedia.com/arts/educational-magazines/boahen-adu-1932-2006.

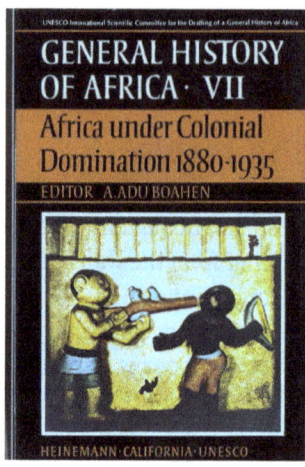

Fig. 1: Jacket for GHA Vol VII (1985).

that he had pursued in his widely read textbooks on the history of West Africa published between 1960 and 1987.[77] Like many of his generation of African historians, Boahen believed that the role of the historian was not only to educate, but also to create relevant knowledge for Africa's newly independent nations. Boahen thus incarnated the spirit of the GHA.

For Boahen, the aspiration to contribute to post-colonial nation-building through writing and teaching history involved a reinterpretation of the colonial period. This reinterpretation was conveyed in the jacket illustration. Africans had been resourceful and engaged in developing strong states before the late-nineteenth century when they encountered the European colonisers supercharged by their industrial tools of empire and ideas of racial superiority. Africans then mobilised deeply rooted cultural and political resources to initiate diverse but according to Boahen united forms of resistance against the colonial oppressors.[78]

This perspective was notable throughout the entire GHA volume. Covering the period 1880 to 1935, it devoted seven chapters to different regions under the headline "African Initiatives and Resistance." "From the inside" in this context meant an emphasis on African initiative and agency. As Boahen summarised in the volume's introduction, history showed that an "overwhelming majority of

---

[77] Toyin Falola, "Adu Boahen: An Introduction," in *Ghana in Africa and the World: Essays in Honor of Adu Boahen*, ed. Toyin. Falola (Trenton, NJ: Africa World Press, 2002), 4.
[78] Adu A. Boahen, *Topics in West African History* (London: Harlow, 1966); Adu A. Boahen, *Ghana: Evolution and Change in the 19th and 20th Centuries* (London: Longman, 1975); Adu A. Boahen, *African Perspectives on Colonialism* (Baltimore: Johns Hopkins, 1987).

African authorities and leaders were vehemently opposed to colonial conquest."[79] From what he called "the African perspective," the colonial period "saw African kings, queens, lineage and clan heads all dominated by one overriding consideration, that of maintaining or regaining their sovereignty, patrimony and culture by the strategy of confrontation or alliance or submission."[80] This interpretation aimed to demonstrate beyond doubt the agency of Africans as they mobilised resources against colonial conquest. Boahen therefore dismissed the use of terms such as "collaboration" and "collaborators" in the colonial encounter as "Africans were all faced with the question of surrendering, retaining or regaining their sovereignty."[81]

The centrality of "the inside" perspective in the volume is underscored further in Boahen's correspondence with contributing authors. A heated exchange with Terence Ranger is particularly illuminating in this respect. The GHA committee commissioned Ranger in 1973 to write an overview of the on-going debate amongst historians about African resistance to colonial rule.[82] Ranger submitted his chapter in 1975 subject to the director's approval.[83] By this time, Boahen was caught up in the political upheavals taking place in Ghana and incarcerated by Acheampong's military regime for his role as a founding member of the People's Movement for Freedom and Justice.[84] Upon his release in 1978, Boahen wrote to Ranger and demanded substantial changes to the chapter. The analysis, Boahen argued, presented "a simplified view" of African responses. He found the title "African Resistance to the Imposition of European Rule: An Overview and Reassessment" highly problematic as it denied "the African of any initiative and puts him always on the defensive or reacting to external stimulus."[85]

Ranger's response was swift and angry. He argued that he had done what had been expected of him, that his interpretation was not influenced by "the psychology of colonialism and neo-colonialism" as Boahen (in Ranger's reading) had implied and that the deadline for changes demanded by Boahen was "absurd after so long a silence."[86] Boahen's reply to Ranger was short. He took

---

79 Boahen, "Africa and the Colonial Challenge," 10.
80 Ibid, 17.
81 Ibid, 18.
82 For one of Ranger's contributions to the longstanding debate over resistance in African history, see Terence Ranger, "The People in African Resistance: A Review," *Journal of Southern African Studies* 4, no. 1 (1977): 125–146.
83 M. Glélé to T. Ranger, 4 March 1975, UNESCO Archives, CLT/CS/7.1.
84 A. Boahen to M. Glélé, 7 Jan. 1979, UNESCO Archives, CLT/CS/7.1.
85 Boahen to Ranger, 15 Dec. 1978, UNESCO Archives, CLT/CS/7.1.
86 Ranger to Boahen, 4 Jan. 1979, UNESCO Archives, CLT/CS/7.1.

strong exception to the tone of Ranger's letter and, referring to the use of the word "absurd," stated that he "never expected that one could use such a word in a letter to a colleague, even if that colleague happens to be an African."[87] Maurice Glélé in the UNESCO secretariat intervened to negotiate a compromise. He reminded Boahen that the committee had in fact previously approved Ranger's chapter.[88] The word collaboration was, however, taken out of the chapter and the title changed to "African Initiative and Resistance in the Face of Partition and Conquest."

This controversy demonstrates the challenge that UNESCO faced to keep the project afloat and the importance attached to the interpretation of "the view from the inside." This was politically committed history. Indeed, the volume offered an interpretation of the colonial period but, as Boahen explained, it also intended to address the question "what the significance of colonialism was for Africa and her history?"[89] In his concluding chapter, Boahen returned to this issue in light of the "inside perspective" which ran through the preceding chapters.[90] In his view, colonialism was certainly not a boon bestowed upon Africans as the defunct colonialist historiography had claimed. Nor was it exclusively the "one-armed bandit" that Walter Rodney had claimed in his chapter of the volume.[91] Colonialism had positive and negative effects politically, socially and economically. The crucial point for Boahen, however, was that the positive effects – which for him included the rise of nationalism and Pan-Africanism as well as science and education – had come about *despite* the intentions of the colonisers. It resulted from the initiative and power of Africans faced with oppressive and technologically advanced European colonisers. The point for Boahen was that Africans had displayed agency and a will to defend their sovereignty in the face of the European oppressors.[92]

---

[87] Boahen to Ranger, 30 Jan. 1979, UNESCO Archives, CLT/CS/7.1. There was also a scholarly disagreement between the two historians as Ranger was an early critic of "history for self-government," which he considered a hinderance to the development of African history. See: Terence Ranger, "Introduction," in *Emerging Themes of African History*, ed. Terence Ranger (Heinemann: Nairobi, 1968), 1–23.
[88] Glele to Boahen, 16 Feb. 1979, UNESCO Archives, CLT/CS/7.1.
[89] Boahen, "Africa and the Colonial Challenge," 19.
[90] Adu A. Boahen, "Colonialism in Africa: Its Impact and Significance," in Boahen, *General History of Africa: Vol. 7*, 782–810.
[91] Walter Rodney, "The Colonial Economy," in Boahen, *General History of Africa: Vol. 7*, 332–351. Boahen agreed that the image of the one-armed bandit was "almost correct" in the economic sphere but less so in political and social spheres.
[92] Boahen, "Colonialism in Africa," 803.

This historical message was relevant for present leaders and peoples in Africa and it was they whom Boahen addressed in the conclusion to the volume. Paraphrasing Ade Ajayi, Boahen claimed that colonialism was indeed "a mere chapter in the numerous chapters of the long history of the continent" but one that:

> Marks a clear watershed in the history of Africa and the subsequent development of Africa, and therefore its history has been and will continue to be very much influenced by the colonial impact on Africa, and destined to take a course different from what it would have taken had there not been any colonial interlude. The most expedient course of action for African leaders to embark upon today, then, is not to write off colonialism but rather to be conversant with its impact, and to try to redress its shortcomings and its failures.[93]

Viewed in this light, Volume 7 of the GHA is testament to the quest for relevance amongst those involved in the project. In this case not least Adu Boahen, a leading representative of the dominant view among the African historians in the GHA project.

Conclusion

Commentators have primarily assessed the GHA in relation to the development of African history as an academic field.[94] In this chapter, however, I have used the GHA to unravel how African intellectuals worked to produce a UNESCO-backed history that they considered relevant to the present and future of the African continent.

UNESCO significantly shaped the GHA with respect to organisational set-up, historical perspective, contributors and memory politics. An important UNESCO influence consisted in the inclusion of important African intellectuals in the transnational engagement with African memory politics. For Diop, Soyinka, Boahen and their generation of historians, historical interpretations had direct and profound impact on the future of independent Africa. The quest for relevance and wholeness among the contributors helps to explain why the GHA was a much more politicised history than the UNESCO History of Mankind. The History of Mankind did not ignore colonialism and decolonisation. Instead, it labelled

---

93 Ibid, 809.
94 In general, the first volumes covering the oldest histories of the continent were most positively reviewed while reviews of the last two volumes covering recent history have been decidedly more mixed.

decolonisation "the most important event of the twentieth century" and devoted more pages to Nkrumah than to Hitler.[95] However, it was a history almost completely devoid of conflict. The GHA differed in this respect with its emphasis on resistance and struggle. The GHA was clearly an ideologically engaged history. Yet the project also expressed a firm belief in the value of science and an equally strong conviction that the politics of memory mattered; that ideas, knowledge and scholarship were prerequisites for coming to terms with a difficult past, for setting the course in the present and for creating a more peaceful future. In this respect, the makers of the GHA were heir to the idealism that had constituted UNESCO's foundation in the first place.

As has been stressed in several chapters in this volume, ideas about the nation, memory and African identity changed fundamentally during the first decades after independence. The ways in which the intellectuals involved in the GHA viewed the project of nation-building also shifted during the decades that the project spanned. An increasingly difficult relationship with what Ki-Zerbo in the late 1990s referred to as the "tropical leviathan" greatly influenced the changing outlook of this generation of intellectuals.[96] As nation-building projects on the continent began to collapse after 1970, it was not possible for historians in Africa to maintain the academic and institutional momentum of the early 1960s when the GHA was launched. As such the GHA project cuts across the rise and decline of African academia and of nation-building more broadly.[97]

Yet in the GHA, the commitment to Pan-Africanism and nation-building continued to resonate. When Volume 8, *Africa since 1935*, was published in 1993, the now older generation of intellectuals and historians wrote about the historical period that had seen the beginning of the GHA project as well as their own youth. A chapter on "Nation-building and Changing Political Structures" written by Mazrui, Boahen, Ki-Zerbo and assistant volume director Christophe Wondji identified the years from 1945 to 1960 as the period during which ideas of nationalism and liberal democracy dominated Africa's political and intellectual scene. They argued that this was followed by an era which from 1960 to 1985 saw the spread of authoritarian rule across the continent.[98] But their chapter ended on a note of temperate hope that democracy and pluralism would again gain momen-

---

95 Betts, "Humanity's New Heritage."
96 Joseph Ki-Zerbo, "African Intellectuals, Nationalism and Pan-Africanism: A Testimony," in Mkandawire, *African Intellectuals*, 78–94.
97 Falola, *Nationalism and African Intellectuals*, 261–295.
98 Joseph Ki Zerbo, Ali Mazrui, Christoph Wondji, and Adu A. Boahen, "Nation Building and Changing Political structures," in *UNESCO General History of Africa Vol 8: Africa since 1935*, ed. Ali Mazrui (London: Heinemann 1993), 468–500.

tum in Africa – not as a side effect of "the *glasnost* and *Perestroika* of Gorbachev or the pressure of international financial institutions such as the World Bank and the IMF or by aid-donors such as the United States, Britain and France" but because of developments and historical trajectories within the continent:

> Herein lies the heart of the democratic revolution sweeping through Africa in the early 1990s. What Africans are demanding, then, is a return not only to liberal democratic values but also to those values embodied in and symbolized by their national mottoes, anthems and flags: national unity, development, freedom and social justice.[99]

Viewed in the *longue durée*, continental perspectives presented in the GHA, the struggle for national integration and state-building in Africa had, according to the authors, only just begun.

Bibliography

Andersen, Casper. "Capacity Building, Scientific Independence, and the Establishment of UNESCOs Science and Technology Agenda for Africa." *Canadian Journal of African Studies* 50, no. 3 (2017): 379–393.

Andersen, Casper. "The Zero Hours of Technology and the Founding of UNESCO." In *Zero Hours: Conceptual Beginnings Vol. 2*, edited by Hagen Schulz Forberg, Chapter 6. Oxford: Palgrave Macmillan, 2021.

Barbosa, Muryatan Santana. "The Construction of the African Perspective: A History of the General History of Africa." *Revista Brasileira de História* 32, no. 64 (2012): 195–214.

Betts, Paul. "Humanity's New Heritage: UNESCO and the Rewriting of World History." *Past & Present* 228, no. 1 (2015): 249–285.

Bhabha, Homi. "Of Mimicry and Man: The Ambivalence of Colonial Discourse." *Discipleship: A Special Issue on Psychoanalysis* 28 (1984): 125–133.

Bhambra, Gurminder, Gebrial Dalia, and Nişancıoğlu, Kerem (eds.) *Decolonising the University*. London: Pluto Press, 2018.

Boahen, Adu A. *Topics in West African History*. London: Harlow, 1966.

Boahen, Adu A. *Ghana: Evolution and Change in 19th and 20th Centuries*. London, Longman 1975.

Boahen, Adu A. "Africa and the Colonial Challenge." In *General History of Africa. Vol. 7: Africa under Colonial Domination, 1880–1935*, edited by Adu A. Boahen, 1–19. London: Heinemann, 1985.

Boahen, Adu A. "Colonialism in Africa: Its Impact and Significance." In *General History of Africa. Vol. 7: Africa under Colonial Domination, 1880–1935*, edited by Adu A. Boahen, 782–810. London: Heinemann, 1985.

Boahen, Adu A. *African Perspectives on Colonialism*. Baltimore: Johns Hopkins, 1987.

---

99 Ki Zerbo et al., "Nation Building," 492.

Brattain, Michelle. "Race, Racism, and Antiracism: UNESCO and the Politics of Presenting Science to the Postwar Public." *American Historical Review* 112, no. 5 (2007): 1386–1413

Connell, Raewyn, Fran Collyer, Fran, Maia João and Morrell, Robert. *Knowledge and Global Power. Making New Sciences in the South*. Clayton: Monash University Press 2019.

Cooper, Frederick. "Conflict and Connection: Rethinking African History." *American Historical Review* 99, no. 5 (1994): 516–1545.

Davidson, Basil. "The Rediscovery of Africa." *The UNESCO Courier* 12, no. 10 (1959): 4–9.

Denoon, Donald, and Adam Kuper. "Nationalist Historians in Search of a Nation: The 'New Historiography' in Dar-es-Salaam." *African Affairs* 217 (1980): 329–349.

Derricourt, Robin. *Inventing Africa: History, Archaeology and Ideas*. London: Pluto Press, 2011.

Dike, Kenneth O. "The Scientific Study of Africa." *The UNESCO Courier* 20, no. 6 (1967): 8–13.

Diop, Cheikh Anta. *Nations Négres et Culture*. Dakar: Présence Africaine, 1955.

Diop, Cheikh Anta. *The African Origins of Civilization: Myth or Reality*. Westport: Laurence Hill, 1974.

Diop, Cheikh Anta. "Origin of Ancient Egyptians." In *General History of Africa: Vol 2: The Ancient civilizations of Africa*, edited by G. Mokhtar, 27–58. London: Heinemann, 1983.

Duedahl, Poul. "Selling Mankind: UNESCO and the Invention of Global History, 1945–76." *Journal of World History* 22, no. 1 (2011): 101–133.

Elzinga, Aant. "UNESCO and the Politics of Scientific Internationalism." In *Science and Internationalism*, edited by Aant Elzinga and Catharina Landström, 89–132. London: Taylor Graham, 1996.

Fage, John D. "The Development of African Historiography." In *General History of Africa: Vol 1: Methodology and African Prehistory*, edited by Joseph Ki-Zerbo, 25–43. London: Heinemann, 1983.

Falola, Toyin. *Nationalism and African Intellectuals*. Rochester: The University of Rochester Press, 2004.

Falola, Toyin. "Adu Boahen: An Introduction." In *Ghana in Africa in the World, Essays in Honour of Adu Boahen*, edited by Toyin Falola, 2–10. Trenton New Jersey: Africa World, 2004.

Falola, Toyin, and Kwame Essien. *Pan-Africanism, and the Politics of African Citizenship and Identity*. Oxford: Routledge, 2014.

Hazard, Anthony Q. "A Racialized Deconstruction? Ashley Montagu and the 1950 UNESCO Statement on Race." *Transforming Anthropology* 19, no. 2 (2011): 174–186.

Howe, Stephen. *Afrocentrism. Mythical Pasts and Imagined Homes*. London and New York: Verso, 1998.

Jabobitti, Edmund E., ed. *Composing Useful Pasts. History as Contemporary Politics*. New York: State of New York University Press, 2000.

Jewsiewicki, Bogumil, and David Newbury, eds. *African Historiographies: What History for Which Africa?* Beverly Hills: Sage, 1986.

Ki Zerbo, Joseph. "General Introduction." In *General History of Africa: Vol 1: Methodology and African Prehistory*, edited by Joseph Ki-Zerbo, 1–25. London: Heinemann, 1983.

Ki Zerbo, Joseph. "African Intellectuals, Nationalism and Pan-Africanism: A Testimony." In *African Intellectuals: Rethinking Politics, Language, Gender and Development*, edited by Thandika Mkandawire, 78–94. London: Zed Books, 2005.

Ki Zerbo, Joseph, Ali Mazrui, Christoph Wondji, and Adu A. Boahen. "Nation-building and Changing Political Structures." In *UNESCO General History of Africa Vol 8: Africa since 1935*, edited by Ali Mazrui, 468–500. London: Heinemann, 1993.

Mama, Amina. "Gender Studies for Africa's Transformation." In *African Intellectuals: Rethinking Politics, Language, Gender and Development*, edited by Thandika Mkandawire, 94–117. London: Zed Books, 2005.

M'Bow, Amadou-Mahtar. "Preface." In *General History of Africa: Vol 1: Methodology and African Prehistory*, edited by Joseph Ki-Zerbo, xvii–xxiii. London: Heinemann, 1983.

Matasci, Damiano. "Assessing Needs, Fostering Development: UNESCO, Illiteracy and the Global Politics of Education (1945–1960)." *Comparative Education* 53, no. 1 (2017): 35–53.

Matasci, Damiano, Jerónimo, Miguel Bandeira and Dores, Hugo Gonçalves. *Education and Development in Colonial and Postcolonial Africa: Policies, Paradigms, and Entanglements, 1890s–1980s*. London: Springer Nature, 2020: 14–18.

Mazrui, Ali. *Africa's International Relations: The Diplomacy of Dependency and Change*. Chicago: Westview Press, 1977.

Mazrui, Ali. *The Africans: A Triple Heritage*. Boston: Little Brown & Co., 1986.

Mazrui, Ali. "Pan-Africanism: From Poetry to Power." *A Journal of Opinion* 23, no. 1 (1995): 35–38.

Mazrui, Ali. "Pan-Africanism and the Intellectuals: Rise, Decline, Revival." In *African Intellectuals: Rethinking Politics, Language, Gender and Development*, edited by Thandika Mkandawire, 56–78. London: Zed Books, 2005.

Martinez, Fernando Valderrama. *A History of UNESCO*. Paris: UNESCO publishing, 1995.

Maurel, Chloé. *Histoire L'Unesco. Les trente Premiére Annnées 1945–74*. Paris: L'Harmatten: 2008.

Maurel, Chloé. "L'histoire Générale de l'Afrique de l'Unesco: Un projet de coopération intellectuelle transnationale d'esprit afro-centré (1964–1999)." *Cahiers d'Études Africaines* 54 (2014): 715–737.

Meskell, Lynn. "UNESCO's World Heritage Convention at 40: Challenging the Economic and Political Order of International Heritage Conservation." *Current Anthropology* 54, no. 4 (2013): 483–494.

Mkandawire, Thandika. "African Intellectuals and Nationalism." In *African Intellectuals: Rethinking Politics, Language, Gender and Development*, edited by Thandika Mkandawire, 10–55. London: Zed Books, 2005.

Mogensen, Mads K., and Ivan. L Christensen. "Report on: Making a Difference: Seventy Years of UNESCO Actions UNESCO Anniversary Conference, UNESCO, Paris, 28–29 October. 2015." *UNESDOC Digital Library*, 2015, accessed 28 November 2019. https://unesdoc.unesco.org/ark:/48223/pf0000244030.

Montagu, Ashley. *Statement on Race: An Annotated Elaboration and Exposition of the Four Statements on Race Issued by the United Nations Educational, Scientific, and Cultural Organization*. Paris: UNESCO Publishing, 1972.

Ndlovu-Gatsheni, Sabelo J. "Decoloniality as the Tuture of Africa." *History Compass* 13, no. 10 (2015): 485–496.

Ndlovu-Gatsheni Sabelo J., and Zondi Siphamandla (eds.). *Decolonizing the University, Knowledge Systems and Disciplines in Africa*. Durham, North Carolina: Carolina Academic Press, 2016.

Ngũgĩ, wa Thiong'o. *Decolonizing the Mind. The Politics of Language in African Literature*. London: James Curry, 1986.
Ngũgĩ, wa Thiong'o. *Something Torn and Something New: An African Renaissance*. New York: BasicCivitas Books, 2009.
Nordholt, Larissa Schulte. "From Metropole to Margin in UNESCO's General History of Africa– Documents of Historiographical Decolonization in Paris and Ibadan." *History in Africa* 46 (2019): 1–10.
Ochwada, Hannington. "Historians, Nationalism and Pan-Africanism. Myths and Realities." In *African Intellectuals: Rethinking Politics, Language, Gender and Development*, edited by Thandika Mkandawire, 193–208. London: Zed Books, 2005.
Ogot, Bethwell A. "Towards a History of Kenya." *Kenya Historical Review* 4, no. 1 (1976): 1–9.
Ogot, Bethwell A. "Description of the Project," In *General History of Africa: Vol 1: Methodology and African Prehistory*, edited by Joseph Ki-Zerbo, xxiii–xxvii. London: Heinemann, 1983.
Ogot, Bethwell A. "Rereading the History and Historiography of Epistemic Domination and Resistance in Africa." *African Studies Review* 52, no. 1 (2009): 1–22.
Ralston, Richard D., with sections on Latin America and the Caribbean by Albuquerque Maura. "Africa in the New World." In *General History of Africa. Vol. 7: Africa under Colonial Domination, 1880–1935*, edited by Adu A. Boahen, 746–782. London: Heinemann, 1985.
Ranger, Terence. "Introduction." In *Emerging Themes of African History*, edited by Terence Ranger, 1–23. Heinemann: Nairobi, 1968.
Ranger, Terence. "The People in African Resistance: A Review." *Journal of Southern African Studies* 4, no. 1 (1977): 125–146.
Renoliet, Jean-Jacques. *L'UNESCO: La Société des Nations et la Coopération Intellectuelle (1919–1946)*. Paris: UNESCO publishing, 1999.
Rodney, Walter. "The Colonial Economy." In *General History of Africa. Vol. 7: Africa under Colonial Domination, 1880–1935*, edited by Adu A. Boahen, 332–351. London: Heinemann, 1985.
Sluga, Glenda. "UNESCO and the (One) World of Julian Huxley." *Journal of World History* 22, no. 3, (2010): 393–418.
Soyinka, Wole. "The Arts in Africa during the Period of Colonial Rule." In *General History of Africa. Vol. 7: Africa under colonial domination, 1880–1935*, edited by Adu A. Boahen, 539–564. London: Heinemann, 1985.
UNESCO. "Africa and African Genius." *The UNESCO Courier* 20, no. 6 (1959): 24–29.
UNESCO. *Guide for the Preparation of the General History of Africa*. Paris: UNESCO Publishing, 1971.
UNESCO. *Ten-year Plan for the Study of African Oral Traditions and the Promotion of African Languages*. Paris: UNESCO Publishing 1972.
UNESCO. *Conference: Meeting of Experts on Historical Contacts between East Africa and Madagascar on the One Hand, and South East Asia on the Other, across the Indian Ocean, GHA Sources and Documents*. Paris: UNESCO Publishing, 1974.
UNESCO. *The Peopling of Ancient Egypt and the Deciphering of Meroitic Script; proceedings*. Paris: UNESCO publishing, 1978.

UNESCO. "Annex to Chapter 1: Deciphering of the Meiotic Script." In *General History of Africa: Vol 2: The Ancient Civilizations of Africa*, edited by G. Mokhtar, 59–84. London: Heinemann, 1983.

Vansina, Jan. "Oral Tradition and its Methodology." In *General History of Africa: Vol 1: Methodology and African Prehistory*, edited by Joseph Ki-Zerbo, 142–166. London: Heinemann, 1983.

Vansina, Jan. "UNESCO and African Historiography," *History in Africa* 20 (1993): 337–352.

II **Political Commemoration & Memory**

Edward Goodman
Remembering Mzee: The Making and Re-making of "Kenyatta Day," 1958–2010

Abstract: While a concern with memory, in particular of the Mau Mau rebellion, has a well-established place in Kenya's historiography, little attention has yet been paid to the postcolonial Kenyan state's official memory regime, to what Kenya's citizens have been asked to remember. The following chapter aims to fill this gap. It traces the origins of "Kenyatta Day," celebrated from 1964 onwards on 20th October each year, and the four successive stories that were told about it by first its proponents, figures associated with the KANU government and the state, and then its critics in parliament and civil society whose attainment of power led to the re-dedication of the day as "Heroes Day" in 2010, when Kenya's "Second Republic" was inaugurated by a new constitution.

In the early hours of the morning of 20th October 1952, British security services in Kenya set in motion the plan codenamed "Operation Jock Scott," a strategy devised over the course of the previous few days, with the intention of decapitating the so-called Mau Mau movement.[1] The rounding-up of around 150 Kenya African Union (KAU) activists would, it was hoped, leave the movement rudderless, allowing security services the opportunity to regain control in the increasingly fraught circumstances of Kenya's Central Province and Rift Valley. At the top of the list (and by the time of his arrest, apparently aware of what was coming) was the name of Jomo Kenyatta, leader of the KAU, author of *Facing Mount Kenya*, and future president of independent Kenya.[2] So began the Emergency, which was to last eight long years.

The roundup was followed by a show trial of Kenyatta and five other men, Fred Kubai, Bildad Kaggia, Paul Ngei, Kungu Karumba and Achieng' Oneko, ac-

---

[1] For an introduction to successive understandings of Mau Mau, see John Lonsdale, "Foreword," in *Mau Mau from Below*, ed. Greet Kershaw (Oxford: James Currey, 1997), xvi–xxx.
[2] On Operation Jock Scott, see David Anderson, *Histories of the Hanged: Britain's Dirty War in Kenya and the End of Empire* (London: W.W. Norton, 2005), 62–63. For an introduction to the tense situation in Central Province and the Rift Valley, see Ch.1. See also David Throup, *Economic and Social Origins of Mau Mau* (London: James Currey, 1987); Daniel Branch, *Defeating Mau Mau, Creating Kenya: Counterinsurgency, Civil War, and Decolonisation* (Cambridge: Cambridge University Press, 2009); and Gabrielle Lynch, *I Say to You: Ethnic Politics and the Kalenjin in Kenya* (Chicago: University of Chicago Press, 2011), Chs. 1–2.

∂ OpenAccess. © 2022 Edward Goodman, published by De Gruyter. [CC BY-NC-ND] This work is licensed under the Creative Commons Attribution 4.0 International License.
https://doi.org/10.1515/9783110655315-005

cused by the colonial state of "managing" Mau Mau. Kenyatta, according to Ransley Thacker, a former Kenyan High Court Judge and Attorney-General of Fiji, brought out of retirement to preside over the case, was the "master mind" behind Mau Mau, the man who had "let loose upon this land a flood of misery and unhappiness affecting the daily lives of all the races in it, including," he made clear, "those of your own people." The KAU's leader, he insisted, had taken "fullest advantage of the power and influence" which he held, the product, according to Thacker, of his education and long immersion in British society, where he had lived from the early 1930s to the mid-1940s. He had done so, the judge claimed, in order to turn back the "progress that had been made" under colonial tutelage "towards an enlightened civilisation" amongst his people, preying on "the primitive instincts which you know lie deep down in their characters," plunging these dupes "back to a state which shows little of humanity," and persuading them "in secret to murder, to burn and to commit evil atrocities which it will take," the judge gravely intoned, "many years to forget." Convinced of his guilt, Thacker sentenced Kenyatta, and the other five, to seven years' hard labour.[3] The future president was to remain in detention until August 1961.

Over the course of the last 60 years, it has been the movement that Kenyatta was convicted (quite wrongly) of managing that has stood "[a]t the heart of Kenya's modern history."[4] Mau Mau has been the central concern of those interested in the question of how "a conscious sense of the past, as something meaningfully connected to the present, is sustained and developed within human individuals and human cultures," the imperative – etched onto the memorial to the self-declared state of Somaliland's experience of war under General Siad Barre, and described in this volume by Mohamed Haji Ingriis – to "respect and remember."[5] Marshall Clough, for example, has traced "the elusive, chang-

---

[3] Judgement of the Crown vs. Jomo Kenyatta *et al*, [1952], Court of the Resident Magistrate at Kapenguria, 8 April 1953, 97–98. On Kenyatta's trial, see John Lonsdale, "Kenyatta's Trials: Breaking and Making an African Nationalist," in *The Moral World of the Law*, ed. Peter Coss (Cambridge: Cambridge University Press, 2002), 196–239; and Anderson, *Histories*, 65–68. On imaginations of Mau Mau more generally, see John Lonsdale, "Mau Mau's of the Mind: Making Mau Mau and Remaking Kenya," *Journal of African History* 31, no. 3 (1990): 393–421.
[4] John Lonsdale, "The Moral Economy of Mau Mau," in *Unhappy Valley: Conflict in Kenya and Africa*, Book Two, ed. Bruce Berman and John Lonsdale (Oxford: James Curry, 1992), 467.
[5] Geoffrey Cubitt, *History and Memory* (Manchester: Manchester University, Press 2007), 9. On Somaliland, see Mohamed Haji Ingriis in this volume. On the imperative to remember, and the need to forget, see also David Rieff, *In Praise of Forgetting: Historical Memory and its Ironies* (New Haven: Yale University Press, 2016). On the postcolonial legacy of Mau Mau, see Nicholas K. Githuku, *Mau Mau Crucible of War: Statehood, National Identity and the Politics of Postcolonial Kenya* (London: Lexington Book, 2016).

ing [and] divisive" memory of Mau Mau in Kenya through successive postcolonial "moments of crisis." The image of the rebellion, he argued, has been mobilised and counter-mobilised at particular times by both opposition forces, a critique of Kenya's post-independence direction, and successive governments, a means to disable the effectiveness of their opponents' arguments and imagery.[6] "[T]he history of Mau Mau, being so evocative," wrote E.S. Atieno Odhiambo, summing up this interest, "is often discussed in public in high enough decibels to be shouted."[7]

Recent writers have been no less impressed by the centrality of representations of Mau Mau in postcolonial Kenya, nor by the difficulty posed by the rebellion. But, in light of the violence that accompanied the 2007 general election, harking back to a theme first considered by scholars in the 1960s, they have added a more central emphasis on the apparent failure or unwillingness of successive Kenyan governments to grapple with Kenya's difficult history, to seek to create a genuinely national history at the centre of the story, criticising their tendency to take refuge in "culture heritage" at the expense of history.[8] In the Kenyan case, the need for amnesia has been, according to Annie Coombes, "a persistently repeated refrain" stretching across fifty years of postcolonial history.[9]

Both are significant themes which have an important place in what follows. The Kenyan state did not, however, only forget. Nor was its interest in the cultivation of memory solely reactive. While in other parts of East Africa, scholarly attention has been paid to official memory regimes – the state-led memorialisation of particular aspects of the past – and the way in which they have been used

---

[6] Marshall S. Clough, "Mau Mau and the Contest for Memory," in *Mau Mau and Nationhood: Arms, Authority and Narration*, eds. E.S. Atieno Odhiambo and John Lonsdale (Oxford: James Currey, 2003), 251–267; Marshall S. Clough, *Mau Mau Memoirs: History, Memory and Politics* (Boulder: Lynne Reinner Publishers, 1998), especially Ch.8.
[7] E.S. Atieno Odhiambo, "The Production of History in Kenya: The Mau Mau Debate," *Canadian Journal of African Studies* 25, no. 1 (1992): 304.
[8] See Annie E. Coombes, Lottie Hughes and Karega-Munene, eds., *Managing Heritage, Making Peace: History, Identity and Memory in Contemporary Kenya* (London: Bloomsbury Publishing PLC, 2014), especially Chs. 4 & 5. See also Terence Ranger, "The Politics of Memorialisation in Zimbabwe," in *Nations and their Histories: Constructions and Representations*, eds. Susana Carvalho and François Gemenne (Basingstoke: Palgrave Macmillan, 2009), 62–76.
[9] Annie E. Coombes, "Monuments and Memories: Public Commemorative Strategies in Contemporary Kenya," in *Managing Heritage, Making Peace: History, Identity and Memory in Contemporary Kenya*, eds. Annie E. Coombes, Lottie Hughes and Karega-Munene (London: Bloomsbury Publishing PLC, 2014), 141.

by both government, as a tool of political persuasion,[10] and its critics, little attention has yet been paid to this in Kenya.[11] The following pages aim to begin to fill this gap. Central to this official memory regime, was the 20th October, the date of Kenyatta's arrest, which was enshrined in Kenya's public calendar as "Kenyatta Day" by the Kenya African National Union (KANU) government in the days leading up to independence on 12th December 1963. In this chapter, I trace the origins of this day and the four successive stories that were told about it by, first, its proponents and defenders, figures connected with the KANU government, and then its critics in parliament and civil society (but not beyond[12]), critics whose attainment of power led to the re-dedication of the day as "Heroes Day" in 2010 with the passage of the new constitution, the promulgation of Kenya's "Second Republic."

Colonial Origins

The earliest efforts to mark the 20th October came in 1958, six years after Kenyatta's arrest, as prominent politicians in Nairobi, including Tom Mboya, the leader of the Nairobi People's Convention Party, and the African Elected Members of the Legislative Council, called for the day of Kenyatta's arrest to be commemorated as either "National Day" or "Freedom Day." In the weeks leading up to the date, the question of how exactly the occasion should be marked was a matter of dispute. Consideration was given to the possibility of launching boycotts of "buses and places of amusement" and perhaps even beer and tobacco. The possibility of holding a demonstration to mark the occasion was also mooted. While the desirability and feasibility of such moves were

---

10 A concept explored by Georg Deutsch in: Jan-G. Deutsch, "Celebrating Power in Everyday Life: The Administration of Law and the Public Sphere in Colonial Tanzania, 1890–1914," *Journal of African Cultural Studies* 15, no.1 (2002): 93–103.
11 Felicitas Becker, "Remembering Nyerere: Political Rituals and Dissent in Contemporary Tanzania," *African Affairs* 112, no. 447 (2013): 238–261; and Marie-A. Fouere, "Julius Nyerere, *Ujamaa* and Political Morality in Contemporary Tanzania," *African Studies Review* 57, no. 1 (2014): 1–24.
12 There are other locations from which Kenyatta Day could fruitfully be examined, other stories which could be told, but on which my sources have little to say. See, for example, Becker, "Remembering Nyerere" and Daniel Branch, "The Search for the Remains of Dedan Kimathi: The Politics of Death and Memorialisation in Postcolonial Kenya," *Past and Present* 206, Supplement 5 *Relics and Remains* (2010): 314–318, both of which attempt to integrate the view from one region with both the official view and elite criticism. The difficulty of the recovery of memory from the margins, meanwhile, is, in part, the focus of Natacha Filippi's chapter in this volume.

debated, however (the product, not least, of the haunting fear of a publicly visible lack of interest), it was widely agreed within this circle that the central feature of these commemorations should be widespread fasting in recognition of Kenyatta's prison suffering. Efforts were made to publicise these plans in the Nairobi People's Convention Party's newspaper, *Uhuru* (plans which were, in turn, picked up by the English language press), and in Kenya's rural localities, where they received at least some support. The Luhya politician Wafula Wabuge, for example, instructed a meeting of the Eldoret District Congress, of which he was president, "to observe 20th October as a day of fasting as a sign that Africans recognised KENYATTA as their true spiritual leader."[13] Kenyatta was, on this reading, the leader of Kenya's Africans, imprisoned by a foreign administration bent on the domination of the African population, his release essential to the cause of Kenyan freedom.

It is worth pausing at this point to ask: why Kenyatta and why at this point? While, as we shall see, Kenyatta's life story came to be associated with the farsighted and ultimately successful fight against colonial oppression, in the 1950s his suitability for this role was perhaps less obvious than it might now appear. From 1947 he had been the leader of a political party, the KAU, which failed in its stated goal of representing the whole of Kenya, struggling to build a base of support beyond its point of origin amongst the Kikuyu in Central Province. Historians have not been kind in their judgements of the party.[14] They were hardly the first to lay such criticisms, however. Kenyatta and leadership of the KAU were both subject to criticism and closely associated with this failure in the 1940s. The editor of the Luo-language newspaper *Ramogi*, for example, complained in 1948 that "although we have supported KAU in almost every respect, we do not feel it is too early to voice our views," which were, he made clear, that Kenyatta, as the organisation's "new president," "has not made it his duty to make people in Nyanza and Coast Province realise the Union's activities." As a consequence of this neglect, he insisted, the organisation should be avoided.[15]

---

[13] The National Archives, Kew, London (hereafter TNA) FCO 141/6636, (Kenya: Nairobi People's Convention Party), Office of the Director of Intelligence and Security, "Nairobi People's Convention Party. Freedom Day – October 20th," 18 October 1958. Original emphasis.

[14] The fullest account of the party's history can be found in John Spencer, *KAU, The Kenya African Union* (London: KPI Limited, 1985). For a more sympathetic account, see John Lonsdale, "KAU's Cultures: Imaginations of Community and Constructions of Leadership in Kenya after the Second World War," *Journal of African Cultural Studies* 13, no. 1 (2000): 107–124.

[15] Cited in Spencer, *KAU*, 178. See also Fay Gadsden, "The African Press in Kenya, 1945–52," *Journal of African History* 21, no. 4 (1980): 522.

In the six years following Kenyatta's imprisonment, however, the political scene in the territory was transformed, the product of the working through of the Emergency's impact.[16] This impact was two-fold. In the first place, shocked by rebellion, colonial concern to cultivate a loyal class of Africans led to the development of the two-part Swynnerton Plan in 1954, the first part focussing on Central Province and the second on the rest of the territory.[17] Whatever the intention of its author, the implementation of the plan quickly bred significant discontent as (in brief) land consolidation policies, central to Swynnerton's vision of the future, worried migrants absent in towns that they were to be cheated of their rural land, while paternalistic measures designed to promote environmentally sustainable development caused rapidly escalating conflict, most notably in areas of the Rift Valley.[18]

The impact of these efforts was seen most clearly in the results of the first African elections which took place in Kenya in March 1957. In the 1940s, African politicians and intellectuals, including Kenyatta and the KAU, had shown themselves to be cleared eyed as to the destructive effects of certain colonial policies, petitioning the colonial government to institute changes of various kinds.[19] In short, they understood the issues.[20] But by way of remedy, they had tended to call for reform, rather than colonialism's abolition. Their goal was African paramountcy, a formula which named colonialism's purpose, borrowing its terms

---

[16] This paragraph draws on arguments outlined at greater length in Edward Goodman, "Us in the Time of Strangers: Imagining Community in Colonial Kenya and Tanganyika" (DPhil diss., Oxford University, 2017), Ch. 4.

[17] RJM Swynnerton, *Colony and Protectorate of Kenya: A Plan to Intensify the Development of African Agriculture in Kenya* (Nairobi: Government Printer, 1954), i; Bethwell A. Ogot, "The Decisive Years, 1956–63," in *Decolonisation and Independence in Kenya, 1940–1993*, eds., Bethwell A. Ogot and William Ochieng (London: James Currey, 1995), 48–49; Robert Maxon, *Conflict and Accommodation: The Gusii and the British, 1907–1963* (London, Associated University Presses, 1989), 132–133.

[18] Derek R. Peterson, *Ethnic Patriotism and the East African Revival: A History of Dissent, 1935–72* (Cambridge, Cambridge University Press, 2012), 136–137; and Julie MacArthur, *Cartography and the Political Imagination: Mapping Community in Colonial Kenya* (Athens, OH: Ohio University Press, 2016), 195–196; TNA FCO 141/5855, (Kenya: Coast Provincial Intelligence Summaries), Coast Provincial Intelligence Summary for the Month of May 1956, 3; Coast Provincial Intelligence Summary for the Month of June 1956, 3; Coast Provincial Intelligence Summary for the Month of July 1956, 4; David Anderson, *Eroding the Commons: The Politics of Ecology in Baringo District, 1890s-1963* (Oxford: Oxford University Press, 2002), Ch. 7.

[19] See TNA CO 53/537/21 (Memorandum by the Kenya African Union, 1946–1947).

[20] Lonsdale, "KAU's Cultures," 110–111.

from the Devonshire Declaration of 1923, rather than repudiating it.[21] From the mid-1950s, in the face of these pressures, however, African thinkers recast the potential of colonial rule, insisting on its ultimate destructiveness, and demanding that it be removed, a novel call. In the course of those elections, then, all but two of the sitting African members of the Legislative Council, nominees of the colonial administration, were rejected by the newly constituted electorate in favour of politicians who, whatever their differences, shared an emphasis on the absolute necessity of independence or *uhuru*.[22]

This development took place, to develop the second significance of the Emergency, in a Kenya politically divided by Emergency-era policies. The colonial government, convinced of the subversive intent of the KAU, banned African political organisations in 1953. In 1955, such organisations were re-allowed, but only at the district level, leaving territory-wide parties out-of-bounds. Politically, then, Kenya was fragmented.[23] In this context, as calls for *uhuru* became increasingly loud, nationalist politicians at the centre of the colony, hemmed in by the restrictions of the 1950s, looked to the symbolic plane in their efforts to bring some sense of common purpose to the people of the colony.[24] Kenyatta's long history of involvement with African political organisations, as well as his national and international profile, made him a useful choice. It was, above all, the position he occupied at the time of his arrest that was emphasised, while the movement he was convicted in 1953 of managing, and his relationship with it, were glossed over.[25] In Tanganyika, where such restrictions did not apply, the politics of the period prior to the formation of the Tanganyika African National Union in 1954, in many respects similar to those of their northern neighbour, were largely forgotten, as a national movement was built (if not a sense of a shared national identity, which had deeper roots) through the restless movement of the party's leadership unfettered by the restriction to operate only at the local level. In Kenya, in a situation of enforced immobility, the image of Kenyatta, the

---

21 The Devonshire Declaration of 1923 stated that "if and when the interests of the indigenous people conflict with those of the immigrant races, those of the former shall prevail."
22 On constitutional reform generally in 1950s Kenya, see Robert M. Maxon, *Britain and Kenya's Constitutions* (Amherst: Cambria Press, 2011). On the election, see Ogot, "The Decisive Years," 57–58; Maxon, *Britain and Kenya's Constitutions*, 118–121; Lynch, *I Say to You*, 60–61; and Branch, *Defeating Mau Mau*, 155–158.
23 On the politics of the period, see Keith Kyle, *The Politics of the Independence of Kenya* (Basingstoke: Palgrave, 1999), Ch. 4.
24 On the nationalist movement and the need for a symbol, see Tom Mboya, *Freedom and After* (London: Andre Deutsch Limited, 1963), 62–63.
25 Republic of Kenya, The National Assembly Official Report (*Hansard*), First Session, 1961, lxxxvii, 87 and 94–102.

imprisoned political leader of Kenya's African people, as Oginga Odinga told the Legislative Council in 1958, was pushed to centre stage.[26]

The image of Kenyatta, and the cause of his freedom, figured centrally in Kenyan politics over the following three years, as his incarceration continued. In the spring of 1961, for example, delegations of African politicians made well-publicised efforts to visit Kenyatta in detention.[27] His release, indeed, became the central issue of the election held in the April of that year, following which the largest African political party, KANU – the leadership of which Kenyatta assumed on his liberation in the following August – refused to form a government until Kenyatta was released.[28] And while their opponents in the Kenya African Democratic Union (KADU), proved willing to form a minority government with Kenyatta still detained, they justified their actions, in part, on the grounds that it was easier to fight for Kenyatta's release from a position of strength, and chastised their opponents for their apparent attempts to turn a national symbol – their "beloved leader" Kenyatta – to party political ends.[29]

After his release, Kenyatta's image became no less central. Half a century before students in South Africa and (then) Britain insisted that Rhodes Must Fall, and similarly animated by the need to Africanise the symbolic landscape, to cultivate an environment befitting an independent African nation, a rebuke to colonial racism and an assertion of the dignity of all human beings, the KANU government made moves in the weeks preceding Kenya's independence on 12th December 1963, to remove statues of colonial figures in Nairobi and to erase their names from Kenya's roads, moves which raised not a whisper of (public) dissent.[30] In this effort, Kenyatta's name and image figured centrally.[31] What

---

26 Oginga Odinga, *Not Yet Uhuru: An Autobiography* (London: Heinemann, 1967), 156–157. See also *Hansard*, First Session, 1961, lxxxvii, 85, & 87–88. On Tanganyika, see G.G. Hajivayanis, A.C. Mtowa and John Iliffe, "The Politicians: Ali Ponda and Hassan Suleiman," in *Modern Tanzanians: A Volume of Biographies*, ed. John Iliffe (Nairobi: East African Publication House, 1973), 227–253.
27 Kyle, *Politics of the Independence of Kenya*, 127.
28 Odinga, *Not Yet Uhuru*, Ch. 11; David Anderson, "'Yours in Struggle for *Majimbo*': Nationalism and the Party Politics of Decolonisation in Kenya, 1955–64," *Journal of Contemporary History* 40, no. 3 (2005): 552–553.
29 *Hansard*, First Session, 1961, lxxxvii, 71, 105 & 122–124.
30 For an introduction to the aims of these movements, see Amit Chaudri, "The Real Meaning of Rhodes Must Fall," *The Guardian*, 16 March 2016, accessed 2 December 2020, https://www.theguardian.com/uk-news/2016/mar/16/the-real-meaning-of-rhodes-must-fall; And specifically for South Africa, see https://jwtc.org.za/resources/docs/salon-volume-9/RMF_Combined.pdf; And for Britain, see RMFOxford #RhodesMustFall, accessed 2 December 2020, https://rmfoxford.wordpress.com/about/. On the need to place the demand that the statues be removed into his-

had been Delamere Avenue in central Nairobi, for example, named in honour of Kenya's most famous settler, became Kenyatta Avenue in time for independence day, named in honour of Kenya's most famous son.[32] And, likewise, the postcard designed to commemorate Kenya's *uhuru*, an independent nation's literal greeting to the wider world, depicted Kenyatta dressed in a pinstripe suit, with hat and tie in national colours, sat on a chair clutching his famous fly whisk in his beringed hands, while the *Daily Nation*'s independence day edition opened with a similar full page portrait of Kenya's leader, the very embodiment of the new nation.[33]

In these final years of empire, occasional reference was made to 20th October and its significance. On his return from the final Lancaster House Conference in 1963, which coincided with the anniversary of his detention, for example, Kenyatta told a rally of, reportedly, 150,000 people, that "October 20 was the most important day in the history of Africa in general and of Kenya in particular." On this day "eleven years ago," he explained, "the imperialists felt that they had silenced the Kenyans never to shout *Uhuru* any more [sic]."[34] Nonetheless, beyond such rhetoric, in the years after 1958 little effort had been made to mark the occasion. As independence approached, however, the KANU government promulgated the day as a national holiday, designated no longer as Freedom Day or National Day, but as *Kenyatta* Day, to be celebrated from 1964 onwards, an occasion that came, over the course of the following almost fifty years, to be marked by a remarkable continuity in ritual and form.[35]

---

torical perspective, see David Priestland, "The University of Cape Town is Right to Remove its Cecil Rhodes Statue," *The Guardian*, 13 April 2015, accessed 2 December 2020, https://www.theguardian.com/commentisfree/2015/apr/13/cape-town-remove-cecil-rhodes-statue.

31 As, for example, did Kwame Nkrumah's in Ghana. On this, and the subsequent history of this image, see Kodzo Gavua, "Monuments and Negotiations of Power in Ghana," in Peterson, Gavua, and Rassool, *The Politics of Heritage in Africa*, 97–112. In Tanzania, by contrast, Julius Nyerere's name only came to be used in this way after his presidency and, in particular, after his death in 1999. Similarly, the public holiday which bears his name marks the day of his passing (14th October). See: Fouere, "Julius Nyerere," 7–8; "Nyerere Resists Renaming of Street," *Tanzanian Affairs*, 148 (1994) accessed 14 March 2021, https://www.tzaffairs.org/1994/05/nyerere-resists-renaming-of-street/.

32 "Delamere Avenue No More," *Daily Nation*, 5 December 1963, 1.

33 Photo, no title, *Daily Nation*, 5 December 1963, 5; Photo, no title; *Daily Nation*, 12 December 1963, 1. On Kenyatta's rings, see interview with his wife, Mama Ngina: C. Mwagiru, "Kenyatta the Family Man," *Daily Nation*, 20 October 1994, Kenyatta Day Special Supplement, 2–3.

34 "150,000 Roar a Welcome to *Mzee*," *Daily Nation*, 21 October 1963, 1.

35 "Delamere Avenue No More," *Daily Nation*, 5 December 1963, 1.

The First Liberation: Proponents

Rituals of state remembrance were, then, a prominent feature of postcolonial Kenyan life, Kenyatta Day inscribed in the national calendar as a public holiday even before the formal arrival of independence and celebrated each year by an elaborate state ritual. Around its edges, the day was marked by various sporting events bearing Kenyatta's name, including the Kenyatta Cup. It also became associated with an initiative, originating with the Ministry of Health on the occasion of the first Kenyatta Day in 1964, to persuade people to donate blood – giving "blood for Kenya – 1964 style," as the *Daily Nation* described it, a post-independence counterpart to the sacrifices of their forbearers.[36] The heart of the annual celebrations, however, was a series of state-led rallies. On a timetable that changed little between the mid-1960s and the late 2000s, a presidential motorcade wended its way through central Nairobi, in its early years, cheered by significant crowds, stopping briefly after 1978 so that Kenyatta's successor might visit his mausoleum.[37] At its destination, the President delivered the speech that was the centre point of the day, outlining some theme judged to be significant to the coming year.[38] These celebrations in Nairobi were replicated across the country, with smaller rallies held in administrative centres and sports stadiums, where local dignitaries and officials made speeches to mark the occasion, their details reported in brief in the national press, and where one local official or another read the President's speech to the assembled crowd. In their form, these rallies drew on longstanding tradition of *barazas*, in theory a colonial adaptation of an indigenous practice, *local* meetings at which technical or state officials conveyed information to those called to the meeting, a form widely used by both colonial and postcolonial administrations.[39] There was no colonial precedent, however, for the coordination of these meetings in this way, for a "national *baraza*," a truly postcolonial innovation. As we shall see, however, the significance of this symbolism shifted with the stories that were told about Kenyatta Day and its meaning.

---

36 T. Hall, "The Tribute," *Daily Nation*, 20 October 1964, 2.
37 "Kenya Turns Out to Cheer Premier," *Daily Nation*, 21 October 1964, 2. "Joyous Drive Through the City," *Daily Nation*, 21 October 1968, 11.
38 Initially this destination was the Kamukunji stadium, the site of Kenya's independence day celebrations, before the event moved to *Uhuru* Park in the late 1960s and to the *Nyayo* stadium in the 1980s.
39 Angelique Haugerud, *The Culture of Politics in Modern Kenya* (Cambridge: Cambridge University Press, 1993), Ch.4.

Four successive stories about Kenyatta and the day dedicated to him were developed between independence and the late 1990s, two by figures associated with the state and two by their critics. Each of these stories had a particular focus on the 1950s, and each reworked elements of older stories, adding new significances and new understandings, as layers, rather than outright or directly replacing earlier versions. The following two sections trace the contours of these stories as they appeared in the pages of national newspapers, the circumstances in which they were offered, and by whom, and the ends which it was hoped they would serve.

At independence, the new Kenyan government faced an apparently urgent problem: how to shore up, or perhaps even create, a widely shared sense of national identity, the necessary glue of the "unity" that was widely understood to be essential if the people of the newly independent state were to maintain a true independence in the modern world of superpowers.[40] This need was rendered more urgent still in Kenya by the divisiveness of the 1950s and its legacies. Kenya in the wake of Mau Mau was a post-conflict society, the legacy of rebellion a potential social fissure. Recruitment of both Kikuyu and members of other ethnic groups into the "loyalist" Home Guard created obvious social divisions. Many people, moreover, accepted the British "tribalist" argument that Mau Mau sought to eject the British in order to install their own ethnocracy, while the image of the oath, and the spectre of sorcery it invoked, led some to fear that the Kikuyu took "illegal oaths" and therefore "we do not know… what they do at night."[41] Social trust was hard to build. Nor, indeed, did the divisiveness of the final years of colonial rule end with the Emergency. In the almost four years between the first Lancaster House conference in January 1960 and Kenya's achievement of independence on 12th December 1963, the battle between the two political parties which fought for control of the independent state, KANU and KADU, was rancorous, plagued by prophecies of civil war, a future "ocean of blood,"[42] as one correspondent told the Regional Boundaries Commission in 1962, the fear that

---

40 See e.g. Mboya, *Freedom and After*, 87; R. Day, "What is Dividing Them," *Daily Nation*, 28 November 1961, 6; J.B.A. Ohanga, "Forum," *Jicho*, 27 July 1960, 3; S.K. Kimalel, "Tribal Groups," *East African Standard*, 1 July 1960, 3.

41 John Lonsdale, "Moral and Political Argument in Kenya," in *Ethnicity and Democracy in Africa*, eds. Bruce Berman, Dickson Eyoh and Will Kymlicka (Oxford: James Currey, 2004), 85; Branch, *Defeating Mau Mau*, 179–180. C K. Mulela et al., 'Hatutaki Ubeberu Mwingine," *Taifa Leo*, 27 February 1961, 3; TNA CO 897/7, "Meeting with a delegation from the Kalenjin Political Alliance," 29 August 1962, 150.

42 TNA CO 897/4, (Kenya Regional Boundaries Commission: Papers. Memoranda Nyanza Province Vol.1 Nos. 1–68), Memorandum of the Nyanza and Rift Valley Uasin Gishu Union to the Governor of Kenya, 20 July 1962, 2.

Kenya might become a second Congo, East Africa's tragedy.[43] This history was, as Kenyatta frequently suggested, difficult.[44] There was much that seemed worth forgetting.[45]

There were deeper questions, too, about how a national identity could be legitimately constructed, questions which underpinned the battle between KANU and KADU. The Kenyan postcolonial state was a latecomer in the game of identity making, the fate of communities the central topic of public argument across the previous two decades. In that period, thinkers in Kenya had imagined the existence of a range of communities. In general, however, they had argued that the most significant and demanding were ethnic.[46] Kenya was, as Kenyatta put it in 1964, the "United Nations in miniature."[47] In this context, in the early 1960s, the central question in Kenyan political thought was: how to create a sustainable unity in the face of honourable and legitimate diversity? As independence approached, supporters of both parties made clear that the accepted need for Kenyan unity could not be allowed to write out of existence legitimate ethnic difference, difference which was widely seen to be both valuable in itself and the only possible basis for the creation of a moral and prosperous Kenyan state, peopled by citizens concerned with corporate flourishing and prepared to work hard for the future. "[I]f governments tried to destroy tribal cultures and customs, languages and ethnical [sic] groupings," wrote Tom Mboya in 1963, giving voice to this consensus, "they would create such a vacuum that the African might find he had nothing to stand upon and [would, therefore,] become a most bewildered person in this modern world." Cosmopolitan liberalism, on this view, threatened only anarchy. Belonging was the necessary basis of creative moral agency. Provided, therefore, that "negative tribalism" was avoided, Mboya argued, "the structure of interdependence within the [ethnic] community, where each man knows he has certain responsibilities and duties and where there are certain sanctions against those who do not fulfil expectations" would provide "the discipline, self-reliance and stability needed in new nations."[48] The

---

43 On the Congo, see J.B.A. Ohanga, "Forum," *Jicho*, 27 July 1960, 3; Mboya, *Freedom and After*, 58–59; Kenyatta himself made such a reference in his speech on his return from the Lancaster House Conference in October 1963. See: "150,000 Roar a Welcome to *Mzee*," *Daily Nation*, 21 October 1963, 1.
44 A key theme, for example, in the speech Kenyatta gave on the eve of the first Kenyatta Day, on which see T. Hall, "Kenya's Tribute to the Premier," *Daily Nation*, 20 October 1964, 1.
45 Clough, "Mau Mau and the Contest for Memory," 256.
46 See Goodman, "Us in the Time of Strangers," Chs. 2 & 4 and Peterson, *Ethnic Patriotism*.
47 Jomo Kenyatta, *Suffering Without Bitterness: The Founding of the Kenyan Nation* (Nairobi: East African Publishing House, 1968), 247.
48 Mboya, *Freedom and After*, 67–70.

first story of Kenyatta Day and its significance was shaped by these two pressures.

Between independence and the early 1970s, on the days around 20th October newspapers typically contained potted histories of the key events of the President's life – his role in Kikuyu politics in the 1920s, his activities in England in the 1930s and 1940s, his leadership of KAU, and, in more detail, his detention and trial in 1952 – published pictures of both Kenyatta's life and the Kenyatta Day celebrations, and covered, sometimes including full transcripts, Kenyatta's speech, the centre point of the day. In this period, in a climate in which the government placed huge pressure on the press to support its agenda and avoid opposition, pressure which created a culture of significant press self-censorship, it was left to figures associated with KANU and the state to add the gloss to these accounts, establishing the significance of the day, and the significance of Kenyatta.[49]

In the late 1950s, as nationalists in Kenya promoted the figure of Kenyatta, they had tended to emphasise the negative effects of the incarceration of their legitimate leaders by exploitative foreigners bent on perpetuating their tyranny. In the early years after independence, Kenyatta assumed a new significance. Two aspects were emphasised. In the first place, the President's life showed, as Tom Mboya suggested in 1964, Kenyatta's "consciousness" of Kenya's problems over a long period of time – long, Mboya noted, before he himself (then only in his 30s) had been born. Kenyatta's career stood, Mboya made clear, as a model of service and dedication to the national cause. "Each country has its hero," he asserted, "whose utterances, whose actions, whose very life inspires the youth of the country. For Kenyans," he claimed, "this person is Kenyatta."[50] Kenyatta was, said a KANU spokesman in 1969, as his long career made clear, "the living spirit of unending readiness to sacrifice and work for Kenya's progress, and of faith in the future of our country."[51] Kenyatta stood, therefore, as proof of the possibility that ethnic particularity could be transcended, an inspiration to national service.

The second gloss that tended to be added focussed more closely on the events of 20th October 1952. Oginga Odinga, speaking at a Kenyatta Day rally in Nakuru in 1964, drew attention to the significance of the day when he urged his audience to the "spirit of unity" which, he insisted, had gripped

---

49 On the press, see Mboya, *Freedom and After*, 100–101; and Charles Hornsby, *Kenya: A History Since Independence* (London: I.B. Tauris, 2012), 113–114, 175 & 212.
50 "A Premier to be Proud of," *Daily Nation*, 20 October 1964, 2.
51 "A Symbol of Sacrifice, Faith and Defiance," *Daily Nation*, 20 October 1969, 10.

Kenya in the wake of Kenyatta's arrest.[52] Kenyatta Day was, a party spokesman explained in 1969, developing the idea, "a symbol [...] not merely of the elemental human right which underlies a nation's independence, *but also of all the impulses which must spring from such a moment.*"[53] On this reading, Kenyatta's arrest was a moment of national birth, the inspiration for the actions of (generally) unnamed patriots across Kenya who in its wake dedicated themselves to working for Kenya's independence, Kenyatta the source of the wider, and disparate, energies which brought down colonial rule. In this story, these figures, the detailed history of the 1950s, or sense of the dynamic which brought colonial rule to its end, remained shadowy, elided in favour of what (apparently) united these efforts: the inspirational figure of Kenyatta. Remembering and forgetting, then, were two parts of the same coin. In this way, the story both allowed space for local histories and local initiative, for valued and valuable difference, and avoided the rawness of the divisions which pocked the 1950s. Kenyatta was the figure that demonstrated the possibility of national unity, while the moment of his arrest was the fount of Kenya's sense of nationhood. On this reading, the "national *baraza*" of Kenyatta Day, can be seen, in a sense, as the re-enactment and reendorsement of this dynamic: with Kenyatta at the centre and the nation arranged around him, Kenya was symbolically re-born and re-dedicated on this day.[54]

In the years immediately after independence, then, Kenyatta Day was supposed to help develop a Kenyan national identity. From the early 1970s, however, state sources began to develop a further emphasis, the second story of Kenyatta Day. The background to this new emphasis was the growth of opposition to Kenyatta's regime from the mid-1960s.[55] In 1966, Oginga Odinga left KANU to set up a new political party, the Kenya People's Union (KPU) asserting the need for a more redistributive politics. Ethnic tensions, moreover, flared across the country in 1969, in the aftermath of the assassination of Tom Mboya, the victim, it appears, of an intense jockeying for position in the battle to succeed the elderly Kenyatta. Twice in that year, furthermore, Kenyatta found himself physically at-

---

[52] "'Now a Re-birth of Unity', says Mr Odinga," *Daily Nation*, 21 October 1964, 2. See also "Always Remember This Day," *Daily Nation*, 21 October 1966, 27.
[53] "A Symbol of Sacrifice, Faith and Defiance," *Daily Nation*, 20 October 1969, 10. Emphasis added.
[54] "'Now a Re-birth of Unity', says Mr Odinga," *Daily Nation*, 21 October 1964, 2. "A Symbol of Sacrifice, Faith and Defiance," *Daily Nation*, 20 October 1969, 10. "Why We Celebrate Kenyatta Day," *East African Standard*, 20 October 1972, 8.
[55] On discontent and opposition to Kenyatta's government, see Githuku, *Mau Mau, Crucible of War*, Ch. 5.

tacked by crowds, supporters of the KPU, in one instance, and Luo angry in the wake of Mboya's murder in the other.[56] In 1971, adding to this sense of threat, evidence was uncovered of an imminent, albeit un-credible, coup.[57] And across the first half of the 1970s, a small group of radical MPs, led by the charismatic J.M. Kariuki, attacked the record of the Kenyatta government, while in the wake of J.M.'s murder in 1975, students held spirited demonstrations against the regime – which included efforts by those at Kenyatta University in Nairobi to remove the President's name from the institution's name plaque, much to Kenyatta's disgust.[58]

In these circumstances, Kenyatta's government took various steps to shore up its authority, including placing a new emphasis on the significance of 20th October.[59] "Kenyatta Day," explained the Minister of Commerce, Gikonyo Kiano, in 1975, "serves to remind us of the supreme *sacrifice* that *Mzee* Kenyatta made so that we the people of Kenya might be free from British colonialism."[60] A similar emphasis was placed by KANU's Nairobi branch, which claimed that "It is a result of torture, and persecution through which *Mzee* Kenyatta and the rest underwent…that brought about the *uhuru* we are enjoying now [sic]."[61] Kenyatta, it was emphasised, had "suffered so that Kenyans can be free." This sacrifice, it was implied, bred an obligation of personal loyalty to the President, a debt incurred by Kenya's population, and the 20th October was cast as "a day to re-demonstrate their loyalty, love and respect for the man who inspired the struggle for *Uhuru*."[62] Kenyatta Day was, as a 1972 editorial in the *East African Standard* put it, "a personal day. Personal to President Kenyatta."[63]

This emphasis on loyalty was, from the early 1970s, a central part of the commemoration. While occasional examples of the genre can be found before this point, from the early 1970s and throughout the 1980s, bridging the divide

---

56 Daniel Branch, *Kenya: Between Hope and Despair, 1963–2011* (New Haven: Yale University Press, 2011), 78–81 and 87–88.
57 Ibid, 102.
58 Hornsby, *Kenya*, 223–224, 270, 274 & 283–286. Branch, *Kenya*, 117. Githuku, *Mau Mau Crucible of War*, 267–276. Kenyatta's parliamentary critics featured prominently in the speech he gave on Kenyatta Day in 1972, on which see: F. Nyanga and O. Mak'Onyango, *East African Standard*, "President Hits [sic] at MPs Who Belittle Kenya," 21 October 1972, 1.
59 On their wider efforts, see Branch, *Kenya*, 102–103 & 118. Hornsby, *Kenya*, 211–212.
60 "Thousands to Attend Big *Uhuru* Park Rally," *Daily Nation*, 20 October 1975, 1. Emphasis added.
61 "All Set for Rally," *Daily Nation*, 20 October 1975, unnumbered back page.
62 "A Proud Day for Kenyans," *Daily Nation*, 20 October 1975, 9. See also *Hansard*, Fourth Session, 1973, xxxi, 1288–1289, and Githuku, *Mau Mau Crucible of War*, 273.
63 "Day of Re-Dedication," *East African Standard*, 21 October 1972, 8.

between the Kenyatta and Moi regimes, the *Daily Nation* often carried prominent declarations of loyalty, sometimes on the front page of the newspaper, from figures associated with the state – ministers, diplomats and so on – the public display of these declarations intended to offer to the wider public a model for their own behaviour and to convince them of the futility of opposition.[64] And in 1989, the connection between remembrance and loyalty was cemented as 10th October, the anniversary of Moi's ascension to the presidency, was designated a national holiday in the name of Kenyatta's successor.[65] In this era then, the "national *baraza*" of Kenyatta Day, looked to be less about the enacting of horizontal bonds than the ceremonial acclamation of a glorious leader, a reinforcement of hierarchy.[66] As we shall see in the next section, however, in the 1990s this emphasis became the subject of vociferous criticism.

The Second Liberation: Critics

Authoritarian as they were, the Kenyatta and Moi regimes had never succeeded in silencing their critics. Central to the thinking of successive opponents of the government, from the KPU in the second half of the 1960s, to J.M. Kariuki and Ngũgĩ wa Thiong'o in the 1970s, had been the memory of Mau Mau and, in particular, the claim that Mau Mau fighters had been disregarded and left impoverished by Kenya's postcolonial governments, the means by which critics of those governments had drawn attention to the inequality that marked Kenyan society and to their wider calls for the greater redistribution of wealth.[67] In the 1990s in Kenya, as in other parts of the world, however, arguments about the nature of the past took on both a new urgency and a new focus in the course of the (at-

---

[64] For an early example, see "Armed Forces Greet the President," *Daily Nation*, 20 October 1966, 1. For typical later examples see, e.g. "Thousands to Attend Big *Uhuru* Park Rally," *Daily Nation*, 20 October 1975, 1; R. Irungu, "Kiambu is Behind KANU All the Way," *Daily Nation*, 20 October 1975, un-numbered back page; "*Mzee* Remembered: Kenyatta Day Messages Galore," *Daily Nation*, 20 October 1983, 4; "President Receives Congratulations," *Daily Nation*, 20 October 1985, 1. See also *Daily Nation*, 20 October 1986, 12; and Hornsby, *Kenya*, 401.
[65] See: *Daily Nation*, 10 October 1989.
[66] On the political economy of authoritarianism, see Daniel Branch and Nic Cheeseman, "Democratization, Sequencing and State-Failure in Africa: Lessons from Kenya," *African Affairs* 108, no. 430 (2008): 1–26.
[67] Clough, "Mau Mau and the Contest for Memory," 256–259. Branch, "Search for the Remains," 308–310.

tempted) democratic transition, Kenya's "second liberation."[68] The memory of the rebellion continued to be mobilised by critics of Moi's regime, not now principally as a prop to arguments about the need for economic redistribution, but, as the heart of a somewhat wider pantheon of independence heroes, with a new emphasis on the dangerous absences that marked Kenya's state memory regime.[69] For roughly the first thirty years of Kenya's postcolonial history, then, it was voices connected with the state which publicly defined the significance of 20th October. From the early 1990s, in the context of political flux, new actors began to develop new narratives, the third and fourth stories of Kenyatta Day.

As Moi's regime became increasingly oppressive and authoritarian in the tough economic conditions of the 1980s, opposition, associated most closely with the Law Society of Kenya and the National Council of Churches in Kenya (NCCK), began to grow.[70] Kenya's single party state, Oginga Odinga claimed in 1987, breaking his long public near silence and giving voice to this opposition, "stifled" "public debate of national issues" and "genuine constructive criticism of the Government." If the KANU government would not allow space for criticism within the party, he asserted, then room should be created for alternative political parties, a necessary step, it came to be argued in a state that had not seen multi-party politics since 1969, to make government accountable to the people, the servant rather than the master.[71] While momentum initially proved difficult to build, opponents of Moi were galvanised in the early 1990s by the fall of the Soviet Union, an event which both inspired opposition forces across the world to believe that authoritarian regimes could collapse and fall, and changed the global geo-political landscape, encouraging critics of Moi internally and externally. When, asked Rev. Timothy Njoya, in a sermon delivered on 1st January 1990, would the changes seen in Eastern Europe make themselves felt in Kenya?[72]

---

[68] See Duncan Bell, "Introduction: Memory, Trauma and World Politics," in *Memory, Trauma and World Politics: Reflections on the Relationship Between Past and Present*, ed. Duncan Bell (Basingstoke: Palgrave Macmillan, 2006), 19–20; and Branch, "Search for the Remains of Dedan Kimathi," 310–311.
[69] For compelling critiques of Mau Mau's central place, see Bethwell A. Ogot, "Mau Mau and Nationhood: The Untold Story," in *Mau Mau and Nationhood*, eds. E.S. Atieno Odhiambo and John Lonsdale (Oxford: James Currey, 2003), 8–36; and Lottie Hughes, "Memorialisation and Mau Mau: A Critical Review," in *Dedan Kimathi on Trial: Colonial Justice and Popular Memory in Kenya's Mau Mau Rebellion*, ed. Julie MacArthur (Ohio: Ohio University Press, 2017), 339–374.
[70] See Branch, *Kenya*, 162. For a detailed consideration of both the Churches and opposition to Moi more generally, see Githuku, *Mau Mau Crucible of War*, Ch. 6.
[71] Hornsby, *Kenya*, 405, 471–472, 475, 478 & 480. Githuku, *Mau Mau Crucible of War*, 335–337.
[72] Hornsby, *Kenya*, 471–472.

The minister's prayers were soon answered. In the post-Soviet world, external patrons, and above all the United States, began to look more critically at African regimes, including Kenya's, convinced now that economic sclerosis was the progeny of authoritarian politics. External pressure for reform, meanwhile, emboldened Moi's domestic opponents, and in early 1991 the first attempts were made to create opposition political parties. In turn, the Moi regime's clampdown on their internal critics, infamously on *saba saba*, the bloody 7th July 1990, provoked international censure, most seriously for the incumbent government in November 1991, when the announcement that aid would be suspended pending internal reform, quickly led Moi to officially re-allow multi-party politics and to announce that elections would be held in the following year.[73]

As public opposition to Moi's regime grew and multi-party politics was conceded, opponents of the government began to rethink Kenyatta Day, and the nation's public remembrance more widely, breaking the state's monopoly on the story of the day's significance. The press itself was an important part of this process, as the culture of self-censorship which characterised the first three decades of Kenya's independence broke down, and the *Daily Nation* began to emerge as the informal voice of the opposition, happier now both to uncover scandal and voice dissenting opinions.[74] One symptom of this shift was the erosion in the press of the imagery of the "national *baraza*" of Kenyatta Day, with the president at the centre and the nation arranged around him, which had in the past stood as a support to the horizontal bonds of national unity and the vertical bonds of loyalty to the state that the day was supposed to foster. In the 1990s, by contrast, local celebrations, so important in the ritual of the day, came to be represented as contested sites, occasions at which political opponents, or factions, battled, while the very appearance of reports on provincial events in the national press became increasingly dependent on the public playing out – often with a significant element of farce – of these disputes. In 1992, for example, the *Daily Nation* reported that "members of the public" walked out of Kenyatta Day celebrations at Kangema Stadium as a local official began to read the President's speech.[75] Two years later, a report described how a KANU official and a chief fought publicly after the "former was denied time to address *wananchi* at [the] Baricho Stadium in Kirinyanga."[76] And in 2000, the *Daily Nation* reported, the mayor of Nakuru was forced to drive to local celebrations in his personal car

---

73 Ibid, 405–487.
74 Ibid, 524.
75 "Occasion Marred by Walk-Out," *Daily Nation*, 21 October 1992, 5.
76 "Chief, KANU Man Exchange Blows," *Daily Nation*, 21 October 1994, 4.

after councillors removed the wheels of his official limousine, accusing him of misusing it.[77]

More broadly, while in the early 1990s, coverage of Kenyatta Day in newspapers continued to include histories of Kenyatta's life and career, space began to be given to new, non-state, voices to outline the significance of the day. Strikingly, in 1992, as the first multi-party elections in a generation loomed, the *Daily Nation* carried extensive interviews with members of the Kapenguria Six, speaking to them about both their experiences in the 1950s and their thoughts on contemporary Kenya and the territory's postcolonial trajectory.[78] Given the multiple voices involved, there was space in these accounts for tensions and disagreements in their subject's understanding of the world in which they lived and its formation. But, across these interviews, in both their form – the novelty of the decision to seek out these voices on this occasion – and their content, a recurring and significant theme was beginning to be developed: that Kenya's ritual of remembrance was inadequate, that the nation's heroes had been *officially* forgotten. As Achieng' Oneko, for example, "described" the situation in his interview, "the freedom fighters who are alive today are a disillusioned lot, who have to toe the line to win favours and recognition from the Government" – an old complaint now given a fresh significance.[79]

In the state's 1960s version of Kenyatta Day, as we have seen, this was a conscious absence. In the 1990s it was recast as an ethical failure, the abandonment, specifically and importantly by the postcolonial elite, of the battle for in-

---

[77] "Leaders in War of Words at Meeting," *Daily Nation*, 21 October 2000, 3. See also "Leaders Told Not to Incite Public," *Daily Nation*, 21 October 1992, 4; "Chaos Mar [sic] PC's Speech," *Daily Nation*, 21 October 1997, 4; "Mayor in Struggle with DO at Rally," *Daily Nation*, 21 October 2000, 2. Contrast with, e.g., "Kenyans United in Hailing President," *Daily Nation*, 21 October 1968, 4; "Parades, Dances and Speeches Mark Kenyatta Day in Provinces," *East African Standard*, 21 October 1972, 9.

[78] See G. Njihia, "Harbour No Bitterness, Urges *Uhuru* Veteran," *Daily Nation*, 20 October 1992, Kenyatta Day Special Supplement, 2–3; J. Githinji, "Down But Not Out…," *Daily Nation*, 20 October 1992, Kenyatta Day Special Supplement, 19; W. Nderitu, "A Widow Reflects on the Lot of Forgotten Heroes," *Daily Nation*, 20 October 1992, Kenyatta Day Special Supplement, 21 and 23. The newspaper also carried an interview with Michael Blundell, see T. Sittoni, "A Look into the Past, Present and the Future," *Daily Nation*, 20 October 1992, Kenyatta Day Special Supplement, 15, 16 and 17. See also the interview with Fred Kubai published on Moi Day: M. Njuguna, "Heroes of *Uhuru* Suffering Without Bitterness," *Daily Nation*, 10 October 1992, 16–17.

[79] G. Njihia, "Harbour No Bitterness, Urges *Uhuru* Veteran," *Daily Nation*, 20 October 1992, Kenyatta Day Special Supplement, 2. On the history of the complaint, see E.S. Atieno Odhiambo, "*Matunda ya Uhuru*, Fruits of Independence: Seven Theses on Nationalism in Kenya," in *Mau Mau and Nationhood*, eds. E.S. Atiento Odhiambo and John Lonsdale (Oxford: James Currey, 2003), 38–39; and Hughes, "Memorialisation and Mau Mau," 348.

dependence, the most significant episode in Kenya's history, and, it followed, of the national interest more generally, their unwillingness to acknowledge their debts to history, in whose shadow they paled, linked to their alleged failures in the contemporary world. In an important sense, this forgetfulness was not merely symptomatic of the ills opposition figures diagnosed in contemporary Kenya, but *constitutive* of them: state elites, they held, abandoned the nation's past, and so its present and future, any sense of national community.

This injunction to remember, and its significance, the attempted recovery of a past officially forgotten, quickly exploded in the Kenya of this time, and continued to be publicly lamented by Moi's critics across the decade and beyond.[80] Above all, this lamentation was marked by a new concern with not only the lives of so-called national heroes, but with their deaths. Opposition MPs in parliament, for example, influenced in part by on-going arguments in other parts of the continent,[81] made recurring calls for this failure to be rectified through the dedication of a "Heroes Acre" or "Square" in Nairobi, where, as an MP put it in 1993, "all prominent Kenyans, including politicians, should be buried," honouring those who had served the nation with distinction.[82] The search for the remains of Dedan Kimathi, the Mau Mau field marshal executed by the British in 1957, and buried in a mass grave, began at this time, the cause taken up by civil society and MPs, and pursued across the next decade and half, all with the intention of giving him a fitting interment – "a state burial with due pomp and ceremony," as an MP put it in Parliament in 1993 – recognition in death.[83] And, reinforcing the link between remembering the past and right conduct in the present, the Law Society of Kenya, along with the Churches the vanguard of opposition to Moi's regime, in a statement made in late January 1994, reacting to the death of Oginga Odinga, took up both issues, "urg[ing] the Government to set aside land for the burial of national heroes," and noting that "the remains of the late freedom fighter Dedan Kimathi still lay in an unmarked grave."[84]

The emphasis on official amnesia which emerged in the early 1990s remained the keystone of interest in Kenyatta Day into the next decade. From the mid-1990s, though, critics of Moi's regime, disappointed by the failure to lever him from power in the elections of 1992 and 1997, developed a new concern

---

80 See also Ogot, "Mau Mau and Nationhood," 8–9.
81 For example, in Namibia and Zimbabwe, on which see: Ranger, "Politics of Memorialisation," 64–65, 69–71, and Coombes, "Monuments and Memories," 143.
82 *Hansard*, Second Session, 1993, ii, 1419.
83 *Hansard*, Second Session, 1993, ii, 1420. On Kimathi, see Branch, "Search for the Remains of Dedan Kimathi," 301–320.
84 "Honour Heroes, Says LSK," *Daily Nation*, 25 January 1994, 2.

with both the origins of, and the intentions behind, this amnesia, the final story of Kenyatta Day. Multi-party politics alone, it seemed, was not enough to ensure the country's "second liberation." Attention increasingly focussed on the arrogation of power in the hands of the president, and the process by which this had occurred, a recurring theme, for example, in articles reflecting on Kenya's postcolonial trajectory in the *Daily Nation*'s special Kenyatta Day supplement in 1997.[85] Constitutional reform, some form of devolution designed to break the monopoly of power exercised by the Office of the President, and on the agenda of opposition forces since the mid-1980s, came in this context to acquire an ever greater significance, a necessary step, it was held, to permanently break Kenya's authoritarian postcolonial mould.[86] It was as part of these wider reflections on the power of the incumbent government in the wake of electoral defeat, that Moi's critics came to view, and attack, Kenyatta and Moi Days as an institutionalised form of non-recognition. While in 1992, the first article that appeared in the *Daily Nation*'s Kenyatta Day special supplement could confidently begin with the assertion that the day, "could as well have been named 'heroes day' for October 20 commemorates the culmination of Kenya's struggle against colonial domination," following their electoral defeats, Moi's critics came increasingly to argue that the failure of recognition they identified was not an accident, but a deliberate concealment woven into the very fabric of remembrance.[87] If Kenya was to be permanently freed, then changes were needed in the nation's calendar of remembrance.

This institutional failure of recognition had, Moi's critics in civil society argued, two significant impacts. Giving voice to the first, in a lecture organised by the Citizen's Coalition for Constitutional Change (4Cs), the Kenya Human Rights Commission, and Muslims for Human Rights, clearly linking the event to wider demands for political reform in Kenya, and delivered in Mombasa on the eve of Kenyatta Day in 1997, the scholar Ali Mazrui demanded that "the Government do away with 'unnecessary' national holidays like the Kenyatta and Moi days," which were, he suggested "like the Queen's birthday." If, he went on, "the days were to be celebrated [...] *they should be renamed.*" "This naming of holidays *to celebrate individual achievements or lack of them,*" he insisted, "is an

---

[85] *Daily Nation*, 20 October 1997, Kenyatta Day Special Supplement, 10–15.
[86] Godwin R. Murunga, Duncan Okello and Anders Sjogren, "Towards a New Constitutional Order in Kenya: An Introduction," in *Kenya: The Struggle for a New Constitutional Order*, eds., Godwin R. Murunga, Duncan Okello and Anders Sjogren (London: Zed Books, 2014), 1–6; Branch, *Kenya*, 182.
[87] P. Ngugi, "Nationalists Remembered," *Daily Nation*, 20 October 1992, Kenyatta Day Special Supplement, 1.

overflow of the Executive powers initiated during the post-colonial period. Naming a national day after a President who is still alive," he lamented, "gives him enormous symbolic power. It should," Mazrui concluded, "only be admissible under a constitutional monarchy, which Kenya is definitely not."[88] The same point underpinned the public unwillingness of civil society organisations, including the "National Convention Executive Council and Church-led Ufungamano reforms initiative," both centrally involved in the struggle for constitutional change, to recognise Kenyatta Day three years later.[89] The occasion – which they called "Mau Mau Day" and, in that year, dedicated to Bildad Kaggia – was, they claimed, "being celebrated in total disregard of those who participated in the fight for [the] country's liberation."[90] Pluralism, political and ritual, was the key to the future.

The official idolisation of the figures of Kenyatta and Moi, according to their civil society critics, not only gave authoritarian governments symbolic power but, by ignoring the wider history of the 1950s, deprived Kenya's citizens of the critical resources they needed to defend their liberties, a double blow. The power of Kenya's independence struggle was suggested, for example, by the lawyer, MP and longstanding critic of both the Kenyatta and Moi regimes, Wanyiri Kihoro, in a book titled *The Kapenguria Six* and quoted from at length in the *Daily Nation* on Kenyatta Day in 2006.[91] In the story, which began and ended with a child asking the question "Why is today called Kenyatta Day?" a family was brought to tears as the curator of a museum narrated the histories of the five other men imprisoned with Kenyatta, an emotional reaction which suggested the power of the past to influence behaviour in the present.[92] This history was far from mere dusty antiquarianism.

The connection was perhaps most clearly expressed by Willy Mutunga, an academic, founding member of 4Cs, stalwart of the opposition to Moi's regime, and later chief justice, in his foreword to the recent book *Dedan Kimathi on Trial:*

---

[88] F. Thoya, "Govt. Incapable of Freedom – Mazrui," *Daily Nation*, 20 October 1997, 32. Emphasis added. Whether or not this symbolic power was as effective as Mazrui, and others, assumed, is far from clear. Further research – a study of "Kenyatta Day from below" – is needed.

[89] On these organisations, see Wanjala S. Nasong'o, "'Revisiting 'the Two Faces of Civil Society' in Constitutional Reform in Kenya," in *Kenya: The Struggle for a New Constitutional Order*, eds., Goodwin R. Murunga, Duncan Okello and Anders Sjogren (London: Zed Books, 2014), 97–115.

[90] "Plea to Honour *Uhuru* Heroes," *Daily Nation*, 21 October 2000, 2. See also M. Wachira, "Kenyans Remember Freedom Heroes as Calls for Name Change Persist," *Daily Nation*, 20 October 2006, 7.

[91] On Kihoro, see Hornsby, *Kenya*, 416 & 464.

[92] M. Wachira, "Kenyans Remember Freedom Heroes as Calls for Name Change Persist," *Daily Nation*, 20 October 2006, 7.

Colonial Justice and Popular Memory in Kenya's Mau Mau Rebellion.[93] "As Kenya looks to its future," he wrote, "it must also look to its past and return dignity and honour to the freedom fighters *whose struggle for justice and human rights we carry on in the present.*"[94] On this understanding, those who fought in the 1990s and beyond against authoritarianism and for a new constitutional order continued the work of, and were inspired by the example of, their ancestors. The ability of Kenya's people to affect change in the present, their agency as citizens, was, on this reading, the product of their historical consciousness. Thinking in his 1938 ethnography *Facing Mount Kenya* about the corrosive impact of colonialism on African life, Jomo Kenyatta had written that it was "the culture he inherits that gives man his human dignity [...] teaches him his mental and moral values and makes him feel it is worth while [sic] to work and fight for liberty."[95] For Moi's critics sixty years later, engagement with a storied history, now focussed on the years immediately preceding independence, was, likewise, the foundation stone of active citizenship.[96]

Both the need for pluralism and a galvanising history led Moi's critics to demand that the state's pattern of remembrance was re-dedicated and re-made, that Kenyatta Day give way to Heroes Day. Alongside the call that the nation's heroes should be recognised through the dedication of Heroes' Square, this demand came to be frequently articulated in the late 1990s and early 2000s, before the victors of the 2002 election, longstanding critics of the Moi government, inscribed the re-dedication of 20th October to the nation's heroes in the both the draft constitution that was offered and rejected in a 2005 referendum and the version that was ultimately accepted in 2010, at which point, Kenyatta Day was no more.[97]

---

[93] On Mutunga, see Nasong'o, "'Revisiting 'the Two Faces of Civil Society' in Constitutional Reform in Kenya," 101 & 110.
[94] Willy Mutunga, "Introductory Note," in *Dedan Kimathi on Trial: Colonial Justice and Popular Memory in Kenya's Mau Mau Rebellion*, ed. Julie MacArthur (Athens, OH: Ohio University Press, 2017), xi. Emphasis added.
[95] Jomo Kenyatta, *Facing Mount Kenya* (New York: Random House, 1965), 304.
[96] Contrast with the attitude of the aid industry and "developers" to history described in Terence Ranger, "Africa in the Age of Extremes: The Irrelevance of African History," in *Rethinking African History*, eds. Simon McGrath, Charles Jedrej, Kenneth King and Jack Thompson (Edinburgh: Centre of African Studies, 1997), 269–291.
[97] For the linking of the two demands, see, e.g. *Hansard*, 2 November 2006, 3370–3372. On links with constitutional reform, see, e.g., K. Mutunga, "The Essential Jomo Kenyatta," *Daily Nation*, 20 October 2006, Weekend Supplement, 2; Robert Nyagah, "Kenyans to Celebrate First *Mashujaa* Day," *Daily Nation*, 19 October 2010, accessed 2 December 2020, http://www.nation.co.ke/

Conclusion

Kenyatta and his connection to 20th October first came to prominence in 1958, as African thinkers recast the potential of colonial rule as the impact of the second colonial occupation bit and, in the shadow of Emergency-era restrictions, sought a national symbol that could unite Kenya's people. In 1963, the day was declared a national holiday by the KANU government, dedicated to Kenyatta. In these early postcolonial years, the state hoped the figure of Kenyatta would stand as proof of the viability of Kenyan nationhood, of the possibility of transcending ethnic difference, skirting the divisions of the 1950s, while leaving principled room for local initiatives and local histories. As Kenyatta's government came under pressure from the late 1960s, the target of growing opposition, his regime added a further gloss: Kenyatta had suffered so that Kenya's people might be free. This past, they insisted, bred an obligation of loyalty, an emphasis which came to characterise the period between the early 1970s and late 1980s, bridging the divide between the Kenyatta and Moi eras. In the 1990s, as opposition to Moi's regime burst into the open, the regime's critics, breaking the state's monopoly, and no less awed by the weight of history's ethical significance, recast again the day's meaning. The nation's heroes, figures beyond Kenyatta, they claimed, had been forgotten by postcolonial governments, this forgetfulness both evidence of and feeding their abandonment of the national interest, their turn to an authoritarian selfish individualism. Stung by their failure in successive elections to lever Moi from power, from the mid-1990s critics of his regime came to see this postcolonial failure of recognition not as a mere accident, but as woven into the very fabric of national commemoration. Days dedicated to Kenyatta and Moi were a deliberate ploy by authoritarian governments to symbolically reinforce their authority at the expense of the critical discussion, the opposition, that healthy society required. The ghosts of Kenyatta's loyalists might have nodded in acknowledgement. The key to the future, Moi's critics suggested, was pluralism, something which required not only the devolution of power and the smashing of the dominance of the Office of the President, but a symbolic democratisation and the cultivation of historical consciousness. Moi and Kenyatta Days, it was argued, should be cast into oblivion, and in their place a more inclusive Heroes' Day raised up, as it was with the promulgation of the 2010 con-

---

news/1056-1036222-15ao6qs/index.html. On the search for hero(ine)s, see Coombes, "Monuments and Memories."

stitution. Whether their high hopes of this symbolic re-dedication of 20th October will be met, however, remains to be seen.[98]

Bibliography

[photo, no title]. 5 December 1963, *Daily Nation*, 5.
[photo, no title]. 12 December 1963, *Daily Nation* 1.
"150,000 Roar a Welcome to *Mzee*." *Daily Nation*, 21 October 1963, 1.
"A Premier to be Proud of." *Daily Nation*, 20 October 1964, 2.
"A Proud Day for Kenyans." *Daily Nation*, 20 October 1975, 9.
"A Symbol of Sacrifice, Faith and Defiance." *Daily Nation*, 20 October 1969, 10.
"All Set for Rally." *Daily Nation*, 20 October 1975, unnumbered back page.
"Always Remember This Day." *Daily Nation*, 21 October 1966, 27.
Anderson, David. *Eroding the Commons: The Politics of Ecology in Baringo District, 1890s-1963*. Oxford: Oxford University Press, 2002.
Anderson, David. *Histories of the Hanged: Britain's Dirty War in Kenya and the End of Empire*. London: W.W. Norton, 2005.
Anderson, David. "'Yours in Struggle for *Majimbo*': Nationalism and the Party Politics of Decolonisation in Kenya, 1955–64," *Journal of Contemporary History* 40, no. 3 (2005): 547–564.
"Armed Forces Greet the President." *Daily Nation*, 20 October 1966, 1.
Atieno-Odhiambo, E.S. "The Production of History in Kenya: The Mau Mau Debate," *Canadian Journal of African Studies* 2, no. 2 (1992): 300–307.
Atieno-Odhiambo, E.S. "*Matunda ya Uhuru*, Fruits of Independence: Seven Theses on Nationalism in Kenya," In *Mau Mau and Nationhood: Arms, Authority and Narration*, edited by Atieno Odhiambo and John Lonsdale, 37–45. Oxford: James Currey, 2003.
Becker, Felicitas. "Remembering Nyerere: Political Rituals and Dissent in Contemporary Tanzania," *African Affairs* 112, no. 447 (2013): 238–261.
Bell, Duncan. "Introduction: Memory, Trauma and World Politics," In *Memory, Trauma and World Politics: Reflections on the Relationship Between Past and Present*, edited by Duncan Bell, 1–5. Basingstoke: Palgrave Macmillan, 2006.
Branch, Daniel. *Defeating Mau Mau, Creating Kenya: Counterinsurgency, Civil War, and Decolonisation*. Cambridge: Cambridge University Press, 2009.
Branch, Daniel. "The Search for the Remains of Dedan Kimathi: The Politics of Death and Memorialisation in Postcolonial Kenya," *Past and Present* 206, Supplement 5 *Relics and Remains* (2010): 301–320.
Branch, Daniel. *Kenya: Between Hope and Despair, 1963–2011*. London: Yale University Press, 2011.
Branch, Daniel, and Nic Cheeseman. "Democratization, Sequencing and State-Failure in Africa: Lessons from Kenya." *African Affairs* 108, no. 430 (2008): 1–26.
"Chaos Mar [sic] PC's Speech." *Daily Nation*, 21 October 1997, 4.

---

[98] On these hopes, see Willy Mutunga, "Foreword: Timothy is Leah and Leah is Timothy," in *We the People: Thinking Heavenly, Acting Kenyanly*, T. Njoya (Nairobi: WorldAlive Publishers, 2017).

Chaudri, Amit. "The Real Meaning of Rhodes Must Fall." *The Guardian*, 16 March 2016, accessed 2 December 2020, https://www.theguardian.com/uk-news/2016/mar/16/the-real-meaning-of-rhodes-must-fall.

"Chief, KANU Man Exchange Blows." *Daily Nation*, 21 October 1994, 4.

Clough, Marshall S. *Mau Mau Memoirs: History, Memory and Politics*. Boulder, Lynne Rienner Publishers, 1998.

Clough, Marshall S. "Mau Mau and the Contest for Memory." In *Mau Mau and Nationhood: Arms, Authority and Narration*, edited by E.S. Atieno Odhiambo and John Lonsdale, 251–267. Oxford: James Currey, 2003.

Coombes, Annie E. "Monuments and Memories: Public Commemorative Strategies in Contemporary Kenya." In *Managing Heritage, Making Peace: History, Identity and Memory in Contemporary Kenya*, edited by Ann E. Coombes, Lottie Hughes and Karega-Munene, 139–184. London: Bloomsbury Publishing Plc, 2014.

Coombes, Annie E., Lottie Hughes, and Karega-Munene, eds. *Managing Heritage, Making Peace: History, Identity and Memory in Contemporary Kenya*. London: Bloomsbury Publishing Plc, 2014.

Cubitt, Geoffrey. *History and Memory*. Manchester: Manchester University Press, 2007.

"Day of Re-Dedication." *East African Standard*, 21 October 1972, 8.

Day, R. "What is Dividing Them." *Daily Nation*, 28 November 1961, 6.

"Delamere Avenue No More." *Daily Nation*, 5 December 1963, 1.

Deutsch, Jan-G. "Celebrating Power in Everyday Life: The Administration of Law and the Public Sphere in Colonial Tanzania, 1890–1914," *Journal of African Cultural Studies* 15, no. 1 (2002): 93–103.

Fouere, Marie-A. "Julius Nyerere, *Ujamaa* and Political Morality in Contemporary Tanzania," *African Studies Review* 57, no. 1 (2014): 1–24.

Gadsden, Fay. "The African Press in Kenya, 1945–52," *Journal of African History* 21, no. 4 (1980): 515–535.

Gavua, Kodzo. "Monuments and Negotiations of Power in Ghana." In *The Politics of Heritage in Africa: Economies, Histories and Infrastructures*, edited by Derek R. Peterson, Kodzo Gavua and Ciraj Rassool, 97–112. Cambridge: Cambridge University Press, 2015.

Githinji, Job. "Down But Not Out…" *Daily Nation*, 20 October 1992, Kenyatta Day Special Supplement, 19.

Githuku, Nicholas K. *Mau Mau Crucible of War: Statehood, National Identity and the Politics of Postcolonial Kenya*. London: Lexington Books, 2016.

Goodman, Edward. "Us in the Time of Strangers: Imagining Community in Colonial Kenya and Tanganyika." DPhil diss., Oxford University, 2017.

Hajivayanis, G.G., A.C. Mtowa, and John Iliffe. "The Politicians: Ali Ponda and Hassan Suleiman." In *Modern Tanzanians: A Volume of Biographies*, edited by John Iliffe, 227–253. Nairobi: East African Publication House, 1973.

Hall, Tony. "Kenya's Tribute to the Premier." *Daily Nation*, 20 October 1964, 1.

Hall, Tony. "The Tribute." *Daily Nation*, 20 October 1964, 2.

Haugerud, Angelique. *The Culture of Politics in Modern Kenya*. Cambridge: Cambridge University Press, 1993.

"Honour Heroes, Says LSK." *Daily Nation*, 25 January 1994, 2.

Hornsby, Charles. *Kenya: A History Since Independence*. London: I.B. Tauris & Co Ltd., 2012.

Hughes, Lottie. "Memorialisation and Mau Mau: A Critical Review." In *Dedan Kimathi on Trial: Colonial Justice and Popular Memory in Kenya's Mau Mau Rebellion*, edited by Julie MacArthur, 339–371. Ohio: Ohio University Press, 2017.
Irungu, Robert. "Kiambu is Behind KANU All the Way." *Daily Nation*, 20 October 1975, unnumbered back page.
"Kenya Turns Out to Cheer Premier." *Daily Nation*, 21 October 1964, 2.
"Kenyans United in Hailing President." *Daily Nation*, 21 October 1968, 4.
"Kenyatta Day Special Supplement." *Daily Nation*, 20 October 1997, 10 & 14, 11 & 13, 12 & 15.
Kenyatta, Jomo. *Facing Mount Kenya*. New York: Random House, Inc., 1965.
Kenyatta, Jomo. *Suffering Without Bitterness: The Founding of the Kenyan Nation*. Nairobi: East African Publishing House, 1968.
Kimalel, S.K. "Tribal Groups." *East African Standard*, 1 July 1960, 3.
Kyle, Keith. *The Politics of the Independence of Kenya*. Basingstoke: Palgrave, 1999.
"Joyous Drive Through the City." *Daily Nation*, 21 October 1968, 11.
"Leaders in War of Words at Meeting." *Daily Nation*, 21 October 2000, 3.
"Leaders Told Not to Incite Public." *Daily Nation*, 21 October 1992, 4.
Lonsdale, John. "Mau Mau's of the Mind: Making Mau Mau and Remaking Kenya." *Journal of African History* 31, no. 3 (1990): 393–421.
Lonsdale, John. "The Moral Economy of Mau Mau." In *Unhappy Valley: Conflict in Kenya and Africa*, Book Two, edited by Bruce Berman and John Lonsdale. Oxford: James Currey, 1992.
Lonsdale, John. "Foreword." In *Mau Mau from Below*, edited by Greet Kershaw, xvi–xxx. Oxford: James Currey, 1997.
Lonsdale, John. "KAU's Cultures: Imaginations of Community and Constructions of Leadership in Kenya after the Second World War," *Journal of African Cultural Studies* 13, no. 1 (2000): 107–124.
Lonsdale, John. "Kenyatta's Trials: Breaking and Making an African Nationalist." In *The Moral World of the Law*, edited by Peter Coss, 196–239. Cambridge: Cambridge University Press, 2002.
Lonsdale, John. "Moral and Political Argument in Kenya." In *Ethnicity and Democracy in Africa*, edited by Bruce Berman, Dickson Fyoh and Will Kymlicka, 73–95. Oxford: James Currey, 2004.
Lynch, Gabrielle. *I Say to You: Ethnic Politics and the Kalenjin in Kenya*. Chicago: University of Chicago Press, 2011.
MacArthur, Julie. *Cartography and the Political Imagination: Mapping Community in Colonial Kenya*. Athens, OH: Ohio University Press, 2016.
Maxon, Robert. *Conflict and Accommodation: The Gusii and the British, 1907–1963*. London: Associated University Presses, 1989.
Maxon, Robert. *Britain and Kenya's Constitutions*. New Jersey: Cambria Press, 2011.
"Mayor in Struggle with DO at Rally." *Daily Nation*, 21 October 2000, 2.
Mboya, Tom. *Freedom and After*. London: Andre Deutsch Limited, 1963.
Mulela, C. K., et al. "Hatutaki Ubeberu Mwingine." *Taifa Leo*, 27 February 1961, 3.
Murunga, Godwin R., Duncan Okello, and Anders Sjogren. "Towards a New Constitutional Order in Kenya: An Introduction." In *Kenya: The Struggle for a New Constitutional Order*,

edited by Goodwin R. Murunga, Duncan Okello and Anders Sjogren, 1–16. London: Zed Books Ltd., 2014.
Mutunga, Kamau. "The Essential Jomo Kenyatta." *Daily Nation*, 20 October 2006, Weekend Supplement, 2.
Mutunga, Willy. "Introductory Note." In *Dedan Kimathi on Trial: Colonial Justice and Popular Memory in Kenya's Mau Mau Rebellion*, edited by Julie MacArthur, 1–35. Athens, OH: Ohio University Press, 2017.
Mutunga, Willy. "Foreword: Timothy is Leah and Leah is Timothy." In *We the People: Thinking Heavenly, Acting Kenyanly: Timothy Njoya: Memoir*, T. Njoya. Nairobi: WorldAlive Publishers, 2017.
Mwagiru, Ciugu. "Kenyatta the Family Man." *Daily Nation*, 20 October 1994, Kenyatta Day Special Supplement, 2–3.
"*Mzee* Remembered: Kenyatta Day Messages Galore." *Daily Nation*, 20 October 1983, 4.
Nasong'o, Wanjala S. "Revisiting 'the Two Faces of Civil Society' in Constitutional Reform in Kenya." In *Kenya: The Struggle for a New Constitutional Order*, edited by Godwin R. Murunga, Duncan Okello and Anders Sjogren, 97–118. London: Zed Books Ltd., 2014.
Nderitu, Wanjohi. "A Widow Reflects on the Lot of Forgotten Heroes." *Daily Nation*, 20 October 1992, Kenyatta Day Special Supplement, 21, 23.
Ngugi, Patrick. "Nationalists Remembered." *Daily Nation*, 20 October 1992, Kenyatta Day Special Supplement, 1.
Njihia, Gichuru. "Harbour No Bitterness, Urges *Uhuru* Veteran." *Daily Nation*, 20 October 1992, Kenyatta Day Special Supplement, 2–3.
Njuguna, Michael. "Heroes of *Uhuru* Suffering Without Bitterness." *Daily Nation*, 10 October 1992, 16–17.
"'Now a Re-birth of Unity,' says Mr Odinga." *Daily Nation*, 21 October 1964, 2.
Nyagah, Robert. "Kenyans to Celebrate First *Mashujaa* Day." *Daily Nation*, 19 October 2010, accessed 2 December 2020, http://www.nation.co.ke/news/1056-1036222-15ao6qs/index.html.
Nyanga, F. and O. Mak'Onyango. "President Hits at [sic] MPs Who Belittle Kenya." *East African Standard*, 21 October 1972, 1.
"Nyerere Resists Renaming of Street." *Tanzanian Affairs*, 148, (1994), accessed 14 March 2021, https://www.tzaffairs.org/1994/05/nyerere-resists-renaming-of-street/.
"Occasion Marred by Walk-Out." *Daily Nation*, 21 October 1992, 5.
Odinga, Oginga. *Not Yet Uhuru: An Autobiography*. London: Heinemann, 1967.
Ogot, Bethwell A. "The Decisive Years, 1956–63." In *Decolonization and Independence in Kenya, 1940–93*, edited by Bethwell A. Ogot and William Ochieng. 48–79. London: James Currey, 1995.
Ogot, Bethwell A. "Mau Mau and Nationhood: The Untold Story," In *Mau Mau and Nationhood*, edited by E.S. Atieno Odhiambo and John Lonsdale, 46–75. Oxford: James Currey, 2003.
Ohanga, J.B.A. "Forum." *Jicho*, 27 July 1960, 3.
"Parades, Dances and Speeches Mark Kenyatta Day in Provinces." *East African Standard*, 21 October 1972, 9.
Peterson, Derek R. *Ethnic Patriotism and the East African Revival: A History of Dissent, 1935–72*. Cambridge: Cambridge University Press, 2012.
"Plea to Honour *Uhuru* Heroes." *Daily Nation*, 21 October 2000, 2.

"President Receives Congratulations." *Daily Nation*, 20 October 1985, 1.

Priestland, David. "The University of Cape Town is Right to Remove its Cecil Rhodes Statue." *The Guardian*, 13 April 2015, accessed 2 December 2020, https://www.theguardian.com/commentisfree/2015/apr/13/cape-town-remove-cecil-rhodes-statue.

Ranger, Terence. "Africa in the Age of Extremes: The Irrelevance of African History." In *Rethinking African History*, edited by Simon McGrath, Charles Jedrej, Kenneth King and Jack Thompson, 269–291. Edinburgh: Centre of African Studies, University of Edinburgh, 1997.

Ranger, Terence. "The Politics of Memorialisation in Zimbabwe." In *Nations and their Histories: Constructions and Representations*, edited by Susana Carvalho and François Gemenne, 62–75. Basingstoke: Palgrave Macmillan, 2009.

Republic of Kenya. *Hansard*. First Session, 1961, *lxxxvii*, 87, 94–102.

Republic of Kenya. *Hansard*. First Session, 1961, *lxxxvii*, 85, 87, 88.

Republic of Kenya. *Hansard*. First Session, 1961, *lxxxvii*, 71, 105, 122–124.

Republic of Kenya. *Hansard*. Fourth Session, 1973, *xxxi*, 1288–1289.

Republic of Kenya. *Hansard*. Second Session, 1993, ii, 1419.

Republic of Kenya. *Hansard*. Second Session, 1993, ii, 1420.

Republic of Kenya. *Hansard*. 2 November 2006, 3370–3372.

Rieff, David. *In Praise of Forgetting: Historical Memory and its Ironies*. New Haven: Yale University Press, 2016.

Sittoni, Toni. "A Look into the Past, Present and the Future." *Daily Nation*, 20 October 1992, Kenyatta Day Special Supplement, 15–17.

Spencer, John. *KAU, The Kenya African Union*. London: KPI Limited, 1985.

Swynnerton, RJM. *Colony and Protectorate of Kenya: A Plan to Intensify the Development of African Agriculture in Kenya*. Nairobi: Government printer, 1954.

"Thousands to Attend Big *Uhuru* Park Rally." *Daily Nation*, 20 October 1975, 1.

Thoya, Francis. "Govt. Incapable of Freedom – Mazrui." *Daily Nation*, 20 October 1997, 32.

Throup, David. *Economic and Social Origins of Mau Mau*. London: James Currey, 1987.

Wachira, Muchemi. "Kenyans Remember Freedom Heroes as Calls for Name Change Persist." *Daily Nation*, 20 October 2006, 7.

"Why We Celebrate Kenyatta Day." *East African Standard*, 20 October 1972, 8.

Mohamed Haji Ingiriis

Southern Somalia's "Glorious Days Are Our Nightmare": The Performance of Political Memory and Contestations of Commemoration in Northern Somalia (Somaliland)

Abstract: This chapter makes a critical intervention into the academic and popular discussions about political memory in Somalia. Focusing on contestations of political memory and disputes over what occurred in the past as well as why, when and where they took place, the chapter foregrounds the importance of memory and commemoration for the Somaliland state-building project. By presenting a new perspective on the making of the breakaway region in northern Somalia that declared itself independent Somaliland in 1991, the chapter offers insights into how memories of trauma function as a political resource that could crystallise conflict and confrontation. Furthermore, in the case observed, judicious deployment of political memory elicited sympathy and solidarity locally and amongst diasporic Somaliland people in the pursuit of the separatist state-building project in Somaliland. Drawing on fieldwork conducted in Somaliland at intervals between 2016, 2018 and 2019 that relied on ethnographic observations and interviews with men and women, the chapter explores how the independence project in Somaliland was constructed through accumulated collective historical grievances. These were used to strengthen the case in favour of seeking recognition for a separate state allowing the collapse of the Somali state. Supposedly collective community suffering was rooted in how the military regime – bent on the protection and preservation of specific clans – mistreated the Isaaq, the predominate clan in Somaliland. Building upon previous studies of political memory, the chapter reveals how particularistic historical grievance shaped – and continues to shape – the process of legitimising separatism in Somaliland.

On one early evening at the end of April 2018, Hassan Mohamud Dagaal "Jaafaa," a grey-haired, middle-aged, former soldier living in Gebiley, a small town located 58 kilometres west of Hargeysa, the capital of northern Somalia (in the autonomous region of Somaliland), sat with me for an interview. He recollected the horrific days that aptly characterise the last decade of the military regime under General Mohamed Siad Barre, who ruled Somalia between October 1969 and January 1991.¹ Jaafaa, employed as a bodyguard of a notorious senior army officer during the 1980s, began to recall key locations and incidents under his watch. He sobbed while recounting his experiences. The most harrowing incident that still haunts him took place in 1981. Yusuf Abdi Ali, nicknamed "Tukeh," then a Lieutenant Colonel in Siad Barre's army, was transferred to the northern 26th military sector where he was given instruction to lead the Fifth Brigade. Tukeh had just returned from the United States where he had undertaken a three-month intensive course in military high command. Upon his return, Tukeh suddenly separated his brigade along clan lines: Isaaq and non-Isaaq. The Isaaq were then, as they are now, the predominant clan in Somaliland. Jaafaa recollected that 180 Isaaq men were lined up, disarmed, and their weapons shelved. They were subsequently taken to prison and treated like hostages.² In the end, 82 of them were released, but the rest disappeared. They were last seen somewhere between Hargeysa and Gebiley. Jaafaa knew nothing of their whereabouts. Those who were lucky enough to have been spared this "disappearance" were saved by non-Isaaq military officers who claimed to have been related to them in one way or another. "We committed no crime," Jaafaa, himself an Isaaq, said with a soft voice.³ The US-based Center for Justice and Accountability fought for years on behalf of Isaaq victims to bring Tukeh who now lives in Virginia to justice in US courts.⁴

In contemporary news reports as well as in much of the existing academic literature, substantial attention is given to the fall of the military regime in January 1991, when the regime was ousted and all state structures disintegrated as a result of a popular uprising that rocked the capital city Mogadishu in December 1990. Especially during the 1980s, Siad Barre's military regime left an enduring legacy of pain, which is regularly and repeatedly recounted in local and diaspor-

---

1 Interview with Hassan Mohamud Dagaal "Jaafaa," Gebiley, Somaliland, 27 April 2018.
2 Ibid.
3 Ibid. Author's translation. See also "Pointers – Somalia: Siad Barre's Foes," *Africa Confidential* 22, no. 9 (22 April 1981): 7; "Somalia: Somalia Barre Hangs on," *Africa Confidential* 24, no. 5 (2 March 1983): 5–7; and "Somalia: Generals on the Move," *Africa Confidential* 25, no. 10 (9 May 1984): 7–8.
4 The Center for Justice and Accountability, "Mass Atrocities in Northern Somalia: Warfaa V. Ali (Col. Tukeh)," accessed 13 September 2018, https://cja.org/what-we-do/litigation/warfaa-v-ali-col-tukeh/.

ic Somali communities, both in private and in public as well as political debate.[5] Similar to conflict-ridden contexts elsewhere on the African continent at the end of the Cold War, such as the Congo where political fissions gave way to violence,[6] the era witnessed state collapse and clan warfare in Somalia. This volatile situation made it difficult for victims of state crimes committed in the 1980s to receive any redress. The repercussions included political violence becoming not only an ordinary occurrence, but also a socially accepted form of expressing contestation for power amongst various armed groups. Although the implications of the war are often debated in popular media outlets, academic literature on the politics of memory remains almost non-existent in Somali studies.[7] Given that memories of the "civil" war remain central to divisions in Somali national identity, it is surprising that the intersection of memory, state power, politics and history has received little attention in scholarship on Somalia. Thus, fundamental questions remain: what scars do violent military regimes leave and why? How do political memories influence and shape post-conflict war-torn societies, state-building, and avenues of redress? Also, in which ways are specific political memories being challenged?

This chapter presents a new perspective on the making of the breakaway region in northern Somalia that declared itself independent Somaliland. It focuses on contestations of political memory and disputes over what occurred in the past as well as why, when and where they took place. Drawing on fieldwork conducted in Somaliland during July and August 2016, April and May 2018 and November and December 2019 using ethnographic observations and interviews with men and women, the chapter offers insights into how memories of trauma function as a political resource that could crystallise conflict and confrontation. Furthermore, in the case observed, judicious deployment of political memory elicited sympathy and solidarity locally and in the diaspora among the Isaaq elites in

---

5 For a detailed study on the politics, policies, practices and performances of the military regime, see Mohamed Haji Ingiriis, *The Suicidal State in Somalia: The Rise and Fall of the Siad Barre Regime, 1969–1991* (Lanham, MD: University Press of America, 2016).
6 Michael Niemann, "War Making and State Making in Central Africa," *Africa Today* 53, no. 3 (2007): 21–39.
7 There are only a few exceptions. See Francesca Declich, "When Silence Makes History, Gender and Memories of War Violence from Somalia," in *Anthropology of Violence and Conflict*, eds. Bettina Schmidt and Ingo Schröder (London: Routledge, 2001), 161–175; Mohamed Haji Ingiriis, "Many Somalia(s), Multiple Memories: Remembrance as Present Politics, Past Politics as Remembrance," *African Identities* 14, no. 1 (2016): 348–369; Mohamed Haji Ingiriis, "How Somalia Works: Mimicry and the Making of Mohamed Siad Barre's Regime in Mogadishu," *Africa Today* 63, no. 1 (2016): 57–83; and Mohamed Haji Ingiriis, "State Violence and Clan Violence in Somalia," *African Conflict and Peacebuilding Review* 8, no. 1 (2018): 73–96.

the pursuit of the separatist state-building project in Somaliland.⁸ The local elites in Somaliland are diverse but they are primarily dominated by Isaaq who consist of political players and businessleaders, many of whom returned from the diaspora. Because Somaliland was constructed through accumulated collective historical grievances, local elites drew on these aspects of political memory to strengthen the case in favour of seeking recognition for a separatist state allowing the collapse of the Somali state – an especially viable option given the new international order post-1990. Supposed collective community suffering was rooted in how the military regime, bent on the protection and preservation of specific clans, mistreated the Isaaq clan in particular.

Building on previous studies of political memory, the chapter reveals how particularistic historical grievance shaped – and continues to shape – the process of legitimising the state in Somaliland.⁹ At the same time non-Isaaq inhabitants of Somaliland, as well as regular people and the younger generation, have challenged this process of legitimisation. To blend the past with the present so as to interrogate the power and politics of memory as it attached to the separatist statehood, the chapter adopts historical as well as contemporary comparative approaches.¹⁰ Historian Arno Mayer contends that the "comparative perspective helps to broach new questions, such as the role of vengeance; to bring to light and challenge unspoken scholarly assumptions, such as the anomaly and mon-

---

8 It should be noted that the Isaaq elites abhor the term "secessionism" contending that Somaliland did not secede from Somalia, but rather had reclaimed sovereignty. The term "separatism," which also suggests something similar to secessionism, is also not appreciated, but this study opts to use it anyway. Field interviews and observations in Hargeysa, November-December 2019.
9 The concept of political memory has different meanings that have been used in various ways. See Ifi Amadiume and Abdullahi An-Na'im, eds., *The Politics of Memory: Truth, Healing & Social Justice* (London: Zed Books, 2000); James M. Mayo, "War Memorials as Political Memory," *Geographic Review* 78, no. 1 (1988): 62–75; and Susana Kaiser, "Escraches: Demonstrations, Communication and Political Memory in Post-Dictatorial Argentina," *Media, Culture and Society* 24, no. 4 (2002): 499–516.
10 My late supervisor Jan-Georg Deutsch taught me how to compare and to contrast historical circumstances, which has left a deep influence on my approach to researching the present and past history of Somali society. My own positionality as a researcher, especially one from southern Somalia doing research in northern Somalia (Somaliland) did not lead to a perception that I was "part of the story," apparently because my family was not affiliated with the military regime. As Catherine Besteman points out that, 'A primary goal of anthropological fieldwork is to gain an understanding of how those being studied make sense of their world'. Catherine Besteman, *Making Refuge: Somali Bantu Refugees and Lewiston, Maine* (Durham: Duke University Press, 2016), 7.

strosity of violence."¹¹ Besides, and with particular relevance for this volume, comparative analysis, Mayer argues, "facilitates identifying the importance of historical legacies and memories."¹²

In contrast to southern Somalia where diverse competing groups still vie for power, the Isaaq elites in Somaliland have sought to coalesce around a separation project bolstered by clan-based historical grievances. Even if this has not always been a smooth process in terms of nation-building, of late the Somaliland state-building project has made progress. The unrecognised state in Somaliland, unlike the recognised state in southern Somalia, was legitimised on the basis of a narrative of clan-based victimhood that has unsurprisingly struggled to attract a wider communal and cohesive solidarity apart from the Isaaq clan, an indication of failure to bring about one national identity inclusive of other groups living in Somaliland.

Identifying how memory and commemoration are used to reframe clan identities, the chapter assesses contested political memory by exploring the historical group grievances upon which the Isaaq base their advocacy for existence as a state separate from the rest of Somalia. It is argued that historical grievances not only lay at the heart of separation from southern Somalia, but more importantly, through contested and conflicting political memories, continue to stabilise and legitimise the separatist state in the eyes of the Isaaq population. This is not because the Isaaq population is more prone to refer to grievance-based political memory than other clans in Somaliland, but because a dominant Isaaq group portrays other Somalis, especially those from southern Somalia, as oppressors as a result of the atrocities committed during the latter years of the Barre era.¹³ The conclusion from historian Uzi Rabi on tribal societies – according to which the state in clan conflicts is not a "political actor" but a "political field" – is relevant in this case.¹⁴ As Marleen Renders observed of Somaliland, the state and the clan have proven to be "part of the same story, part of the same political dynamics."¹⁵ The interplay between the state and the clan came to follow what Carole Nagengast calls "a dialectical relationship."¹⁶

---

11 Arno J. Mayer, *The Furies: Violence and Terror in the French and Russian Revolution* (Princeton: Princeton University Press, 2000), 14.
12 Ibid.
13 Field interviews and observations in Hargeysa, April-May 2018.
14 Cited in Alice Hills, "Somalia Works: Police Development as State Building," *African Affairs* 113, no. 945 (2014): 92.
15 Marleen Renders, *Consider Somaliland: State-Building with Traditional Elders and Institutions* (Leiden: Brill, 2012), 57.

To make these arguments, this chapter will briefly discuss political memory in relation to Somaliland from a theoretical perspective. It will then detail the historical background that forms the basis for the formulation of these political memories. The final two sections consider the construction of identity as people of Somaliland and how this construction is being challenged, followed by a brief conclusion.

Political Memory, Grievance and Commemoration

Post-colonial-states are constructed through a selection of myriad memories and sustained on contextual commemoration. Casper Andersen's chapter in this volume, as well as that of Ed Goodman's, are pertinent here by analysing decolonisation and political memory. The preservation of a political memory creates a baseline for the state to foster solidarity within its citizenry. In examining the politics of memory in Eritrea, Daniel Mekonnen reveals how specific, selective, and contested memories of the past in Asmara are preserved to promote post-conflict state-building.[17] Moreover, political memory plays a decisive role in forming and constructing states within states, where antagonism between local communities and the state exist, as for instance in a conflict-ridden political landscape. Discussing the memorialisation policies of the Western Balkans, Israel and Palestine, Lee David argues that "memory construction is quite often used to define and reinforce [political] boundaries."[18]

Political memory also blends group grievances in the context of severely war-torn settings. In the case of conflict and post-conflict settings, Ernest Renan emphasised that "griefs are of more value than triumphs, for they impose duties, and require a common effort."[19] Political memory in war-torn societies can be more heavily contested than in societies unburdened by violent conflict. People memorialise the aftermath of a war differently through various groups, subgroups and close-knit communities. As evident in Natacha Filippi's chapter in this volume, public communal outcry against and close community-held

---

16 Carole Nagengast, "Violence, Terror, and the Crisis of the State," *Annual Review of Anthropology* 23 (1994): 117.
17 Daniel Mekonnen, "Contested Versions of Collective Memory in Postindependence Eritrea," *African Conflict & Peacebuilding Review* 3, no. 2 (2013): 151–170.
18 Lee David, "Holocaust and Genocide Memorialisation Policies in the Western Balks and Israel/Palestine," *Peacebuilding* 5, no. 1 (2017): 51–66.
19 Ernest Renan, "What is a Nation," in *Nation and Narration*, ed. Homi K. Bhabha (London: Routledge, 1990), 19.

grievances about selective commemoration that legitimise certain contemporary political projects or historical narratives are common in politically-charged settings. As Stephen Ellis suggested: "It is far better to find models of what they are or were, in other words to identify structures or ideas that have been central to the historical experience of these societies."[20]

Rebuilding a (post-conflict)-state to include communities in both northern and southern Somalia has proven a challenge from the moment of complete state collapse in 1991.[21] In light of contested political memories and historical group grievances, and since many Somalis have long been in a state of traumatic transition, a Somali-wide negotiated political settlement as part of a broader post-war recovery remains out of reach. Instead, stratified patterns of political memory connect past and present political realities in Somaliland. Protracted armed conflict over state power and resources between the military regime and its opponents since the late 1970s produced a legacy which compartmentalised Somalis, and even non-Somalis who study them, along clan lines. Somalis, as well as non-Somalis who write about them, often find a reason to debate the basic facts of the civil war, such as when hostilities began.[22] Similar divisions are found when dealing with other conflict-ridden and post-conflict societies. But not only is it necessary to avoid the pitfall of propagating one clan's historical narratives as the preferential or official one, but also a just account demands that the political histories of an array of groups (or clans) be considered equally. In reviewing Lidwien Kapteijns' controversial book about the 1991 clan-based wars in Somalia, Ken Menkhaus finds that "[a]s in many other post-war settings, a critical dimension of historical grievance narratives is all about when one begins the story." He concluded: "Intentionally or not, Kapteijns' book provides one clan... much more ammunition in its grievance narrative than others, and

---

20 Stephen Ellis, "The Mutual Assimilation of Elites: The Development of Secret Societies in Twentieth Century Liberian Politics," in *The Powerful Presence of the Past: Integration and Conflict along the Upper Guinea Coast*, eds. Jacqueline Knörr and Wilson Trajano Filho (Leiden: Brill, 2010), 185.
21 "Move by Hassan Sheikh Unites Somaliland Tribes against Him," *The Indian Ocean Newsletter*, no. 1429 (17 June 2016).
22 See Ingiriis, "Many Somalia(s)," 348. Daniel Companon recalls his attempt to remain politically neutral during the armed conflict in Somalia in the 1990s: "I have been trying to keep a line that is not biased in favor of one clan. I was told by the former editor of *Horn of Africa* that my early article on the opposition fronts made many Northerners especially Isak [Isaaq] people very unhappy. I am proud of it because this allowed me to publish later an article (in *Politique Africaine*) explaining the secession of Somaliland as a legitimate process (although it was opposed by sections of the non-Isak clans in the North). In the long run, I retained some credibility." Daniel Compagnon, email communication, 24 Jan 2014.

for that reason [it] will be heavily contested."²³ In order to better understand the nuanced historical trajectories of political memories and the state-building project in Somaliland, it is imperative to reflect on how these crucial themes relate to the political and cultural construction of historical group grievances in this context, and what connects certain groups to the past.

Siad Barre and Somaliland

The former British Protectorate of Somaliland joined the former *Somalia Italiana* (Italian Somalia) in 1960, the year of African Independence, to form the Somali Republic.²⁴ The merger was initially conducted peacefully, but the subsequent dispensation of power – where both powerful positions of the Presidency and the Prime Minister's office went to southern politicians – angered Isaaq elites who had expected one of their own to assume the relatively powerful post of the Prime Minister. This dissatisfaction ultimately manifested in an aborted military coup led by relatively young Isaaq military officers in December 1961.²⁵ The aborted coup did not lead to a popular uprising, even when some were killed and others wounded, but its consequences added to the mosaic of Isaaq historical grievance in the long run on grounds of a coherent victimhood commemoration. An independent judicial process in a Mogadishu criminal court presided over by a British judge, Indian lawyers and Italian prosecutors acquitted the coup plotters.²⁶ The desperate Isaaq political situation went hand-in-hand with growing socio-economic underdevelopment of the Isaaq region, as euphemistically expressed in a melancholic 1962 poem by one prominent Isaaq poet,

---

23 Ken Menkhaus, "Review: Clan Cleansing in Somalia: The Ruinous Legacy of 1991 by Lidwien Kapteijns. Philadelphia, PA: University of Pennsylvania Press, 2013," *The Journal of Modern African Studies* 52, no. 2 (2014): 679–681.

24 Amina H. Adan, "Somalia: An Illusory Political Nation-State," *South Asia Bulletin* 14, no. 1 (1994): 99–109.

25 "Documentary – Taariikh Nololeedka Cabdilaahi Koongo Qaybtii 9aad," (between min. 00:21–04:53), accessed 26 August 2014, https://www.youtube.com/watch?v=36e9oM9Or7Q; "Documentary – Taariikh Nololeedka Cabdilaahi Koongo Qaybtii 10aad," (between min. 00:31–08:43), accessed 26 August 2014, https://www.youtube.com/watch?v=EsANwflCoYM; "Documentary – Taariikh Nololeedka Cabdilaahi Koongo Qaybtii 11aad," (between min. 00:28–09:22), accessed 26 August 2014, https://www.youtube.com/watch?v=-1s7DkF1T2E; and "Documentary – Taariikh Nololeedka Cabdilaahi Koongo Qaybtii 12aad," (between min. 00:28–09:57), accessed 26 August 2014, https://www.youtube.com/watch?v=pMNZSVWRF_c.

26 Ibid.

"*adduunyo Hal baan lahaa, Hashii horor baa la tagay, haan maran baan sidaa*" (of all the world possessions, I had only but one She-camel and the She-camel was robbed by a beast, so I'm holding an empty vessel).[27] Isaaq elites played a less important role in politics until the change in administration in July 1967. At that point, the post of Prime Minister went to Mohamed Haji Ibrahim Egaal, the Isaaq's most prominent politician. The elation of many Isaaq that one of their own had finally assumed the position of Prime Minister would last no more than two years and three months.

The successful military coup of October 1969, which followed a few days after the assassination of President Abdirashid Ali Sharmarke, interrupted Egaal's efforts to defuse Isaaq public grievances towards the government in Mogadishu.[28] The first years of General Siad Barre's rule saw important achievements, including literacy campaigns, massive developmental projects, and improvements to health care and education. These achievements remain central for the memory and commemoration of the Siad Barre regime in southern Somalia. Indeed, at first, Siad Barre made crucial promises to repair the socio-political injustices and corrupt practices that had characterised the previous civilian administration. These promises proved empty, however, as he increasingly adopted clan-oriented policies, favouring one clan over the other to consolidate his power.[29]

The General's increasingly repressive measures gave rise to armed opposition movements – the Isaaq-dominated Somali National Movement (SNM) was founded in 1981 – and the emergence of these movements further fuelled the repression. Feeling threatened, Siad Barre, in the late 1980s, allowed his ground and air forces (including mercenaries from South Africa) to target civilians belonging to the clans from which the leaders of the armed insurgent movements hailed. In northeast Somalia (present-day Puntland), Siad Barre's army destroyed the powerbase of the armed opposition within a few years. However, in northern Somalia (present-day Somaliland), the situation was more dire and prolonged.[30] The Isaaq's northern regions of Waqooyi Galbeed (Northwest) and much of Togdheer were hard hit by Siad Barre's forces during the armed

---

27 "Cali Sugulle iyo Heestii 'Hiddiidiiyooy Hidii (1962)," (between min. 0:01–7:31), accessed 28 April 2020, https://www.youtube.com/watch?v=QMFaFE-HDK8.
28 Mohamed Haji Ingiriis, "Who Assassinated the Somali President in October 1969 The Cold War, the Clan Connection or the Coup d'État," *African Security* 10, no. 1 (2017): 1–24.
29 "Pointers – Somalia: Siad Barre's Foes," *Africa Confidential*; "Somalia: Somalia Barre Hangs on," *Africa Confidential*; and "Somalia: Generals on the Move," *Africa Confidential*.
30 Michael Simmons, "Thousands of Somalis Reported Dead in Genocide Attacks," *The Manchester Guardian Weekly*, 15 January 1989.

struggle spearheaded by the SNM, which aimed to defeat and depose the military regime.[31] The war between Siad Barre and the SNM intensified and climaxed in 1988 when Siad Barre enacted a supposedly peaceful accord with Colonel Mengistu Haile Mariam, his Ethiopian counterpart. The two dictators agreed to cease hostilities that were born out of the disputed Somali region in Ethiopia. They also promised to stop providing support to each other's armed opposition groups.[32]

The SNM established a temporary military base in Ethiopia's Somali region. Fearful of expulsion by Mengistu, the opposition group hastened to move to northern Somalia in what, from a military perspective, came close to suicide.[33] This desperate military measure was conducted clandestinely. As soon as they crossed the border into Somalia, SNM forces began to storm Siad Barre's army in the two most populated Isaaq towns in the northern region, Hargeysa and Bur'o. Siad Barre's military authorities, anticipating that the agreement with Mengistu would bring about the SNM's demise, were caught by surprise. They had seriously underestimated that, as Michael Walls writes, the SNM "was formed with a strong sense of grievance that only grew more intense as Siad Barre's government became more brutal and repressive," leading to "consolidated Isaaq solidarity."[34]

The military regime's response to the surprise attacks was devastating. It unleashed a series of devastating campaigns on the Isaaq civilians, most of whom were seen as sympathetic to – and supportive of – the SNM struggle. The campaign further hardened clan divisions, with targeted civilians forced to seek

---

[31] Confidential Cable: "Two Views on Somaliland: Hostile Forces Target Economy, No Return to a Unified Somalia." This cable was sent from US Embassy in Djibouti to the State Department in Washington. Accessed 7 December 2014, http://cables.mrkva.eu/cable.php?id=118293. For the SNM, see Gérard Prunier, "A Candid View of the Somali National Movement," *Horn of Africa* 13–14, no. 3–4 & no. 1–2 (1990): 107–120; Ibrahim Megag Samatar, "Light at the End of the Tunnel: Some Reflections on the Struggle of the Somali National Movement," in *Mending Rips in the Sky: Options for Somali Communities in the 21st Century*, eds. Hussein M. Adam and Richard Ford (Lawrenceville, N.J.: The Red Sea Press, 1997), 21–48; Said S. Samatar, "How to Run an SNM Gauntlet," *Horn of Africa*, 13, no. 1–2 (April & June 1990): 78–87; and Michael Walls, "Liberation Struggle for Regime Change: Somaliland's Transition from Conflict to Civilian Government," in *National Liberation Movements as Governments in Africa*, ed. Redie Bereketeab (London: Routledge, 2017), 218–219.

[32] "Somalia: Tango in the Ogaden," *Africa Confidential*, 27, 11, 21 May 1986, 4; "It is Impossible to Disdain People's Memory, Mr President," *KAAH: A Periodical Journal of the Ogaden National Liberation Front* 111 (July 1988): 15–17.

[33] "Somali National Movement," (between min. 02:35–05:15), accessed 20 May 2014, http://www.youtube.com/watch?v=XWosiLB6YNg.

[34] Walls, "Liberation Struggle for Regime Change," 218. See also Jutta Bakonyi, "Moral Economies of Mass Violence: Somalia 1988–1991," *Civil War* 11, no. 4 (2009): 434–454.

the protection of the SNM, no matter if they previously supported their cause. As a result, in the late 1980s much – if not almost all – human and material infrastructure of Waqooyi Galbeed (the Northwest) region was destroyed. Human rights reports warned that "a long-term human rights crisis" loomed amidst heavy "human rights abuses," even "civil war in the north," well before the armed conflict turned into full-blown civil war throughout Somalia.[35] International observers writing for *The Guardian* and *The Times* of London bolstered the argument that the military regime aimed to obliterate the Isaaq clan as the era of Siad Barre was fading.[36]

Following heavy bombardment in May 1988 from both Somali levies and non-Somali mercenaries, the most important Isaaq town of Hargeysa came to resemble Beirut in the 1970s or Berlin in the 1940s. Somaliland elites also refer to Hargeysa as the "Dresden of Africa." The reference is indicative of their attempt to make the suffering legible to a foreign audience. Therefore, it does not primarily serve to commemorate the events in Somaliland itself but rather to legitimise the secession project abroad. During this period, the Isaaq population was turned into or, in the eyes of the military regime, made themselves "second-class citizens in their own homeland," in the words of a former diplomat of the Siad Barre regime.[37] As the armed conflict dragged on and intensified, most Isaaq civilians fled to the Ethiopian border to escape the military regime's war machines.[38] Still, death and destruction awaited many on the road. Country reports documented that Siad Barre's forces used landmines "to threaten the ci-

---

[35] Africa Watch, *Human Rights Abuses and Civil War in the North: A Report from the U.S. General Accounting Office* (New York: Africa Watch, 1989); Amnesty International, *Somalia: A Long-Term Human Rights Crisis* (New York: Amnesty International, 1988); and Amnesty International, *Somalia: Imprisonment of Members of the Isaaq Clan Since Mid-1988* (New York: Amnesty International, 1988). On the geographies of the genocide and the magnitude of the crisis, see Mohamed Haji Ingiriis, "'We Swallowed the State as the State Swallowed Us': The Genesis and Genealogies of Genocide in Somalia," *African Security* 9, no. 3 (2016): 237–258; and Sarah G. Philips, "Proximities of Violence: Civil Order Beyond Governance Institutions," *International Studies Quarterly* 63, no. 3 (2019): 680–691.

[36] "Somali Military Bid to Obliterate Clan as Barre Era Fades," *The Times*, 2 July 1987; and "Somali Troops in 'Massacres and Bombings," *The Guardian*, 24 June 1988. See also "Somalia: Civilians Massacred," *The Indian Ocean Newsletter*, no. 321 (27 February 1988), 4; and "Somalia: Thousands Dead," *The Indian Ocean Newsletter*, no. 340 (9 July 1988), 1.

[37] Abdullahi Dool, "Good Governance: Self-Administering Regions within a Democratic Union," *Somalia* 4 (June 2001): 9. See also "Somalia: The Forgotten Men," *New African*, April 1988.

[38] Africa Watch, *A Government at War with Its Own People: Testimonies About the Killings and the Conflict in the North* (New York: Africa Watch, 1990).

vilian population and protect military installations."[39] The heavy-handed military pressure imposed on the Isaaq brought about a proliferation of armed resistance movements as other clans became convinced that the only way to depose of the military regime would be by way of a violent takeover.[40]

The legacy of this war remains one of trauma for the Isaaq population. It also resulted in the commemoration of the "sacred" separation of Somaliland from Somalia. The eventual fall of Siad Barre enabled Isaaq political players to recreate the colonial border that demarcated what used to be British Somaliland and Italian Somalia. They initially argued not for separation, but for the "restoration of sovereignty lost in the 1960 merger with Somalia."[41] They further used claims of abuses of power, the autocratic exploitation of state resources, and the military regime's policy of targeting Isaaq civilians during the period of armed insurgency as the driving force behind this push for separation. Nowhere was this more plainly emphasised than in the June 1996 paper of the Somaliland government that sought official recognition of Somaliland. That explicitly connected separation with the political memory of the Isaaq people. The paper is replete with a selective historical narrative of genocide, massacre and torture.[42]

In recent years, a more detailed and nuanced picture of Siad Barre's regime has been presented in order to understand the causes and consequences of what has been called a genocidal campaign by Isaaq leaders as well as foreign observ-

---

[39] Megan Wertz, "Country Profile: Somaliland," *Journal of Conventional Weapons Destruction* 10, no. 1 (2006): 38. See also Robert Gersony, *Why Somalis Flee: Synthesis of Accounts of Conflict Experience in Northern Somalia by Somali Refugees, Displaced Persons and Others* (Washington: State Department, 1989); Robert Gersony, "Why Somalis Flee: Conflict in Northern Somalia," *Cultural Survival Quarterly* 13, no. 4 (1989): 45–58; and "Thousands Flee as Somali Soldiers Massacre Civilians," *The Observer*, 3 July 1988.

[40] For discussion of the formation of armed opposition movements, see Daniel Compagnon, "Somali Armed Movements: The Interplay of Political Entrepreneurship and Clan-Based Factions," *African Guerrillas*, ed. Christopher Clapham (Oxford: James Currey, 1998), 73–89; Daniel Compagnon, "The Somali Opposition Fronts: Some Comments and Questions," *Horn of Africa* 13, no. 1–2 (January-June 1990), 29–54; Daniel Compagnon, "Dynamiques de Mobilisation, Dissidence Armée et Rébellion Populaire: Le Cas du Mouvement National Somali (1981–1990)," *Africa* 47, no. 4 (1992): 502–530; Marcel Djama, "Sur la Violence in Somalie: Genése et Dynamique des Formations Armées," *Politique Africaine* 47 (1992): 147–152; Mohamed Haji Ingiriis, "Between the Devil and the Deep Blue Sea: The Birth and the Breakdown of the Somali Armed Movements, 1976–1999," in *National Liberation Movements as Governments in Africa*, ed. Redie Bereketeab (London: Routledge, 2017), 233–248; and Walls, "Liberation Struggle for Regime Change."

[41] Field interviews and observations in Hargeysa, April-May 2018.

[42] *The Republic of Somaliland*, Submission on Statehood and Recognition of Republic of Somaliland, Hargeisa, June 1996.

ers.[43] Through a lens of clan versus clan tension, military regime authorities sought to destroy the SNM by targeting Isaaq civilians who shared clan affiliation with armed opposition movements. The presence of a single dominant clan at the top of the military regime helped political players from other clans to rally their supporters to revolt.[44] Since it sanctioned state-sponsored violence, the Siad Barre state – unlike, for instance, the Sierra Leonean state[45] – became a significant point of contention for different clans. After Siad Barre was overthrown, clans who benefitted from his regime refused to accept that they were no longer in control, while those clans oppressed by his military regime could not be convinced to share power with those who had been friendly towards the state.[46] Over time the conflict escalated from disputes about the distribution of state spoils to one pertaining to its survival as a single entity. As human rights organisations described, this was a complete transformation of the nature of violence.[47] The political memory sustaining the Somaliland separation traces its roots to what the Isaaq elites remember as the "Hargeysa Holocaust" perpetrated against them in 1988 by the military regime,[48] though this portrayal is not shared in the south. Somali President Farmaajo, for example, uses the term "atrocities" to describe the event.

Amidst the geopolitics of the Cold War, Siad Barre acted with impunity as a "gate-keeper" between the West and the East, initially allying for eight years with the Soviets and then switching sides to join the United States. The years during which his regime allied with the West were the most brutal of his rule.[49] The re-

---

43 Ingiriis, *The Suicidal State in Somalia*; Ingiriis, "'We Swallowed the State'"; Ingiriis, "How Somalia Works"; Ingiriis, "Between the Devil and the Deep Blue Sea"; and Ingiriis, "State Violence and Clan Violence."
44 Ingiriis, *The Suicidal State in Somalia*, 194. See also Pierre Englebert, *Africa: Unity, Sovereignty & Sorrow* (Boulder: Lynne Rienner Publishers, 2009), 23.
45 David Keen, *Conflict & Collision in Sierra Leone* (Oxford: James Currey, 2005), 105.
46 Field interviews and observations in Hargeysa, July-August 2016.
47 Africa Watch, *A Government at War with Its Own People*; Africa Watch, *Human Rights Abuses*; Amnesty International, *Somalia*; and Amnesty International, *Somalia*. For additional analysis, see Daniel Compagnon, "State-sponsored Violence and Conflict under Mahamed Siyad Barre: The Emergence of Path Dependent Patterns of Violence," World Peace Foundation Occasional Papers, 22 October 2013, accessed 23 December 2013, http://sites.tufts.edu/reinventingpeace/2013/10/22/state-sponsored-violence-and-conflict-under-mahamed-siyad-barre-the-emergence-of-path-dependent-patterns-of-violence/.
48 Ingiriis, "'We Swallowed the State.'"
49 Box 4, folder "Somalia – President Mohammed Siad Barre" of the National Security Adviser's Presidential Correspondence with Foreign Leaders Collection, Gerald R. Ford Presidential Library. For an interesting analysis on the US-Siad Barre relationship, see Mohamed Diriye Abdullahi, "In the Name of the Cold War: How the West Aided and Abetted the Barre Dictatorship

gime received massive military aid, which fuelled and prolonged the armed conflict and introduced the automatic modern weaponry that still remains in use in Somalia today. Some Siad Barre military officers confirmed to American authorities in Mogadishu that their forces, as well as their "allies," used US military equipment to break the Isaaq powerbase during the brutal campaigns against that community.[50] The "allies" were local non-Isaaq clan militia in the North fighting on behalf of the Siad Barre military regime.

State policy declared that to survive in the pool of dissenting armed opposition movements that emerged from the 1970s, the military regime worked under a system of patronage and patrimonialism to reward one clan and punish another, with the assistance of other allied clans. Officers of the military regime were also ordered to execute members of clans that opposed Siad Barre.[51] In the southern regions, this only affected people temporarily but in the northern regions, punishing the communities from which armed opposition groups hailed was an extensive process because local civilians assisted their youth joining the insurgency.[52]

An over-reliance on clan punishment caused clans not only to fight for the spoils of the state to compensate for the military regime's brutality but also to exact revenge on each other. Refugees from the Somali region in Ethiopia were for this reason targeted during the 1991 clan-based wars. Local communities targeted them in retribution for contributing to the regime-sponsored campaigns of punishment against the local clans in the south in the 1980s.[53] The Siad Barre regime also targeted the Somali Patriotic Movement (SPM), an Ogaadeen-dominated armed resistance group in Kismaayo, Jubada Hoose (Lower Juba), and the United Somali Congress (USC), a Hawiye-dominated armed resistance group in the country's central and southern regions as well as Mogadishu. The collective clan punishment campaigns asserted through brutal military measures eventually led to the collapse of the military regime in January 1991, set the stage for the 1991 clan-based wars after Siad Barre's fall and

---

of Somalia," in *Genocide, War Crimes & The West: History and Complicity*, ed. Adam Jones (London: Zed Books, 2004), 241–259.

50 Cable from US Embassy in Mogadishu to Washington, "Sub: Peace Breaking Out in the North?," accessed 31 August 2014, https://wikileaks.org/cable/1990/03/90MOGADISHU2527.html.
51 Ibid.
52 Interview with S. A. A., Gebiley, 28 November 2019.
53 "Somalia: The Ogadeni's Misfortune," *Africa Confidential* 25, no. 21 (1984): 5–7. See also *Keydmedia*, "Baladweyne: Qaxootigii Ogaadeenka oo Ciidam[a]da Maxamad Siyaad Barre ay Hubeeyeen!," (between min. 00:25–05:13), accessed 26 July 2014, http://www.youtube.com/watch?v=Dt1pqsZ2R-I.

flight, and culminated in heated historical grievances held by each Somali clan as political memory in its own right.[54]

Political Memory and Construction of Identity

After the fall of the Siad Barre regime, SNM leaders in May 1991 convened a conference at which representatives of clans from the northern regions proclaimed an independent Somaliland state. The subsequent separatist state-building project to come would not prove an easy task, however, with years of internecine fighting between sub-clans of the Isaaq following the declaration. Some supported the separation and others opposed it until the mid-1990s, when a relative peace was achieved with grand conferences in the towns of Borame and Sheikh.

Beyond the region, Isaaq in the diaspora who witnessed the war first-hand also carried the scars inflicted by the Siad Barre regime and wartime atrocities. Somaliland's declared separation thus garnered considerable moral and financial contribution from many diasporic Isaaq communities traumatised by the protracted and bitter armed struggle. The Isaaq diaspora mobilised the issues of political marginalisation, economic exclusion and genocidal campaigns perpetuated by Siad Barre's regime to engender a sense of unity, which made reaching consensus locally easier than in southern Somalia. Even when Somaliland encountered a torturous conflict within the clan, the Isaaq diasporic communities invested significant energy and resources to resolve local disputes and ensure separatism.[55]

The immediacy with which Isaaq elites proclaimed independence for the Somaliland state after the fall of the military regime testifies to how Siad Barre's regime was seen as central to the practice of political memory. In conversations on the streets of Hargeysa, many Isaaq men and women in their everyday engagement with the Somaliland question evoke the scorched-earth campaigns committed by the Siad Barre regime to promote the case for international recognition for their separatist state.[56] As Compagnon aptly observed in the early 1990s, "*L'attitude de la population [I]saaq trouve son fondement dans la guerre civile qui débuta dans le Nord avec la lutte armée*" (the attitude of the Isaaq population is rooted in the civil war that began in the North with the armed strug-

---

54 Ingiriis, *The Suicidal State in Somalia*.
55 Stephanie R. Bjork, *Somalis Abroad: Clan and Everyday Life in Finland* (Chicago: University of Illinois Press, 2017), 109.
56 Field observations, Hargeysa, 26 July 2016.

gle).⁵⁷ The colonial and post-colonial outlook of the Isaaq today stands markedly apart from the traditional Somali nation-state conception based on one unified greater Somalia statehood comprising all five Somali zones in the Horn of Africa.

Every year, many Isaaq gather in Somaliland towns and in cities like London and Nairobi to commemorate 18 May 1991, the day when Somaliland independence was declared. In these commemoration ceremonies, the Isaaq people, whether in the diaspora or back home, assert pride, most notably with regard to Somaliland's relative stability in contrast to the continued violent character of politics in southern Somalia. There, the pretence of an "armed peace" protected variously by Ethiopian, Kenyan or other African forces predominates, while in Somaliland the practice of an "unarmed peace" unaccompanied by physical foreign presence prevails. The contrast is the main reason, apart from clan sentiments, why in southern Somalia people still refer to Siad Barre's maintenance of relative calm until the civil war reached the capital in Mogadishu in December 1990 as *xilligii nabadda* (the peaceful era). As one Isaaq female intellectual in Hargeysa pointed out, "their [southern Somalia's] glorious days are our nightmare. For example, they think Siad Barre was their saviour when he was our destructor."⁵⁸ Both Radio Mogadishu and the Somali National Television eulogise the era of the military regime by replaying interviews and programmes released while Siad Barre was in power.⁵⁹ Overall, people in southern Somalia and even elsewhere in Puntland recall Siad Barre and his regime in ways distinctly different to those in Somaliland.

A number of episodes at the intersection of politics and commemoration reinforced divisions between Somaliland and southern Somalia. For example, Hassan Sheikh Mohamud, who led southern Somalia from 2012 to 2017, organised a state burial for General Mohamed Ali Samatar, who served as Siad Barre's Vice President, Prime Minister and Minister of Defence. As the *Journal of the Anglo-Somali Society* reported in 2016, Samatar, in a US civil court, "admitted his responsibility for torture, extrajudicial killing, war crimes and other human rights abuses committed against the civilian population during the brutal military dic-

---

57 Author's translation. Daniel Compagnon, 'Somaliland, un Ondre Politique en Gestation?', *Politique Africaine* 50 (June 1993): 10.
58 Interview with S.C.A., Hargeysa, 4 May 2018.
59 *Radio Muqdisho*, "21 Oct.Taariikhdii kacaanka iyo khudbadihi ugu muhiimsana Madaxweyne Siyaad. Keydka R/muqdisho.DHAGEYSO," accessed 9 September 2018, https://www.radiomuqdisho.net/21-oct-taariikhdii-kacaanka-iyo-khudbadihi-ugu-muhiimsana-madaxweyne-siyaad-keydka-rmuqdisho-dhageyso/.

tatorship of the Siad Barre régime."⁶⁰ The (s)election of Mohamed Abdullahi Mohamed 'Farmaajo' to succeed Hassan Sheikh Mohamud as President in Mogadishu through a parliamentary vote on 8 February 2017 also opened old wounds for the Isaaq. Many regarded Farmaajo as part of Siad Barre's regime, in which Farmaajo served as a junior staff member at the Somali Embassy in the United States before defecting to apply for political asylum in America in the late 1980s. Farmaajo's government further triggered this notion of a connection between Farmaajo and Siad Barre when it added the latter's son-in-law to a committee tasked with mediating between the federal government in Mogadishu and leaders in Somaliland. Speaking at the commemoration of Women's Day on 8 March 2018, Somaliland President Muuse Biihi reminded Farmaajo of how "his uncle (Siad Barre) destroyed lives and wealth" in the North.⁶¹ With an emotional speech in which he seemed to shed tears, Biihi's words caused elderly women in his audience to cry out in support. Around that time, at King's Café in Hargeysa, a businesswoman assessed Farmaajo's performance as President after a year in office and reached the same conclusion as Muuse Biihi: "Farmaajo is doing nothing other than imitating his uncle [Siad Barre]."⁶² No matter if we assume that the displayed emotions are completely genuine, or at least partially political theatre, it is clear that people make sense of their position by drawing from historical grievances that reverberate in the present. In this case, "never a predatory state again" serves as a code echoing political memories that caution against any oppressive rule or reproduction of Siad Barre's later reign.⁶³

Commemorations such as these in southern Somalia impede fruitful discussions of how the entire territory might come together as one unified, non-violent nation-state. As renowned historian of Somali society Charles Geshekter noted, it was – conceptually speaking – the Isaaq masses who comprehended that "the railroad train of Somali history had gone around a steep bend in the tracks in 1991, striving the past decades to feed and sustain their administrative state apparatus, while leaving the identification of its historical roots to academics."⁶⁴

---

60 "General Mohamed Ali Samatar, 1931–2016," *Journal of the Anglo-Somali Society* 60 (Autumn 2016): 62.
61 "Madaxweyne Muuse Biixi oo dumar ka ooy siiyay + xuska 8march," *Hadhwanaag News*, March 8, 2018; and "Khudbad Muuse Biixi Cabdi," *Somaliland Television*, 8 March 2018.
62 Interview with S.A.H., Hargeysa, 29 April 2018.
63 Field interviews, Hargeysa, July-August 2016 and April-May 2018.
64 Charles Geshekter, email communication, 24 April 2013; See also Lee Cassanelli, "Reconciliation and Reconstruction: Are there Lessons from Somalia's [R]ecent History?," paper present-

This does not mean that political memory in Somaliland is more legitimate or powerful than in southern Somalia. Rather, it highlights that in the Somaliland case charged political memory supported the cause of political expediency. Each post-Siad Barre government in Somalia developed a special website mainly for propaganda purposes, that is to advance its political project. But none could present a similarly coherent, albeit selective and self-centred, case of historical grievance as that of Somaliland.[65]

Southern Somalia's inability to present an equally (excessively) orderly national myth apparently discourages people in Somaliland from the belief that reuniting with southern Somalis would result in improvement for them.[66] But shifting clan alliances and changing local political conflicts in Somaliland also create conditions for the Isaaq people to re-assess the benefits of separatism without discarding the politics of memory altogether. Whenever a case of genocide denial arises from southern Somalia, both pro-separatist and anti-separatist Isaaq camps take on defensive positions in relation to how Somaliland has or has not principally been subjected to *gumaad* (genocide).[67]

In Hargeysa, the cause of separatism is also present in commemorative practices, such as memorials. A monument celebrating *Daljirka Dahsoon* (the Unknown Soldier) in Hargeysa starkly contrasts with Mogadishu's tribute to *Daljirka Dahsoon*. The latter embodies the unified state in southern Somalia, while the former stands for the separate state in Somaliland. Hargeysa's *Daljirka Dahsoon* evokes a common, grievance-based historical memory of war trauma. It stands in *Kheyriyadda*, the city centre of Hargeysa, a monument depicting a MiG17 war aircraft with a Somali national flag on both sides. This epitomises Siad Barre's warplanes that launched airstrikes on the town while flying from the Hargeysa airport in 1988.[68] The base, symbolising the bombardment, is decorated with representations of the civilians massacred by the military regime, such as a mother carrying her son on her back covered with a waving Somaliland flag. Other drawings show an old man who lost both hands and one leg at the height of the military regime's punitive campaign of an aerial attack on the Isaaq.[69] The

---

ed at the 6th International Congress of Somali Studies, Berlin, 6–9 December 1996; and Simon Horner, "Somalia: Can the Jigsaw be Pieced Together," *ACP-EU Courier* 162 (1997): 46–53.
65 Mohamed Haji Ingiriis, "From Pre-Colonial Past to the Post-Colonial Present: The Contemporary Clan-Based Configurations of Statebuilding in Somalia," *African Studies Review* 61, no. 2 (2018): 55–77.
66 Field interviews, Hargeysa, July-August 2016 and April-May 2018.
67 Field interviews, Hargeysa, November-December 2019.
68 Field observations, Hargeysa, 11 July 2016 and 29 April 2018.
69 Ibid.

monument displays its message with the phrase: *Xus oo Xusuusnow* (Respect and Remember). Monuments of this nature have mushroomed in Hargeysa. They can be seen starting from the entrance of the Egaal International Airport and continuing to a depiction of an armoured tank in the city centre that serves as yet another illustration of how political memory is present on public display. Monuments such as these are used as backdrops for public events, and in particular for the celebration of Somaliland independence day on May 18. Julie MacArthur noted a similar proliferation in her study of late colonial Kenya, highlighting that "public monuments scattered throughout the capital depict an upheld hand gripping the mapped geo-body of Somaliland."[70]

Craving for a separate state is so strong among the Isaaq that political players from the community as well as the northern public use terms such as the "Somali Territories" and "Somali-speaking peoples" to refer to the region and the people living therein.[71] This is not only to avoid any mention of Somalia but also to emphasise the position of Somaliland within the wider Somali states of the Horn. After many years of conflict and negotiations between the Isaaq and the non-Isaaq as well as within the Isaaq, the independence project through grievance-based political memory continues to divide the clans living in Somaliland. For instance, people opposed to separation have charted a new form of identity as "unionists" opposing the "secessionist one clan enclave."[72] Their critics brand them "enemies of the state."[73]

A military schism also divides people into *mujaahid* (holy warrior: plural *mujaahidiin*) and non-*mujaahid*. *Mujaahidiin* are, broadly, those who were part of the SNM struggle. The title of *mujaahid* is specially reserved for military leaders such as Muuse Biihi Abdi, the current President of Somaliland, and his close friend Mohamed Kaahin, the Minister of Interior, both former commanders of the now defunct SNM. The *mujaahid* versus non-*mujaahid* dichotomy sows suspicion among the clans and compounds the alienation of those who are not Isaaq because they did not belong to the SNM. The divide between those who were *mujaahidiin* and those who were not appears to have been lastingly defined during the armed SNM struggle against the military regime.[74] Both grievance-based po-

---

70 Julie MacArthur, *Cartography and the Political Imagination: Mapping Community in Colonial Kenya* (Athens, OH: Ohio University Press, 2016), 229.
71 Ingiriis, "From Pre-Colonial Past to the Post-Colonial Present."
72 Field interviews, Hargeysa, July-August 2016 and April-May 2018.
73 Ibid.
74 For the foreseeable future, Somaliland seems to be politically controlled by Muuse Biihi's powerful clan of the Sa'ad Muuse/Habar Awal of the Isaaq, which will likely compound rising

litical memory and historical commemoration practices in Somaliland contribute to legitimising separatism. However, the ways in which people have manipulated the narratives of the horrors of Siad Barre's rule and the heroic struggle of the SNM *mujaahidiin* also leads to a number of critical challenges, as outlined in the next section.

Challenges to Grievance-Based Separatism

The post-conflict Somaliland state faces internal challenges of nation-building. A major obstacle is that an overarching national identity encompassing of all the clans and communities in Somaliland was not born out of the formation of the separatist state. The conflict over the Isaaq past versus non-Isaaq past still stands. On one hand, despite the developing visions of one united Isaaq political memory as a result of the "defection" of some of Somaliland's political players to Mogadishu, Somaliland authorities are striving to strengthen Isaaq unity by repeatedly bringing up the genocide and the success of the SNM in liberating their people from brutal oppression.[75] On the other hand, while reinforcing the importance of the SNM's achievement, the Isaaq-dominated Somaliland authorities are wary of sanctioning a historical narrative that elevates one clan. They worry that non-Isaaq clans may feel excluded and complain of further political marginalisation by the Somaliland separatism if the SNM political memory is made the only official one. Compared with previous years, historical narratives of the non-Isaaq can increasingly be observed in the public celebrations and gatherings in Somaliland. Most Isaaq officials and intellectuals who delivered speeches in the first Laas Aanood Book Fair held in the heart of the Dhulbahante territory publicly acknowledged the political memory of the anti-colonial Dervish struggle (1899–1920), which non-Isaaq clans like the Dhulbahante frequently glorify in public discourses. Both Dhulbahante political players and their public use this history as a historical counterweight to the more recent, privileged Isaaq historical position.[76]

Distinct from the overwhelming majority of the Isaaq who desire separation from the south, most of the other clans living in Somaliland, such as the Dhulbahante, the Warsangeli, the Gadabiirsi and the Iise clans, continue to contend that they are not supportive of Somaliland. Diasporic groups growing out of

---

local political tensions by reinforcing the alienation of large numbers of the Isaaq, especially the Habar Yoonis.
75 Field interviews, Hargeysa, November-December 2019.
76 Field interviews, Laas Aanood, 10–11 December 2019.

these clans constantly urge their local political players to establish their own clan-states.[77] Thus, whilst the process of state-building was largely successful in the Isaaq-dominated areas in Somaliland, prominent voices among the Dhulbahante in eastern Somaliland and the Gadabiirsi in western Somaliland continue to object to the separatist project.[78] Many influential political players and military officials of these two clans supported the Siad Barre regime in the 1980s, although several others sided with the Isaaq and joined the SNM. Some Isaaq recall when the Siad Barre regime employed Dhulbahante and Gadabiirsi militias to counter the SNM attacks, but most largely refrain from publicly expressing this grievance to avoid inflaming relations with the non-Isaaq living within the Somaliland state.[79] Some Gadabiirsi recall incidents in which the SNM allegedly took revenge on their community in the Awdal region in 1991.[80] Dhulbahante leaders' opposition to the Somaliland separation mainly stems from the common clan genealogy they share with Siad Barre. They also have a different memory of his regime in which they had enjoyed a significant share of the state's spoils, which causes them to wait for power to be taken by another Siad Barre.[81]

The (re)creation of national identity in Somaliland defined – and was itself defined by – the political memory aimed at crafting a new identity amongst those living in the region. However, not only is there no common identity to unite the Isaaq and the non-Isaaq, the Isaaq themselves are absent an all-embracing unified clan ideology to advocate for Somaliland as a nation-state parallel to Eritrea or South Sudan.[82] In Hargeysa, for instance, Isaaq sub-clans have separate quarters and one frequently hears "*daantaas waxaa deggan reer hebel*" (that quarter is populated by that clan). According to conventional clan wisdom, Hargeysa, the capital, is essentially divided into two quarters between

---

77 For discussion of rising separatism around the world, see Tanisha M. Fazal, "Go your Own Way: Why Rising Separatism Might Lead to More Conflict," *Foreign Affairs* (July-August 2018): 113–123.
78 Field interviews, Laas Aanood, 10–11 December 2019 and Boorame, 10–11 August 2016.
79 Field interviews, Hargeysa, July-August 2016 and April-May 2018.
80 "Sh. Xasan Daheeye oo ka sheekaynaya xasuuqii SNM ka samaysay Boorama," (between min. 0:01–11:23), accessed 13 September 2018, https://www.youtube.com/watch?v=_-iNyr2842o. Compare *Arabsiyo News*, 'Xasuuqii ka dhacay Arabsiyo xiligii taliska Siyaad Bare,' accessed 11 December 2017, https://www.youtube.com/watch?v=LB3K0UjoCK0. Northern and southern Somalians have two slightly dissimilar pronunciations of this clan. In the former, it is known as Gadabuursi while in the latter, it is referred to as Gadabiirsi. Since I am a southern Somali, I adopt the southern Somali pronunciation.
81 Field interviews, Laas Aanood, 10–11 December 2019.
82 Field interviews, Hargeysa, July-August 2016 and April-May 2018.

the two main Isaaq sub-clans: *Daanta Sacad Muuse* (the Sa'ad Muuse Quarter) and *Daanta Garhajis* (the Garhajis Quarter). This division has emerged in spite of the fact that other Isaaq clans such as Arap also claim partial ownership of Hargeysa.[83] Beyond the capital, regions populated by non-Isaaq are called *darafyada* (peripheries), reflecting how they are removed from the centre and trail the Isaaq areas in terms of power and resources. People from these peripheral regions, such as Sool and parts of Sanaag and Togdheer, take two routes to challenge Isaaq power: first, by seeking to align with other entities such as Puntland and second, by attempting to form their own mini states.[84] Both strategies seek to weaken the Somaliland separatist project and force negotiations that will drive resources to these marginalised regions.

Prominent political players among the Gadabiirsi clan evince some support for Somaliland separation.[85] In contrast with the Dhulbahante and the Warsangeli as sub-clans of the Harti, Gadabiirsi leaders integrated deeply into the Somaliland state system soon after factions of Dhulbahante and Warsangeli elders joined their Harti co-clansmen in Puntland in 1998.[86] The Gadabiirsi then operated separately from the Harti clan coalition that was formed to promote parochial clan interests contrary to their political alliance in the 1960s under the

---

[83] Field interviews, Habaasweyn, 13 December 2019.
[84] Field interviews, Laas Aanood, 10–11 December 2019.
[85] Field interviews and observations, Boorame and Hargeysa, July-August 2016.
[86] Gadabiirsi academic turned political player Ahmed Samatar once condemned what he called the clan domination of every aspect of life in Somaliland (a euphemism for the Isaaq), including the state system. That he now avidly supports Somaliland suggests that authorities in Hargeysa have accommodated some dissident voices like Samatar and Ali Khaliif Galayr, a senior Dhulbahante political player, thus achieving much greater political clout than they had possessed from the outset. See: "Prof. Ahmed Ismail [S]amatar (Somaliland waa muqadas) oo ka soo laabtey Hargaysa," (between min. 0:51–35:05), accessed 20 July 2016, https://www.youtube.com/watch?v=cSfjo8KPZCU. Compare Samatar's earlier position: "Lewis's interpretations are curiously partisan. Here, for example, Siyaad Barre is excoriated for his dictatorial appetite, while Mohamed Ibrahim Egal, known across the Somali territory for his unmatched malfeasance and animus towards anyone more educated or competent, is handled with a soft touch, if not outright affirmation (284 [sic]). In addition, Lewis is so sold on the 'Somaliland' project that he maligns those Northerners who continue to hold on to their nationalist credo as cohorts driven by self-interest. On the other hand, chauvinistic regionalists bent on dismembering the Somali Republic are portrayed as honourable, and with the right cause to boot. But it was not always like this in Lewis's work. Well into Siyaad Barre's rule, Lewis produced essays that celebrated the new order and what he thought it portended. What is one to make of these drastically shifting optics." Ahmed I. Samatar, "I. M. Lewis, *A Modern History of the Somali: Nation and State in the Horn of Africa*. Athens: Ohio University Press, 2002," H-Net Reviews, December 2013, 2 accessed 27 December 2016, https://www.h-net.org/reviews/showpdf.php?id=8552.

United Somali Party (USP). The primary concern for the Gadabiirsi population in the Awdal region has been to increase their parliamentary seat numbers, insofar as the comparatively few number allocated to them two decades ago limits their influence.[87] The Iise and other peripheral clans like Fiqishinni/Eyr/Habar Gidir either supported or stayed silent on the issue of the SNM struggle.

When the SNM liberated most of Somaliland in February 1991, the organisation chose not to take advantage of the weaker position of the dissenting clans such as the Dhulbahante, Gadabiirsi and Warsangeli by conquering them and forcefully imposing SNM rule. This was partly because various Isaaq political players were focused on competing for power within that clan. With the eventual mediation of Isaaq clan elders who became part of a "hybrid" state system that could accommodate clan tradition and a modern state system, Somaliland came to enjoy a relative peace unknown to southern Somalia in recent years.[88] Persistent peace lessened the possibility that Isaaq political players could resort to violent politics in achieving their ambitions.

However, the unequal power structure between those who hold the power and resources and those who do not created stratifications by clan and by class that invigorated new grievances within the Isaaq. This was demonstrated by the political fissures caused by the new *Jeegaan* alliance of two Isaaq sub-clans, Habar Awal and Habar Je'lo, in the presidential elections. As a result two other Isaaq sub-clans, Habar Yoonis and Edagalle (combined as Garhajis), have been comparatively marginalised.[89] This attests to the fact that historical political memory can eventually be challenged by a political present in which the many intermittent conflicts between and within Isaaq clans predominate.[90]

Some Isaaq intellectuals are beginning to challenge the use of memories of a violent past as the kind of commemoration worthy of upholding separation from the south. For example, during a 2018 interview in Hargeysa, a university lecturer who spoke English with a Kenyan accent after living there for many years insisted that "the past is the past, let's talk to the present and turn to the future. It's wrong to stick to the past. Who is now killing who in Somalia? Monuments

---

87 Field interviews and observations, Boorame, 10–11 August 2016.
88 Field interviews, Hargeysa, April-May 2018.
89 Field interviews, Hargeysa, July-August 2016; and "Qaab-Dhismeedka Ciidanka Qaranka Somaliland, Hogaamada ciidanka iyo beelaha ay ka soo jeedaan," September 2016.
90 *Lughaya*, 'Daawo Xukuumada Somaliland Oo Ka Hadashay Dagaal Khasaaro Gaystay Oo ka Soo Cusboonaaday Ceel-af-wayn', accessed 9 September 2018, http://www.lughaya.com/home/2018/07/24/daawo-xukuumada-somaliland-oo-ka-hadashay-dagaal-khasaaro-gaystay-oo-ka-soo-cusboonaaday-ceel-af-wayn/.

are wrong to display here."[91] Even though the Isaaq grievance-based political memory has long served as the basic justification for Somaliland's separation, local Hargeysa people have already begun to position the military regime differently due to the longevity of the fragmentation along clan lines within Somaliland.

Commemoration of the military regime's oppressive rule follows two distinct trajectories. While some recall the regime with fondness (mostly the Garhajis), others (such as the Habar Awal and some Habar Je'lo) remember this time with bitterness. One Habar Yoonis female cook at a university guesthouse in Hargeysa lamented that, when Siad Barre was in power, the current fragmentation of the Somali state into weak mini-states was never possible.[92] Other people, including some Edagalle elders, contend that Siad Barre's legacies will not soon be forgotten in Somaliland, in spite of anecdotal signs of nostalgia for the days of a unified Somalia.[93] Some young people are beginning to hesitate when it comes to taking positions for either Somalia or Somaliland. This is not entirely surprising, because as times passes, an increasing percentage of the Isaaq population was not yet born when the worst atrocities took place in the late 1980s. People discuss the heated issues of political memory and take sides about the past, but although those who desire separation are still much more numerous than those who prefer the return to southern Somalia, people are beginning to reassess the separation stance.[94]

Although many Isaaq youth have no memory of a unified Somalia, prominent voices among Somaliland youth call for "reunion" with Somalia.[95] Yet authorities in Hargeysa appear to ignore these emerging voices that would embrace either another merger with Somalia or the notion of recreating from Hargeysa a re-unified single Somali nation-state, with the capital relocated from Mogadishu to Hargeysa. More worryingly, authorities continue to suppress the voices of those who prefer unity with southern Somalia rather than Somaliland separation.[96] This occurred when a young Isaaq woman went to Mogadishu in 2016,

---

91 Conversations with A.F.C., Hargeysa, 2 May 2018.
92 Conversation with F.H.S., Hargeysa, 22 July 2016.
93 Field interviews, Hargeysa, November-December 2019.
94 Field interviews and observations in Hargeysa, July-August 2016.
95 "Gabdho Reer Hargaysa ah oo Amaan Kala Dul dhacay Muqdisho Iyo Somali Weyn," *Cagaaran*, accessed 11 December 2017, https://www.youtube.com/watch?v=Her3UPmpJ-s; "Gabadh re[er] Hargaysa oo Somaali Jacayl la ilmaysay," *Daljire*, accessed 11 December 2017 https://www.youtube.com/watch?v=4-QUNrBeaOI&feature=youtu.be; and "Gabadh re[er] Burco ah oo Jawab Kulul siisay Islantii Farmaajo werartay," accessed 11 December 2017, *Daljire*, https://www.youtube.com/watch?v=0ID7RAD553s..
96 Field interviews, Hargeysa, July-August 2016 and April-May 2018.

condemned the separatist Somaliland state while commending the Siad Barre regime, and was arrested in 2018.[97] In July that year, an elderly Isaaq man living in the United Kingdom received threatening comments from other Isaaq after he recorded and posted on YouTube a video in which he praised Siad Barre. The man recounted the former president's childhood "bravery" as well as the leader's family history characterised by an ability to survive against all odds. He denounced the SNM struggle and contended that SNM fighters were conspirators working for Ethiopia.[98] For this anti-Somaliland narrative, he would have faced arrest if he ever went to Somaliland without retracting his statements. A third case came in May 2019 when a young Isaaq man wore the blue Somali national flag in the Hargeysa market. Photos of his arrest by the local police were disseminated on various anti-Somaliland websites.[99] Six months later, in November, Farmaajo invited the young Isaaq man to Villa Somalia (the presidential palace) in Mogadishu to give him an award for his bravery.[100]

The developments in Somaliland suggest that the unity of a people cannot be maintained solely on the basis of past political memory, however charged. Rather, the state has to serve a purpose in the present. In other words, the state must deliver social services and development. Young people in Hargeysa are to some extent proud of their city, but they also share with their counterparts in Mogadishu and elsewhere in southern Somalia the push to emigrate to Europe via the Mediterranean Sea to make a living.[101] The fact that Somaliland possesses no major industries that could lessen unemployment exacerbates the situation. Somaliland authorities seek to overcome their lack of natural resources by negotiating with Arab investors from the Gulf States to create local jobs. An acute condition of unemployment exists because since 1991, preoccupation with separation has isolated Somaliland's people from the rest of Somalia even in terms of resource-sharing, making the gap between the haves and

---

97 "Somaliland oo xukuntay Gabar Abwaanad aheyd," Midnimo, accessed 9 September 2018, http://midnimo.com/2018/04/15/somaliland-oo-xukuntay-gabar-abwaanad-aheyd/.
98 "Siyaad Barre geesi waddaniya ayuu ahaa, Allaah hawnaxariisto," (between min. 0:13–18:50), accessed 13 September 2018, https://www.youtube.com/watch?v=te55tOPLtoU; and "Taariikhdii M, Siyaad Barre qaybtii 2 AAD," (between min. 0:13–29:21), accessed 13 September 2018, https://www.youtube.com/watch?v=IS2ewjxdT54.
99 "Daawo Sawirro: Madaxweyne Farmaajo oo caawa la kulmay Wiilkii Hargeysa loogu xiray dareyska Somaliya," Halqaran.com, 20 November 2019; and "MUUQAAL: Wiilkii Hargeisa Calanka Loogu xidhay oo ka Warbixiyey Soo Dhowayntii Madaxwayne Farmaajo," *Kalshaale.ca*, 21 November 2019.
100 "Wiil ku labistay dhar laga sameeyey calanka Soomaaliya oo maanta la xidhay," *Hiiraan Online*, 14 May 2019.
101 Field interviews, Hargeysa, July-August 2016 and April-May 2018.

have-nots in Somaliland much wider than in southern Somalia.[102] Due to poor infrastructure, water and electricity are only available to affluent families who have access to state resources or private companies. Both Somaliland and southern Somalia rank as two of the poorest states in Africa.

Somaliland has also witnessed a worsening security condition, especially in the eastern part of the country. Recurring armed conflicts between the Isaaq and the non-Isaaq, but also within the Isaaq, became a daily feature of life. The extent of the insecurity reached worrisome levels when a colonel in the Somaliland army defected with his forces in 2018 and declared the establishment of an armed rebel front in eastern Somaliland. Colonel Said Awil Jama, better known as Colonel Aarre, a Habar Yoonis commander, fell out with Somaliland military leaders in Hargeysa whom he accused of clannism – the tendency to favour their clans at the expense of other clans.[103] Aarre himself was accused by the Somaliland military commanders of killing ten civilians and embezzling the salaries of the forces he had commanded. Aarre denied any wrongdoing and instead emphasised his role as one of the initial founders of the Somaliland army.[104] A viable peace-building process was agreed upon between the two sides of the Isaaq clan to avert armed political conflict among them, yet Aarre's forces reengaged in some parts of the eastern Somaliland between 2018 and 2019. A deterioration of security was not only negatively affected local conditions; it threatened to erode international goodwill and recognition of Somaliland that depended on having a largely peaceful process of state-building.[105]

Conclusion

Post-colonial Somalia was a society that endured prolonged armed conflict that ravaged the once unified state. Riven by a brutal civil war consisting of years of inter- and intra-clan conflicts, exacerbated by contestation of the commemoration of historical grievances, war-torn Somalis came up with various political memories to secure divergent political positions of power. As Besteman stated: "Anthropologists recognize that memories play tricks, that current experiences reshape recollections of past events, and that stories are told with an eye to their possible future significance."[106] Leaders in Somaliland provided a political

---

102 Ibid.
103 "Colonel Caarre oo iska difaacay eedo loo jeediyey," *Voasomali*, 28 August 2019.
104 Ibid.
105 Field interviews, Hargeysa, July-August 2016 and April-May 2018.
106 Besteman, *Making Refuge*, 30.

memory designed to cement unity among the Isaaq and sustain the existence of a separate state. It started its statehood as a "negotiated state" or a "mediated state" that developed into a state system combining modern and traditional modes of authority.[107] In front of the international community, historical grievances gave legitimacy to the Somaliland insistence on becoming a separate state from Somalia.[108] The Somaliland state came into being on the basis of a shared memory of political victimhood experienced by the Isaaq clan. This historical grievance will pose a challenge for any future rapprochement for the two nations. Negotiated solutions to the political conflicts among the clans, especially the separation project, failed to capture the confidence of non-Isaaq clans who had been erased from the common political memory over past events, especially of the Siad Barre regime, being disseminated by Isaaq elites. The fact that Somaliland remains unrecognised internationally after nearly three decades reinforces Somaliland authorities' frustration with the status quo. In official discourse and local news media in Hargeysa, Somalia is a foreign country with which the 'Republic of Somaliland' wishes to maintain international relations. Conversely, whilst exercising no real control or authority over Somaliland, the Somali Federal Government in Mogadishu attempts to maintain the juridical illusion that Somaliland remains, after all, part and parcel of Somalia. The future will determine how these two contradictory present and past positions will be settled.

Historians writing about the recent past encounter different challenges than those who write about the distant past. People tend to become easily agitated or excited over the recent past or contemporary history. For instance, as Jonah Rubin points out in a case of memory politics in contemporary Spain, "people enact memory politics not only by contesting narratives of the past, but also, first and foremost, by dis- and reassembling the physical, institutional, and social entanglements that undergird democratic politics."[109] In his personal history

---

[107] Tobias Hagmann and Didier Péclard, "Negotiating Statehood: Dynamics in Power and Domination in Africa," *Development and Change* 41, no. 4 (2010): 539–562; Marleen Renders and Ulf Terlinden, "Negotiating Statehood in a Hybrid Political Order: The Case of Somaliland," *Development and Change* 41, no. 4 (2010): 723–746; and Ken Menkhaus, "The Rise of the Mediated State in Northern Kenya: The Wajir Story and its Implications for State-building," *Africa Focus* 21, no. 2 (2008): 23–38.

[108] Brian J. Hesse, "Lessons in Successful Somali Governance," *Journal of Contemporary African Studies* 28, no. 1 (2010): 71–83; and Brian J. Hesse, "Where Somalia Works," *Journal of Contemporary African Studies* 28, no. 3 (2010): 343–362.

[109] Jonah S. Rubin, "How Francisco Franco Governs from Beyond the Grave: An Infrastructural Approach to Memory Politics in Contemporary Spain," *American Ethnologist* 45, no. 2 (2018): 214–227. For how this was the case in other contexts, see T. Fujitani, Geoffrey M. White and Lisa Yoneyama (eds.), *Perilous Memories: The Asia-Pacific War(s)* (Durham, Duke University

of the post-Biafra period, Chinua Achebe contended that victims of violent African conflicts "are often too ready to let bygones be bygones."[110]

However, this was not the case in Somaliland where memories of the horrors of the Siad Barre regime still remain present in the minds of most Isaaq people. A sustainable peace between Somaliland and southern Somalia will only succeed when Isaaq historical grievances are adequately addressed. As Geshekter pointed out, "[t]he memories of the real Siad Barre regime atrocities will not soon be forgotten in Somaliland. The revivalist/reconstructionist energies seem mainly in the south. The north says 'no more Mogadishu.' The world does not know what to do except try and put the fractured, shattered, broken state back together again."[111] Though some Isaaq people disagree with the formation of the Somaliland state (its separation from southern Somalia), very few want to negotiate with Mogadishu as to the rightfulness of the existence of the state in Somaliland representing a clan identity as Isaaq, but rather as members of a broader Somaliland community.

Writing about Somalia in the 1990s, Simon Horner inquired about whether the Somali "jigsaw" – in this case, the chronic conflict – could be pieced together.[112] This chapter has explored the intersection between political memory and state-building projects in post-conflict Somalia. The theme of political memory is an important one, yet it is largely ignored in studies of Somali state-building. The chapter has addressed post-conflict contexts to understand many forms of grievance-based political memory. The recollections of many Somalis camouflage the roots of clan conflicts and the cataclysms caused by the Siad Barre regime. Siad Barre's regime, not unlike the regime of Daniel arap Moi in Kenya, was remembered by many in Somaliland as "a depressing time of political oppression, mismanagement of resources, rising insecurity and increasing corruption." But in southern Somalia people vary between having positive and negative recollections of the era.[113] These divergent political memories have deeply divided inter- and intra-clans, thus illustrating how post-conflict historical grievances generate political divisions among the communities living in Somaliland and southern Somalia. Somaliland was created using a conscious construction of

---

Press, 2001); and Jay Winter, *Remembering War: The Great War between Historical Memory and History in the Twentieth Century* (New Haven: Yale University Press, 2006).
110 Chinua Achebe, *There Was A Country: A Personal History of Biafra* (London: Penguin Books, 2012), 49.
111 Charles Geshekter, email communication, 24 April 2013.
112 Simon. "Somalia," 46–53.
113 Jeong Kyung Park, "Blaming the Moi Era: Memories of Bad Governance among Eastlands Residents in Nairobi, Kenya," *Memory Studies* (2018): 691–707.

past historical grievance to drive the separate state-building project towards attracting international recognition. Past and present grievances illuminate political realities in Somaliland which were primarily built upon political memory that drew from the legacies of the military rule.

Bibliography

"21 Oct.Taariikhdii kacaanka iyo khudbadihi ugu muhiimsana Madaxweyne Siyaad. Keydka R/muqdisho.DHAGEYSO," *Radio Muqdisho*, 22 October 2015, accessed 9 September 2018, https://www.radiomuqdisho.net/21-oct-taariikhdii-kacaanka-iyo-khudbadihi-ugu-muhiimsana-madaxweyne-siyaad-keydka-rmuqdisho-dhageyso/.

Abdullahi, Mohamed Diriye. "In the Name of the Cold War: How the West Aided and Abetted the Barre Dictatorship of Somalia." In *Genocide, War Crimes & The West: History and Complicity*, edited by Adam Jones, 241–259. London: Zed Books, 2004.

Achebe, Chinua. *There Was A Country: A Personal History of Biafra*. London: Penguin Books, 2012.

Africa Watch. *Human Rights Abuses and Civil War in the North: A Report from the U.S. General Accounting Office*. New York, Africa Watch, 1989.

Africa Watch. *A Government at War with Its Own People: Testimonies About the Killings and the Conflict in the North*. New York, Africa Watch, 1990

Amadiume, Ifi, and Abdullahi An-Na'im, eds. *The Politics of Memory: Truth, Healing & Social Justice*. London: Zed Books, 2000.

Adan, Amina H. "Somalia: An Illusory Political Nation-State." *South Asia Bulletin* 14, no. 1 (1994): 99–109.

Amnesty International. *Somalia: A Long-Term Human Rights Crisis*. New York: Amnesty International, 1988.

Amnesty International. *Somalia: Imprisonment of Members of the Isaaq Clan Since Mid-1988*. New York: Amnesty International, 1988.

Anon. "It is impossible to Disdain People's Memory, Mr President." *KAAH, A Periodical Journal of the Ogaden National Liberation Front* 111 (July 1988): 15–17.

"Baladweyne: Qaxootigii Ogaadeenka oo Ciidam[a]da Maxamad Siyaad Barre ay Hubeeyeen!" *Keydmedia*, accessed 26 July 2014, http://www.youtube.com/watch?v=Dt1pqsZ2R-I.

Bakonyi, Jutta. "Moral Economies of Mass Violence: Somalia 1988–1991," *Civil War* 11, no. 4 (2009): 434–454.

Besteman, Catherine. *Making Refuge: Somali Bantu Refugees and Lewiston, Maine*. Durham: Duke University Press, 2016.

Bjork, Stephanie R. *Somalis Abroad: Clan and Everyday Life in Finland*. Chicago: University of Illinois Press, 2017.

Box 4, folder "Somalia – President Mohammed Siad Barre" of the National Security Adviser's Presidential Correspondence with Foreign Leaders Collection at the Gerald R. Ford Presidential Library.

Cable from US Embassy in Mogadishu to Washington. "Sub: Peace Breaking Out in the North?." Accessed 31 August 2014, https://wikileaks.org/cable/1990/03/90MOGADISHU2527.html.

Cassanelli, Lee. "Reconciliation and Reconstruction: Are there Lessons from Somalia's [R]ecent History?," paper presented at the 6th International Congress of Somali Studies, Berlin, December 6–9, 1996.
"Colonel Caarre oo iska difaacay eedeo loo jeediyey," *Voasomali*, 28 August 2019.
Compagnon, Daniel. "The Somali Opposition Fronts: Some Comments and Questions," *Horn of Africa* 13, no. 1–2 (January-June 1990): 29–54.
Compagnon, Daniel. "Dynamiques de Mobilisation, Dissidence Armée et Rébellion Populaire: Le Cas du Mouvement National Somali (1981–1990)," *Africa* 47, no. 4 (1992): 502–530.
Compagnon, Daniel. "Somaliland, un Ondre Politique en Gestation?," *Politique Africain* 50 (June 1993): 9–20.
Compagnon, Daniel. "Somali Armed Movements: The Interplay of Political Entrepreneurship and Clan-Based Factions." In *African Guerrillas*, edited by Christopher Clapham, 73–89. Oxford: James Currey, 1998.
Compagnon, Daniel. "State-sponsored Violence and Conflict under Mahamed Siyad Barre: the Emergence of Path Dependent Patterns of Violence," World Peace Foundation Occasional Papers, October 22, 2013, accessed 23 December 2013, http://sites.tufts.edu/reinventingpeace/2013/10/22/state-sponsored-violence-and-conflict-under-mahamed-siyad-barre-the-emergence-of-path-dependent-patterns-of-violence/.
Confidential Cable. "Two Views on Somaliland: Hostile Forces Target Economy, No Return to a Unified Somalia." U.S. Embassy in Djibouti to the State Department in Washington, 6 August 2017, accessed 20 December 2020, https://web.archive.org/web/20160328033823/http://cables.mrkva.eu/cable.php?id=118293.
"DAAWO SAWIRRO: Madaxweyne Farmaajo oo caawa la kulmay Wiilkii Hargeysa loogu xiray dareyska Somaliya," *Halqaran.com*, 20 November 2019.
"Daawo Xukuumada Somaliland Oo Ka Hadashay Dagaal Khasaaro Gaystay Oo ka Soo Cusboonaaday Ceel-af-wayn," *Lughaya*, accessed 9 September 2018, http://www.lughaya.com/home/2018/07/24/daawo-xukuumada-somaliland-oo-ka-hadashay-dagaal-khasaaro-gaystay-oo-ka-soo-cusboonaaday-ceel-af-wayn/.
David, Lee. "Holocaust and Genocide Memorialisation Policies in the Western Balks and Israel/Palestine." *Peacebuilding* 5, no. 1 (2017): 51–66.
Declich, Francesca. "When Silence Makes History, Gender and Memories of War Violence from Somalia." In *Anthropology of Violence and Conflict*, edited by Bettina Schmidt and Ingo Schröder, 161–175. London: Routledge, 2001.
Djama, Marcel. "Sur la Violence in Somalie: Genése et Dynamique des Formations Armées." *Politique Africaine* 47 (1992): 147–152.
Document. "Qaab-Dhismeedka Ciidanka Qaranka Somaliland, Hogaamada ciidanka iyo beelaha ay ka soo jeedaan." September 2016.
"Documentary – Taariikh Nololeedka Cabdilaahi Koongo Qaybtii 9aad." Accessed 26 August 2014, https://www.youtube.com/watch?v=36e9oM9Or7Q.
"Documentary – Taariikh Nololeedka Cabdilaahi Koongo Qaybtii 10aad." Accessed 26 August 2014, https://www.youtube.com/watch?v=EsANwflCoYM.
"Documentary – Taariikh Nololeedka Cabdilaahi Koongo Qaybtii 11aad." Accessed 26 August 2014, https://www.youtube.com/watch?v=-1s7DkF1T2E.
"Documentary – Taariikh Nololeedka Cabdilaahi Koongo Qaybtii 12aad." Accessed 26 August 2014, https://www.youtube.com/watch?v=pMNZSVWRF_c.

Dool, Abdullahi. "Good Governance: Self-Administering Regions within a Democratic Union." *Somalia* 4 (June 2001): 5–36.
Ellis, Stephen. "The Mutual Assimilation of Elites: The Development of Secret Societies in Twentieth Century Liberian Politics." In *The Powerful Presence of the Past: Integration and Conflict along the Upper Guinea Coast*, edited by Jacqueline Knörr and Wilson Trajano Filho, 185–204. Leiden: Brill, 2010.
Englebert, Pierre. *Africa: Unity, Sovereignty & Sorrow*. Boulder, Colo.: Lynne Rienner Publishers, 2009.
Fazal, Tanisha M. "Go your Own Way: Why Rising Separatism Might Lead to More Conflict." *Foreign Affairs* (July-August 2018): 113–123.
Fujitani, T., Geoffrey M. White and Lisa Yoneyama, eds *Perilous Memories: The Asia-Pacific War(s)*. Durham, Duke University Press, 2001.
"Gabadh re[er] Burco ah oo Jawab Kulul siisay Islantii Farmaajo werartay," *Daljire*, accessed 11 December 2017, https://www.youtube.com/watch?v=0ID7RAD553s.
"Gabadh re[er] Hargaysa oo Somaali Jacayl la ilmaysa," *Daljire*, Accessed 11 December 2017, https://www.youtube.com/watch?v=4-QUNrBeaOI&feature=youtu.be.
"Gabdho Reer Hargaysa ah oo Amaan Kala Dul dhacay Muqdisho Iyo Somali Weyn." *Cagaaran*, accessed 11 December 2017, https://www.youtube.com/watch?v=Her3UPmpJ-s.
"General Mohamed Ali Samatar, 1931–2016," *Journal of the Anglo-Somali Society* 60 (Autumn 2016): 62.
Gersony, Robert. *Why Somalis Flee: Synthesis of Accounts of Conflict Experience in Northern Somalia by Somali Refugees, Displaced Persons and Others*. Washington: State Department, 1989.
Gersony, Robert. "Why Somalis Flee: Conflict in Northern Somalia." *Cultural Survival Quarterly* 13, no. 4 (1989): 45–58.
Geshekter, Charles. Email communication, 24 April 2013.
Hagmann, Tobias, and Didier Péclard. "Negotiating Statehood: Dynamics in Power and Domination in Africa." *Development and Change* 41, no. 4 (2010): 539–562.
Hesse, Brian J. "Lessons in Successful Somali Governance." *Journal of Contemporary African Studies* 28, no. 1 (2010): 71–83.
Hesse, Brian J. "Where Somalia Works." *Journal of Contemporary African Studies* 28, no. 3 (2010): 343–362.
Horner, Simon. "Somalia: Can the Jigsaw be Pieced Together." *ACP-EU Courier* 162 (1997): 46–53.
Hills, Alice. "Somalia Works: Police Development as State building." *African Affairs* 113, no. 945 (2014): 88–107.
Ingiriis, Mohamed Haji. *The Suicidal State in Somalia: The Rise and Fall of the Siad Barre Regime, 1969–1991*. Lanham: University Press of America, 2016.
Ingiriis, Mohamed Haji. "How Somalia Works: Mimicry and the Making of Mohamed Siad Barre's Regime in Mogadishu." *Africa Today* 63, no. 1 (2016): 57–83.
Ingiriis, Mohamed Haji. "'We Swallowed the State as the State Swallowed us': The Genesis and Genealogies of Genocide in Somalia." *African Security* 9, no. 3 (2016): 237–258.
Ingiriis, Mohamed Haji. "Many Somalia(s), Multiple Memories: Remembrance as Present Politics, Past Politics as Remembrance." *African Identities* 14, no. 1 (2016): 348–369.

Ingiriis, Mohamed Haji. "Who Assassinated the Somali President in October 1969?: The Cold War, the Clan Connection or the Coup d'État." *African Security* 10, no. 1 (2017): 1–24.

Ingiriis, Mohamed Haji. "Between the Devil and the Deep Blue Sea: The Birth and the Breakdown of the Somali Armed Movements, 1976–1999." In *National Liberation Movements as Governments in Africa*, edited by Redie Bereketeab, 233–248. London: Routledge, 2017.

Ingiriis, Mohamed Haji. "State Violence and Clan Violence in Somalia." *African Conflict and Peacebuilding Review* 8, no. 1 (2018): 73–96.

Ingiriis, Mohamed Haji. "Clan Politics and the 2017 Presidential Election in Somaliland." *Journal of Somali Studies* 4, no. 1–2 (2018): 117–133.

Ingiriis, Mohamed Haji. "From Pre-Colonial Past to the Post-Colonial Present: The Contemporary Clan-Based Configurations of Statebuilding in Somalia." *African Studies Review* 61, no. 2 (2018): 55–77.

Kaiser, Susana. "Escraches: Demonstrations, Communication and Political Memory in Post-Dictatorial Argentina." *Media, Culture and Society* 24, no. 4 (2002): 499–516.

Keen, David. *Conflict & Collision in Sierra Leone*. Oxford: James Currey, 2005.

"Khudbad Muuse Biixi Cabdi," *Somaliland Television*, 8 March 2018.

MacArthur, Julie. *Cartography and the Political Imagination: Mapping Community in Colonial Kenya*. Athens, Ohio: Ohio University Press, 2016.

"Madaxwayne muuse biixi oo dumar ka ooy siiyay + xuska 8march," *Hadhwanaag News*, March 8, 2018.

Mayer, Arno J. *The Furies: Violence and Terror in the French and Russian Revolution*. Princeton: Princeton University Press, 2000.

Mayo, James M. "War Memorials as Political Memory." *Geographic Review* 78, no. 1 (1988): 62–75.

Mekonnen, Daniel. "Contested Versions of Collective Memory in Postindependence Eritrea." *African Conflict & Peacebuilding Review* 3, no. 2 (2013): 151–170.

Menkhaus, Ken. "The Rise of the Mediated State in Northern Kenya: The Wajir Story and its Implications for State-building." *Africa Focus* 21, no. 2 (2008): 23–38.

Menkhaus, Ken. "Review: *Clan Cleansing in Somalia: The Ruinous Legacy of 1991* by Lidwien Kapteijns. Philadelphia, PA: University of Pennsylvania Press, 2013." *The Journal of Modern African Studies* 52, no. 2 (2014): 679–681.

"Move by Hassan Sheikh Unites Somaliland Tribes Against Him." *The Indian Ocean Newsletter*, no. 1429, 17 June 2016.

"MUUQAAL: Wiilkii Hargeisa Calanka Loogu xidhay oo ka Warbixiyey Soo Dhowayntii Madaxwayne Farmaajo," *Kalshaale.ca*, 21 November 2019.

Nagengast, Carole. "Violence, Terror, and the Crisis of the State." *Annual Review of Anthropology* 23 (1994): 109–136.

Niemann, Michael. "War Making and State Making in Central Africa." *Africa Today* 53, no. 3 (2007): 21–39.

Park, Jeong Kyung. "Blaming the Moi Era: Memories of Bad Governance among Eastlands Residents in Nairobi, Kenya." *Memory Studies* (2018): 691–707.

Philips, Sarah G. "Proximities of Violence: Civil Order Beyond Governance Institutions." *International Studies Quarterly* 63, no. 3 (2019): 680–691.

"Pointers – Somalia: Siad Barre's Foes." *Africa Confidential* 22, no. 9 (April 22, 1981): 7.

"Prof. Ahmed Ismail [S]amatar (Somaliland waa muqadas) oo ka soo laabtey Hargaysa." Accessed 20 July 2016, https://www.youtube.com/watch?v=cSfjo8KPZCU.
Prunier, Gérard. "A Candid View of the Somali National Movement." *Horn of Africa* 13–14: no. 3–4 & no. 1–2 (1990): 107–120.
Renan, Ernest. "What is a Nation." In *Nation and Narration*, edited by Homi K. Bhabha, 8–22. London: Routledge, 1990.
Renders, Marleen. *Consider Somaliland: State-Building with Traditional Elders and Institutions*. Leiden: Brill, 2012.
Renders, Marleen, and Ulf Terlinden. "Negotiating statehood in a hybrid political order: The case of Somaliland," *Development and Change* 41, no. 4 (2010): 723–746.
Rettig, Max. "Gacaca: Truth, Justice, and Reconciliation in Postconflict Rwanda." *African Studies Review* 51, no. 3 (2008): 25–50.
Rubin, Jonah S. "How Francisco Franco Governs from Beyond the Grave: An Infrastructural Approach to Memory Politics in Contemporary Spain." *American Ethnologist* 45, no. 2 (2018): 214–227.
Samatar, Ahmed I. "I. M. Lewis, *A Modern History of the Somali: Nation and State in the Horn of Africa*. Athens: Ohio University Press, 2002." *H-Net Reviews*, December 2013, accessed 27 December 2016, https://www.h-net.org/reviews/showpdf.php?id=8552.
Samatar, Ibrahim Megag. "Light at the End of the Tunnel: Some Reflections on the Struggle of the Somali National Movement." In *Mending Rips in the Sky: Options for Somali Communities in the 21st Century*, edited by Hussein M. Adam and Richard Ford, 21–48. Lawrenceville, N.J.: The Red Sea Press, 1997.
Samatar, Said S. "How to Run an SNM Gauntlet." *Horn of Africa* 13, no. 1–2 (April & June 1990): 78–87.
"Sh. Xasan Daheeye oo ka sheekaynaya xasuuqii SNM ka samaysay Boorama." Accessed 13 September 2018, https://www.youtube.com/watch?v=_-iNyr2842o.
Simmons, Michael. "Thousands of Somalis Reported Dead in Genocide Attacks." *The Manchester Guardian Weekly*, 15 January 1989.
"Siyaad Barre geesi waddaniya ayuu ahaa, Allaah hawnaxariisto." Accessed 13 September 2018, https://www.youtube.com/watch?v=te55tOPLtoU.
"Somali Military Bid to Obliterate Clan as Barre Era Fades," *The Times*, July 2, 1987.
"Somali National Movement." Accessed 20 May 2014, http://www.youtube.com/watch?v=XWosiLB6YNg.
"Somali Troops in Massacres and Bombings," *The Guardian*, June 24, 1988.
"Somalia: Barre Hangs on." *Africa Confidential* 24, no. 5 (1983): 5–7.
"Somalia: Civilians Massacred." *The Indian Ocean Newsletter*, February 27, 1988, no. 321.
"Somalia: Confused Situation Persists." *The Indian Ocean Newsletter*, no. 405 (11 November 1989).
"Somalia: Generals on the Move." *Africa Confidential* 25, no. 10 (1984): 7–8.
"Somalia: The Forgotten Men," *New African*, (April 1988).
"Somalia: The Ogadeni's Misfortune." *Africa Confidential* 25, no. 21 (1984): 5–7.
"Somalia: Tango in the Ogaden." *Africa Confidential* 27, no. 11 (1986): 3–5.
"Somalia: Thousands Dead." *The Indian Ocean Newsletter*, no. 340 (9 July 1988).
"Somaliland oo xukuntay Gabar Abwaanad aheyd," *Midnimo*. Accessed 9 September 2018, http://midnimo.com/2018/04/15/somaliland-oo-xukuntay-gabar-abwaanad-aheyd/.

"Taariikhdii m, siyaad barre qaybtii 2 aad." Accessed 13 September 2018, https://www.youtube.com/watch?v=IS2ewjxdT54.

The Center for Justice and Accountability, "Mass Atrocities in Northern Somalia: Warfaa V. Ali (Col. Tukeh)." Accessed 13 September 2018, https://cja.org/what-we-do/litigation/warfaa-v-ali-col-tukeh/.

The Republic of Somaliland, "Submission on Statehood and Recognition of Republic of Somaliland." Hargeisa, June 1996.

"Thousands Flee as Somali Soldiers Massacre Civilians," *The Observer*, (3 July 1988).

Walls, Michael. "Liberation Struggle for Regime Change: Somaliland's Transition from Conflict to Civilian Government." In *National Liberation Movements as Governments in Africa*, edited by Redie Bereketeab, 218–232. London: Routledge, 2017.

Wertz, Megan. "Country Profile: Somaliland," *Journal of Conventional Weapons Destruction*, 10, no. 1 (2006): 38.

"Wiil ku labistay dhar laga sameeyey calanka Soomaaliya oo maanta la xidhay," *Hiiraan Online*, (14 May 2019).

Winter, Jay. *Remembering War: The Great War between Historical Memory and History in the Twentieth Century*. New Haven: Yale University Press, 2006.

"Xasuuqii ka dhacay arabsiyo xiligii kaidii taliska Siyaad Bare." *Arabsiyo News*, accessed 11 December 2017, https://www.youtube.com/watch?v=LB3K0UjoCK0.

III **Nostalgia – between Social Connection & Social Ordering**

Rouven Kunstmann and Cassandra Mark-Thiesen
The Memory Process in the Commemorations of the Dead in West African Newspapers

Abstract: This chapter considers the memory process in the commemorations of the dead in a sample of newspapers from Nigeria and Liberia from the 1940s to 1960s. At its centre are the obituaries and in-memoriams of middle- to upper-class citizens published by family members and the state. The chapter homes in on how a number of journalistic processes, from "signalling" to "masking" to "controlling," were used to capture specific elements of the past and, more significantly, to guide the present and future self-fashioning of the African elite.

As a fitting part of this *Gedenkschrift*, itself a technology of death culture, this chapter explores practices surrounding death as performed in West African newspapers of the 1940s to 1960s. We examine the printing of death notices and obituaries both as a historically dynamic process and as one of multiple interrelated modes of (both textual and non-textual) social communication and memory-making in Africa. With its emergence in the nineteenth century, the West African press has been at the forefront of forming and reinforcing identities, helping both individuals and institutions to present themselves to a wider audience. In recent times, studies of the practices of self-fashioning in print culture have attracted much attention in Africanist historiography and beyond.[1] This chapter explores the social and political signalling accompanying announcements of death in newspapers. Herein we compare two forms of publicising death, namely in-memoriams and obituaries. In line with Jan-Georg Deutsch's interest in the study of social relations in shaping history, we demonstrate the commemoration expressed in these West African advertisements of death as promoting the solidification of sociopolitical relationships.

For the purpose of this examination of print media, we draw evidence from Nigerian and Liberian newspapers. After the Second World War, both states en-

---

[1] Derek R. Peterson, Emma Hunter, and Stephanie Newell, eds., *African Print Cultures: Newspapers and Their Publics in the Twentieth Century* (Ann Arbor, MI: University of Michigan Press, 2016); Mamadou Diawara, Bernard C. Lategan, and Jörn Rüsen, eds., *Historical Memory in Africa: Dealing with the Past, Reaching for the Future in an Intercultural Context* (New York: Berghahn Books, 2010).

OpenAccess. © 2022 Rouven Kunstmann and Cassandra Mark-Thiesen, published by De Gruyter. This work is licensed under the Creative Commons Attribution 4.0 International License.
https://doi.org/10.1515/9783110655315-007

tered a phase of rapid transformation. Nationalism heightened and urbanisation swelled amidst growth in population and prosperity. Yet, significant differences persisted. In the Nigerian example, on a surface level, in-memoriams published by private citizens in privately-owned dailies are used as a means to broadcast bereavement to a closed circle of family and friends. However, if viewed with a more critical eye, it becomes evident that these death notices, which only reflected the shell of a life lived, had a larger radius of transmission, namely to members of social groups to which the deceased belonged. In the case of Liberia, we analyse obituaries printed by the state in one of its official vehicles, the *Liberia Official Gazette*. At first glance, this case study demonstrates how the state kept alive the memory of purportedly remarkable citizens. However, this veneer of a state-individual relationship simply cloaks acts of elite self-fashioning and communication to promote an idealised vision of the group's identity. Indeed, in journalism and more broadly, control (selection, exclusion, fragmentation) of memory served a critical function when it came to creating these continuity-building, identity-affirming, and future-oriented histories of deceased individuals.[2]

Elite actors in both the independent Liberian state and decolonising Nigerian society promoted at best fragmentary and highly curated pillars of identity in printed advertisements of death. Therefore, in this chapter we argue that these notices commemorating a member of the elite deployed symbolic markers to articulate relationships with state and society directed toward the future, and especially the maintenance of power structures in elite society. Photographs, such as the studio-images used for in-memoriams, added a layer of visual enhancement in such social communication.

These practices of commemoration highlight the agency of different publics, as well as the importance of African political ideologies beyond the state.[3] In spite of the urgency of national politics in the African press during this era, an announcement in commemoration of the dead took up newspaper space serving a purpose apart from disseminating colonial, anticolonial, or nationalist sentiments.[4] Therefore, published by the state (in Liberia) and by journalists and

---

[2] For a discussion on the community-building aspects of the different "modes" of the memory process, see, for example, Mamadou Diawara, Bernard C. Lategan, and Jörn Rüsen, "Introduction," in Diawara, Lategan, and Rüsen, *Historical Memory in Africa*, 3.

[3] Karin Barber, *The Anthropology of Texts, Persons, and Publics* (Cambridge: Cambridge University Press, 2008); Miles Larmer and Baz Lecocq, "Historicising Nationalism in Africa," *Nations and Nationalism* 24, no. 4 (October 2018): 893–917.

[4] Stephanie Newell, "From Corpse to Corpus: The Printing of Death in Colonial West Africa," in Peterson, Hunter, and Newell, *African Print Cultures*, 389–424.

private citizens (in Nigeria), printed advertisements of death allow us to draw further attention to the contested nature and multiple dimensions of nationalist identities as well as to shed light on the crystallisation of new (at times, gendered) professional ideals in the mid-twentieth century. The chapter underlines the value of placing a historical analysis of memory and media at the conjunction of state, society, and individual relationships.

Printing Industries and Journalism in Nigeria and Liberia between the 1940s and 1960s

Beginning in the 1940s, Liberia and Nigeria were two West African states experiencing fast-paced socio-political and economic transformation. Whereas the economic hardship that resulted from the Second World War had propelled political activism among those living in the Colony and Protectorate of Nigeria, leaders in the long independent state of Liberia entered a new phase of nation-building facilitated by rubber wealth. The press added further stimulus to processes of change in both states. As part of this change, remembering the dead in newspapers became part of the self-fashioning of individuals and typically elite social groups.

The Liberian press was founded with the establishment of the *Liberia Herald* in 1830. With an estimated circulation of 500 copies, it became Africa's fifth oldest newspaper.[5] Death notices contributed to the fabric of the *Herald* from the very start, together with announcements of births, marriages, and shipping news. Run by well-educated, religious Caribbean and North American emigrants during its first two decades of its existence, the Liberian press was largely dedicated to supporting the local colonial project by promoting it to black settler families from the African Diaspora. During this time, newspapers published by missionary groups praised religious education and distributed ethnographic reports from the surrounding rural areas. Indeed, a marker of the broader Liberian press was its orientation toward the African diaspora "evident in the inclu-

---

5 The *Liberian Herald* was preceded by Francophone periodicals published in Egypt during the Napoleonic occupation of 1797; the South African *Cape Town Gazette* (1800); *The Royal Gazette* and *Sierra Leone Advertiser* (1801); and *The Royal Gold Coast Gazette* (1822). Carl Patrick Burrowes, *Power and Press Freedom in Liberia, 1830–1970: The Impact of Globalization and Civil Society on Media-Government Relations* (Trenton, NJ: Africa World Press, 2004), 23, 54, 101.

sion of African exotica."⁶ Poems were also routinely printed on the pages of the local press.

Leading into the era of independence in 1847, the campaign in favour of black leadership for the state rose significantly on press agendas. Appeals for more secure avenues of commerce (given tough competition from European traders and foreign political powers) and greater economic, especially agricultural, productivity were weaved into the lines of various articles. According to the scholar of Liberia Carl Patrick Burrowes, during the Republican era between 1847 and 1907, debates concerning civic virtue and citizenship, for instance as they were conditioned upon ownership of property, dominated the Liberian press. These arguments arose in response to the growing number of manumitted slaves with little or no education sent to Liberia directly from their former plantations in the American South. Overall, journalistic opinions tended to align with the outlook of government on the issue of class divisions as they aimed to appeal to "skilled" individuals in the Diaspora in the United States and the Caribbean. The *Liberia Gazette* (later *Liberia Official Gazette*) was first published in 1892.

By the turn of the twentieth century, changes in international relations brought on by European imperialism pushed the discussion further in the way of nation-building. This new internal orientation was strengthened by the first generation of Liberian-born politicians who entered the national stage during this era, and who had close regional allegiances to preserve. Rural development rose on the agenda. Increasingly, a process of modernisation dependent on global integration also became the norm. In particular, after the 1940s, members of the press had to play along in the government's seduction of Western states and corporations for investments, or face harsh consequences, including long-term imprisonment. In spite of these tactics, the public and private Liberian press maintained a discourse about the significance of sovereignty, patriotism and ardour that had been produced with the country's independence. The Liberian government's own newspapers were also deployed for such purposes.⁷

The circulation of newspapers in the 1840s reflected Liberia's small, literate population. Around 2,388 settlers, of whom only 32 percent were literate, resided primarily in settlements along the coast, or on the St. Paul River. *The Weekly Spy* (1898–1902) became the country's first weekly,⁸ and, on 22 May 1950, journalists launched Liberia's first daily newspaper, *The Listener*.⁹ But while the press was blooming, as late as the 1980s national literacy rates remained largely stagnant.

---

6 Burrowes, *Power and Press Freedom in Liberia*, 23.
7 See, for instance: Ibid, 59.
8 Ibid, 65.
9 Ibid, 190.

In Nigeria, early newspapers were strictly missionary endeavours. On 23 November 1859 in Abeokuta, Reverend Henry Townsend from Exeter in England founded the *Iwe Irohin*, a newspaper published in Yoruba with the help of converts. It was published on a bi-weekly basis for eight consecutive years.[10] By the early twentieth century, members of Saro, who were freed slaves from Latin America who reached affluent status in Sierra Leone, and elite families in coastal cities such as Lagos or Port Hartcourt published weeklies.[11] In 1926, the *Daily Times of Nigeria* became the first daily newspaper and from the mid-1930s onwards daily newspapers spread across the country when Nnamdi Azikiwe established the *West African Pilot* and his newspaper group Zik's Press Limited. Other dailies followed and in 1949, the *Nigerian Tribune*, which is still in print today, was launched.[12] Journalists working for these newspapers often addressed the political struggle against the colonial administration by challenging newly introduced constitutions or competing political parties. Individual editions included editorials, feature articles, letters to the editors, and regular columns in which politics were of outmost importance. In addition, topics of daily concerns, from fashion advice to the topical debate about soldiers' resettlement schemes, made up part of the coverage.

The circulation of these newspapers grew significantly between the 1940s and the 1960s. The *Daily Times*' circulation alone increased from 25,000 in 1951 to 55,000 in 1955 and to 96,000 in 1959.[13] Initially, the *WAP* had a circulation of 6,000 in 1937 reaching 9,000 a year later. In 1950, the *WAP* printed 20,000 issues daily.[14] However, there were more readers than issues. Not only did literate

---

10 Fred I.A. Omu, "The 'Iwe Irohin', 1859–1867," *Journal of the Historical Society of Nigeria* 4, no. 1 (1967): 35–44; Oluwatoyin B. Oduntan, "Iwe Irohin and the Representation of the Universal in Nineteenth-Century Egbaland," *History in Africa* 32 (2005): 295–305.
11 David Pratten, "Creole Pioneers in the Nigerian Provincial Press," in Peterson, Hunter, and Newell, *African Print Cultures*, 75–101; Wale Adebanwi, "Colonial Modernity and Tradition: Herbert Macaulay, the Newspaper Press, and the (Re)Production of Engaged Publics in Colonial Lagos," in Peterson, Hunter, and Newell, *African Print Cultures*, 125–150; Omu, "The 'Iwe Irohin', 1859–1867"; Karin Barber, *Print Culture and the First Yoruba Novel: I.B. Thomas's 'Life Story of Me, Segilola' and Other Texts* (Leiden: Brill, 2012).
12 We would like to thank the staff at the *Nigerian Tribune* for their assistance and permission to reproduce the images in this chapter.
13 Rosalynde Ainslie, *The Press in Africa: Communications Past and Present* (London: Gollancz, 1966), 57.
14 Nnamdi Azikiwe, *My Odyssey: An Autobiography* (London: Hurst, 1970), 300–303.

members in cities and villages alike consume newspapers, but they were also known to read them out loud to others.[15]

With the devolution of power, the rise of political parties, and the substantial increase of education in Nigeria, new intellectual and vocationally trained experts, e.g. teachers, lawyers, engineers, and doctors, joined and challenged the established Saro families and those groups who traditionally held prestigious positions in association with the colonial state, such as government clerks.[16] In Liberia, unprecedented economic growth leading into the 1950s and 1960s resulted in more widespread education and professionalisation for many as well. However, the press by and large remained in the hands of educated elite urbanites of black American and Caribbean heritage (disparate communities often lumped together as "Americo-Liberians" in the historiography). And they continued to struggle to gain substantial freedom from government control.[17]

Printing Death in (West) Africa: A Brief overview of the Literature

In this chapter we purposefully distinguish between the obituary and the in-memoriam. Although most of the same information can be contained in both, Lawuyi has contended that burial arrangements are only ever listed in the obituary.[18] Moreover, as can be seen in Figure 5, obituaries were published shortly before the funeral, while in-memoriams were published years after death.[19] Based on the source material under investigation, we note that the obituaries published by the Liberian state were much more extensive than Nigerian in-memoriams as they included biographical information about the deceased at particular stages of life, such as place of birth, education, and career path. As becomes evident in the following sections, these discrepancies carry important implications for conducting historical analysis with such sources. The privately commissioned

---

15 Leonhard Harding, *Geschichte Afrikas im 19. und 20. Jahrhundert* (München: Oldenbourg Verlag, 2013), 74.
16 James S. Coleman, *Nigeria: Background to Nationalism* (Berkeley: University of California Press, 1960), 289.
17 Burrowes, *Power and Press Freedom in Liberia*, 267.
18 Olatunde Bayo Lawuyi, "The Story about Life: Biography in the Yoruba Obituaries," *Diogenes* 37, no. 148 (1989): 93.
19 This was also the case for Rachel Tinu Adebimpe's in-memoriam, which commemorated her death on 6 October 1948, six years later. *Daily Times*, 6 October 1954 (Fig. 5.).

in-memoriams and obituaries published in Nigerian newspapers were shorter. They were also more eye-catching as many included old photographs of the deceased appearing alive and in good health. What connects these forms of printing death are the community-reinforcing processes deriving from their publication. This included the self-fashioning of elite groups by disseminating messages about their past, present, and future.

The important relationship between past, present, and future in public death rituals in Africa, as well as their intermedial and changing nature, has been discussed by a number of Africanist historians. In Thomas C. McCaskie's study of the burial of Asante kings during the nineteenth century, he contended that "the future of society itself depended upon the rigorous enactment of appropriate mortuary rituals," since the death of the *Asantehene* was interlinked with matters of social reproduction and general prosperity.[20] The death and mortuary rituals of an *Asantehene* were about cultural referencing, affirmation, and renewal.[21] A key part of this memory process for participants concerned "reviewing and debating the history of power" and "the shape of [their] future."[22] This defence or critical reflection on the status quo was also visible at broader levels of society. Describing the transforming death rituals of "ordinary" Akan people during the twentieth century, Kwame Arhin portrays the melding of chronologies as follows: "Funeral rites are meant to consolidate a status already enjoyed, or to lay claim to a higher one believed to be attained through higher education, successful business activities or involvement in politics, the three means of social mobility in Ghana."[23] In their participation in the rite, the community "reaffirms its norms and values."[24] Speaking to the idea of ritualistic practices surrounding death as creating space for not only socio-political affirmation, but also contention, John Parker exhibits the Ga (Accra) harvest festival of *Homowo*, which celebrates ancestors who died during a famine, as permitting increasingly potent forms of political contestation by social groups marginal to society by the late nineteenth and early twentieth centuries.[25] Furthermore, in his 2021-monograph, Parker specifically addresses the writing of death as he describes how between

---

20 Thomas C. McCaskie, "Death and the Asantehene: A Historical Meditation," *The Journal of African History* 30, no. 3 (1989): 428.
21 Ibid, 430.
22 Ibid.
23 Kwame Arhin, "The Economic Implications of Transformations in Akan Funeral Rites," *Africa* 64, no. 3 (1994): 317.
24 Ibid.
25 John Parker, "The Cultural Politics of Death and Burial in Early Colonial Accra," in *Africa's Urban Past*, eds. David Anderson and Richard Rathbone (Oxford: James Currey, 2000), 216.

1874 and 1901 Gold Coast newspapers inscribed practices of writing about death within the public sphere as part of a burgeoning cultural nationalism.[26] Obituaries, Parker finds, became a 'formalized genre which sought to publicly record and celebrate the achievements of individuals' in the backdrop of grief and loss.[27]

The memorialisation of the death of individuals in Africa evolved over time next to shifts in urbanisation, understandings of property rights, cross-border migration, new technologies, and appearances of different cadres of national rulers. McCaskie places the emergence of advertisements of death as well as their incorporation into a deep-rooted funeral rite in a sphere of ritualistic and aspirational modernity. According to him, "[t]hey evidenced participation in or aspiration to modernity, but they also built upon a legacy of customary oral practice."[28] One of these tools of mediation was the photograph, appearing in obituaries in Nigerian newspapers since the 1940s, much earlier than in neighbouring Ghana for which Tom McCaskie explains that "[f]ull-page obituaries emerged in the 1960s, and photographs of the deceased became common during the 1970s."[29]

Nozomi Sawada focuses on the period from the 1880s to the 1920s to analyse single instances of portraits of important dignitaries, such as E.W. Blyden, that were placed in public places such as Glover Memorial Hall in Lagos.[30] Newspaper photography in post-war Nigerian newspapers developed a different dynamic since they went out to a diverse readership. Continuing from Sawada's work, the examples of the obituaries in the Nigerian newspapers and the *Liberia Official Gazette* demonstrate how journalism constantly evoked the past to inform the present and the future. This relationship between "what was" and "what could be" was one facet in the dynamic memory process in these advertisements commemorating the dead.

In-memoriams and obituaries also disseminated political ideologies. As Stephanie Newell informs us, these types of announcements have a compelling

---

26 John Parker, *In My Time of Dying: A History of Death and the Dead in West Africa* (Princeton: Princeton University Press, 2021), 228–244.
27 Ibid, 241.
28 Thomas C. McCaskie, "Writing, Reading, and Printing Death: Obituaries and Commemoration in Asante," in *Africa's Hidden Histories: Everyday Literacy and Making the Self*, ed. Karin Barber (Bloomington: Indiana University Press, 2006), 349.
29 Ibid, 358.
30 Nozomi Sawada, "Selecting Those 'Worthy' of Remembering: Memorialization in Early Lagos Newspapers," *Journal of West African History* 2, no. 2 (2016): 79–108.

function of mediation that a focus on death further brings to the fore.[31] A dead person's eternalised representation in print provides access points to the spaces of mediation and highlights how bodies are represented by devices such as "genre, narrative perspective, language, and style."[32] The serial nature of the format and its eventual mass production extended existing practices of remembrance. Moreover, in her work, cultural theorist Aleida Assmann describes a similar process specifically for political and cultural forms of memory, which are designed as transgenerational.[33] This relation of spatiality and temporality constitutes a collective memory. From a journalistic perspective, we can also conceive of advertisements of death in newspapers as fragments of history changing through time and in specific locations.

Death notices and obituaries disseminated social identities to a wide audience. As Rebekah Lee and Megan Vaughan have pointed out, mourning helped the grieving to carry on. Proper mourning relegated the dead to the realm of ancestors, as opposed to turning them into "vengeful ghosts."[34] Amongst other steps, the action of "registering", that is inscribing the personal experience of death into the public sphere via broadcasting it in newspapers, addressed the social group to which the deceased belonged.[35] Printing in-memoriams and obituaries can thus be categorised as one step in a multipronged operation described as the registration of death. Hence, the selected newspapers offered spaces for commemoration, signalling, and the fortifying of communities who sought to associate with the (colonial) state in terms of status, but not necessarily for the purpose of upholding official nationalism.

In-memoriams and Obituaries in Nigerian Newspapers

Nigerian newspapers printed obituaries in different sections but most prominently in a designated space with the title "In Memoriam."[36] In-memoriams appeared

---

31 Newell, "From Corpse to Corpus," 390.
32 Ibid.
33 Aleida Assmann, "Memory, Individual, and Collective," in *The Oxford Handbook of Contextual Political Analysis*, eds. Robert Goodin and Charles Tilly (Oxford: Oxford University Press, 2006), 216.
34 Rebekah Lee and Megan Vaughan, "Death and Dying in the History of Africa since 1800," *The Journal of African History* 49, no. 3 (2008): 342.
35 Lee and Vaughan, "Death and Dying," 342.
36 E.g. *WAP, Daily Times, Nigerian Tribune*.

side by side on a single page. From the late 1940s onwards, obituaries and in-memoriams often included a photograph of the deceased. These portrait photographs, typically taken several years prior to death, showed the deceased in a healthy state of appearance.[37] Captions and text beneath them completed the obituary. The text below the photograph described the circumstances of the death and illuminated specific stages in the life the person had led. The written text expressed the grief of relatives, friends, and colleagues but also praised the achievements of the deceased. In certain cases, obituaries were entirely self-referential: depicting a living relative instead of the deceased, describing the depicted person's achievements while only briefly mentioning the dead person. Prominent identity markers, such as profession, religion, or public offices held, joined the expressions of regret about the circumstances of death and wishes for the afterlife. These personal messages composed by mourning relatives and friends provide a point of contrast to the more levelled state-centred advertisements of death published in the *Liberia Official Gazette*.

As mentioned above, printing in-memoriams was part of a process of registering death within a given social community. Indeed, it was in its indication of the social relationships of the community that the in-memoriams entered the public sphere.[38] Since they were typically designed by and for an elite public, in-memoriams and other advertisements of death included symbols that represented a "ruling class hegemony in a Gramscian sense."[39]

By marking relevant individual achievements, the author attempted to assign meaning to the lived experiences of the deceased, while also signifying values for the present and future in front of the deceased's social group. Put differently, the registration of death in the public sphere mutually informed and reassured the writer as well as intended readers that social and cultural conventions would be maintained. This affirmation of identities involved a variety of practices, such as hiding, masking, displaying, revealing, explaining, and informing, as outlined with the help of examples in the following section.[40]

---

[37] Also see: Stephen F. Sprague, "Yoruba Photography: How the Yoruba See Themselves," *African Arts* 12, no. 1 (1978): 52–59, 107; Charles Gore, "African Photography," *African Arts* 48, no. 3 (2015): 1–5; Charles Gore, "Commemoration, Memory, and Ownership: Some Social Contexts of Contemporary Photography in Benin City, Nigeria," *Visual Anthropology* 14, no. 3 (2001): 321–342.
[38] Olatunde Bayo Lawuyi, "The Social Marketing of Elites: The Advertised Self in Obituaries and Congratulations in Some Nigerian Dailies," *Africa* 61, no. 2 (April 1991): 247–263.
[39] Karin Barber, "Popular Arts in Africa," *African Studies Review* 30, no. 3 (1987): 1–78; Lawuyi, "The Social Marketing of Elites," 247.
[40] Lawuyi, *Story about Life*, 109.

Most of these practices were affirmations of identities that manifested via the fusion of two different forms of media, namely photographs and text, which journalists merged to design the layout of the in-memoriams and obituaries more generally. Photographs published in Nigerian newspapers in the 1940s and early 1950s were often full-length portrait photographs of the deceased. These portrait photographs became a central element in commemorative discourse in newspapers. As will be shown in the examples that follow, as part of this undertaking of shaping and reinforcing of social identities, distinct values and achievements, such as piety and career paths, qualified as contributing to identity formation and aspirational outlooks.

On 7 November 1949, the *West African Pilot (WAP)* reported on the memorial service marking the anniversary of the death of a wealthy Lagosian businessman: J.H. Doherty. Instead of an image of J.H. Doherty, however, the *WAP* printed a portrait photograph of his son, as demonstrated in Fig. 1. The image of R. Ade Doherty, who was a member of the young educated elite, being a lawyer sitting on the Crown Counsel in the Western Provinces, overshadows his father's representation in the newspapers. The transgenerational memory process reflected in this in-memoriam builds on the business success of the father – entrepreneurship being a well-respected career path in the interwar and postwar periods – as well as the son's career in law. While both professions were prestigious, the career in law and his position as Senior Crown Counsel in the Western Provinces unequivocally identified the son as part of the colonial state apparatus. A professional identification with the colonial state, which served as a catalyst for careers in business and public administration, is a repeated subject in obituaries, and stands in contrast to other parts of the newspaper, such as the editorial and feature articles, where journalists directly challenged colonial officials with regularity.

Obituaries did not exclusively reveal or obscure. Rather, they projected a complex relationship between masking and concealing. While the printing of the son's photograph and the caption credits the son's own achievements, the *WAP* simultaneously celebrated Doherty senior, the one-time clerk who had emerged as founder of a large trading enterprise. The high social status of the Doherty family was disseminated to readers by illuminating the combination of entrepreneurial success and legal experience held within this single family unit. The location of the memorial service at the cemetery on Ikoyi Island, one of the most affluent areas of Lagos, further expressed the Dohertys' social ranking.

A successful career, especially in business, carried much weight within the Lagos community. For example, on 3 March 1953, the *Nigerian Tribune* printed the image with caption of Tjiani Badaru on a page reserved for announcements,

Fig. 1: *West African Pilot*, 7 November 1949.

such as celebrations and festivals, where in-memoriams were also published. Apparently, he was a "salesman of the G.B. Ollivant", one of Nigeria's largest trading companies and a subsidiary of the United Africa Company of Nigeria. His photograph appeared next to an article describing how Badaru arranged a "funeral party" to honour his mother's death.[41] While any references to the particular Muslim burial ritual practices of his immediate family were absent – his religious adherence amongst other things being made visible through his style of dress, as seen in Fig. 2 – the announcement broadcasted issues of broader relevance to Baradu's social class, including the extent of his wealth and his adherence to social norms, as seen in the fact that he entertained a large number of guests to honour his deceased mother.[42] Informing others about the profession of deceased family members and showing evidence of their purported wealth were common practices in Nigerian obituaries across different newspapers.

In-memoriams were descriptive but also carried strong sentiments of grief. While most deaths were of natural causes associated with old age, precise details of how death arrived could be concealed. This act of veiling the sad or troubling particulars created suspense for the reader, but also emphasised a feeling of respect and of great loss. Combined with a soft voice of outrage, grief was evermore fervently expressed when the successful and diligent had unexpectedly passed away, that is without having adequately benefited from life's drudgery, or so it was contended. The *WAP* marked the death of Michael Obiora Emodi

---

41 *Nigerian Tribune*, 3 March 1953.
42 Ibid.

Fig. 2: *Nigerian Tribune*, 3 March 1953.

on 10 September 1965 (Fig. 3) with the following words: "Your Labour ended, but you never enjoy the fruit of your Labour. The wicked have done their worst [sic.] Never in [sic.] thousand years will there be another you."[43] Presumably Emodi had encountered death before his retirement. As shown in Fig. 4, another obituary printed just months later used virtually identical phrasing to describe the premature demise of another individual.[44]

Whereas a peaceful afterlife was conditioned upon a successful life, an unexpected death often caused particularly strong expressions of grief. Expressing both diligence and prosperity as motives and achievements of deceased formed an essential part of the commemoration in obituaries and in-memoriams. There were conditions to the display of prosperity and wealth. In the previous examples, family members showed their own wealth when commemorating their late relatives. The commemoration became a platform of display for continued success. In the case that follows, namely that of a person who died before their time (so to speak), those left behind did not seem to be required to display the person's wealth.

While the information given in the previous examples is introspective, not actually appealing to the readership, other writers used obituaries to directly express misdeeds that had occurred within the community. Take for instance the obituary of Ibironke Akanke Akibola published in the *WAP* on 5 September 1965, which stated the following: "We pray that God may protect us from FRIENDS because it is easy to defend ourselves from our enemies. We could spend eternity mourning thee and yet not do justice to our sense of loss [...]. Only those who have suffered the like would realise the silent pains and

---

43 *WAP*, 10 September 1965.
44 *WAP*, 1 October 1965.

Fig. 3: *WAP*, 10 September 1965.   Fig. 4: *WAP*, 1 October 1965.

agony of parting without good-bye."[45] Outsiders to Akibola's community were left to fill in the gaps surrounding the cause of her death which was well-known to those with insider status within her community. The reference to her "friends" implicated close acquaintances in Akibola's death.

The previous examples consist of obituaries published in English. However, further masking and signalling could occur with the deployment of indigenous

---

45 *WAP*, 5 September 1965.

[Reads]

In Memoriam

In evergreen and loving memory of our dearly beloved mother.

MADAM RACHEL
TINU ADEBIMPE

who slept in Christ Jesus on October 6, 1948. Six years have rolled since we missed your motherly care. Rest in peace.

[Names of members of the Adebimpe family]

Fig. 5: *Daily Times*, 6 October 1954.

language. In contrast to in-memoriams, Yoruba was scarcely used in the obituaries printed in English-language newspapers. However, specific phrases received frequent mention. One of these was "*Orun re o*" – a variation of "rest in peace."[46] Captions in Yoruba were common for registering the dead by informing readers, in particular insiders to the community, about the deceased. Signalling to Yoruba middle-class audiences was achieved by publishing half of the obituary's text in vernacular. Figurative and literal references to character traits passed on in the family demonstrated the deceased's value to the community. For example, the in-memoriam of Mrs. Asimowu O. Anigbalawo (Fig. 6), published in the *Nigerian Tribune* on 16 January 1953, pointed to her industriousness, leadership, and carefulness. The translated caption reads:

> To the memory of my beloved mother Asimowu Oladebo Anigbalawo, the child of the one that arrives and everywhere is filled up, the child of the one that fills carriage up with loads, the child of a pacesetter may your heaven be well with you. The child of the neat

---

[46] "Orun re o" translates to "Do have good heaven or May you have a good heaven." Another expression was "Omo Alaiye Ode Lafose Orun re o," which is one of the few ancestral references and means: "The Child of King of Ode Remo land, the Lafose, do have good heaven." See: *Daily Times*, 2 September 1965 and 26 August 1965.

one that walks in the market with gales. It is the dirty ones that walk carelessly in the market. Sleep on well.⁴⁷

A deeper identification with the Yoruba community was created in the incorporation of family praise songs that highlighted the amalgamation of past and newer aspirational rituals of death. These praise songs were figurative and referred to character traits passed down through a lineage. One announcement, for instance, informed readers that the whole family excelled at debate.⁴⁸ As in the example of Asimowu O. Anigbalawo, appeals to a wider community and to a tradition of positive qualities dominated Yoruba language in-memoriams. In spite of the few aforementioned phrases in Yoruba, obituaries published entirely in Yoruba are missing from the English language newspapers and they tended not to include any references to ancestral spirits.

Fig. 6: *Nigerian Tribune*, 16 January 1953.

In spite of the temporal difference between obituaries, published shortly after the death, and in-memoriams, published one to several years later, they both represent a genre which brings together trajectories of the state, society, and individual. Obituaries and in-memoriams therefore helped to create spaces beyond the paradigmatic reading of the colonial public sphere as a purely na-

---

47 Thanks to Joseph Ayodokun who assisted with the translations.
48 *Daily Times*, 5 January 1952, 11.

tionalist or anticolonial space.⁴⁹ Within this space, status gained from careers built on the security and welfare offered to servants of the colonial state fashioned the commemorated individual while associating them with characteristics proffered by his or her community members, such as employability, industriousness, dependability, and ambition leading to prosperity. The process of registering the dead not only shaped and reaffirmed the identity of the deceased, but it also signalled and informed their social group about their relation to society and to the state.

Reading and Printing of Death: The Case of the *Liberia Official Gazette*

For the case of the United States Janice Hume contends that obituaries reinforced myths about the nation in addition to their function for collective memory.⁵⁰ However, when we observe Liberia where no more than a third of the population had immediate access to these announcements, because they could read them, such a grand claim would be mere exaggeration. As this section shows, state officials in Liberia habitually used dead patriots as a means of elite identity-making. The Liberian government entered into journalism in September 1892 with the first publication of the *Liberia Gazette*.⁵¹ Officials used this central organ of the state legislature to publicise the obituaries of prominent public figures with particular professional traits, e. g. those who contributed to politics, education (particularly in the case of women), and the advancement of state-sanctioned religion, reflecting the values of the small population of an educated elite. Obituaries printed in the *Gazette* of the 1950s and 1960s affirm this group's self-fashioning of displaying the proximity to the power of the state.

Known as the *Liberia Official Gazette*, the paper was initially released as a bi-monthly periodical. "The *Gazette* carried no news stories or commentaries and consisted entirely of reports on government revenue, high-level government appointments, [...] passports issued, patents granted, and maritime traffic."⁵² Information for the *Gazette* regularly streamed in from a number of governmental de-

---

49 For a discussion of "beyond spaces" and "paracolonial networks," see Stephanie Newell, "'Paracolonial' Networks: Some Speculations on Local Readerships in Colonial West Africa," *Interventions* 3, no. 3 (2001): 336–354.
50 Janice Hume, *Obituaries in American Culture* (Jackson: University Press of Mississippi, 2000), 9.
51 Burrowes, *Power and Press Freedom in Liberia*, 143.
52 Ibid, 65.

partments.⁵³ In contrast, state-orchestrated obituaries in the *Liberia Official Gazette* were advertisements that were promptly printed, immediately following the death of a purportedly remarkable public figure. Obituaries in the *Gazette* comprised single- or or multipe-page special issues (i.e. *The Liberia Official Gazette: EXTRAORDINARY*). They were printed on demand to minimise the gap between a person's death and the spread of news about the event. These obituaries consisted solely of text; images of the deceased did not feature. However, lengthy, formulaic biography compensated for the absence of visual stimuli. While family members likely related to some of the finer biographical details, these announcements of death were products of the upper class who dominated the administration. The actual authorship behind these obituaries is not entirely clear. A low-level office in the State Department prepared them, however, the signature of the secretary of state (Momolu Dukuly from 1954 until 1960 and Joseph Rudolph Grimes thereafter) gave them official importance.

Special issues of the *Gazette* announced the death of prominent Liberian patriots. Information about the lives of these individuals was compiled in a standardised format and sent to the president's desk after passing the State Department. The next step was circulation.⁵⁴ However, the *Gazette* contained no commercial advertisements and was not expected to turn a profit. Copies were not sold, but rather distributed to the media and political officials, such as the superintendents in the counties surrounding the capital. In 1949, for instance, a superintendent reportedly would be given 50 copies, which he handed out to his subordinates and friends.⁵⁵ An initial audience consisted of government employees and their networks in the urban capital, the coastal areas and selected districts in the interior. There was only limited effort to attract a broad and diverse readership. Spot news reporting events as they occurred and visual images were entirely absent from these periodicals, which had more in common with a colonial Blue Book than a popular journalistic format. In terms of function, the *Gazette* itself intended only to collect and display state affairs to those in immediate proximity of the power of the state. However, in a

---

53 For instance, in 1916 the clerk of the Supreme Court was reported to have sent a docket containing a summary of the proceedings to be reprinted in it. L.M. Ferguson to N.K. Gibson, Assistant Secretary of State, 10 April 1916.
54 See, for example, Journal of the 118th Day's Sitting of the Honourable the Liberian Senate, First Session of the Legislature, Wednesday, 24 July 1968. Legislative/ Senate Journal/ 22 July-7 August 1968.
55 Fifty copies were sent to the Superintendent in Grand Cape Mount in 1949. See, for example, Christie W. Doe, Chief Departmental Clerk, to Superintendent of Grand Cape Mount County, 29 July 1949, Executive/ Executive Mansion/ Grand Cape Mount 1945–1951.

second step, some of the information contained in these periodicals would be reprinted in commercial newspapers accessed by a broader audience. Furthermore, while it is difficult to estimate precisely when this tradition started, the reading out aloud of obituaries at funerals continues in urban areas today.[56]

In contrast to the Nigerian case that was characterised by journalists who reported on death working for privately-owned newspapers, in Liberia, the state recorded the loss. These obituaries were formulaic in terms of content. Each dispatch followed the same progression, typically beginning with the government's "deep regrets" about a sad or tragic event, including the date, time and place of the death. This rehearsal was followed by details about the individual's birthplace, and further social and political genealogy of the deceased. Next came information about their education, memberships in various fraternities and churches, and honours received from the state, such as the Medal of Distinguished Order of Services, Knight officials of the Order of the Star of Africa, amongst others, followed by the names of surviving family members. Details describing the funeral rites, burial location, and procedures of governmental commemoration completed the passage. An understanding of the relationship between the state and these communities as unshakeable thereby entered the public arena.

Collective memories location between history and myth has been addressed by scholars such as Avishai Margalit and Jeffrey Blustein, whose work bears important insights for the study of obituaries.[57] Margalit portrays what he calls "shared memories" as overlapping between "scientific" and "common sense" worldviews. He states that, "Myth, as an embodiment of the enchanted worldview, is populated with wondrous animals, supernatural interventions in nature and history, heroes and gods, and heroes on the way to becoming gods: all charmed and charming in the literal sense of the word."[58] In giving thanks to and simultaneously broadcasting the feats of the dead patriots to the literate Liberian population, officials and elites could further a selective and almost fantastical portrait of their community; one that celebrated concrete narratives of citizenship and civic values. In other words, as with the Nigerian death announcements, the "registering" of death involved appealing to a social strata af-

---

[56] Carl Patrick Burrowes, *Between the Kola Forest and the Salty Sea: A History of the Liberian People before 1800* (Monrovia: Know Yourself Press, 2016), 1.
[57] Avishai Margalit, *Ethics of Memory* (Cambridge: Harvard University Press, 2009), 63–65; Jeffrey Blustein, *The Moral Demands of Memory* (Cambridge: Cambridge University Press, 2008), 188–198.
[58] Margalit, *Ethics of Memory*, 63.

filiated with the deceased.[59] As also shown in the Nigerian examples, these death notices included symbols that represented a ruling ideology.[60] Unequal relationships of wealth and power and the values of elite groups were on full display during this ritual of death. Advertisements of death spoke to the signifiers of social influence, revealing important insights into a process of elite identity formation. In addition, the state affirmed this identity through a variety of practices, such as hiding, masking, displaying, revealing, and concealing.[61]

Journalists exhibited deceased elites' value to and identification with the state in a select number of ways, as will be demonstrated in the following examples. Atop the list were public service, religion, education and rural-urban integration. Still, distinctions were drawn between "important" and "very important" patriots when it came to the state's tributes of respect. The flag of the Republic was flown at half-mast on all public buildings for the duration of one day after a prominent public figure had died. On rare occasions and to signal even greater importance, the flag remained lowered for up to 15 days. Another unmistakable distinction is seen in the different lengths of published obituaries, typically ranging from one to two pages.

Julius Cecil Jones' 1963 obituary referenced his relationship with multiple Liberian presidents. It stated that President Edwin Barclay appointed him Collector of Internal Revenues for Grand Cape Mount county and noted that, "President Tubman was pleased to commission him as Superintendent of Grand Cape Mount County in 1944."[62] Other commemorated professionals included judges and military men, educators, and religious leaders. The wives of government officials were often publicly remembered, signalling both a familial ideal as well as the inherently public nature of their status. The obituary of Mrs. Malvenia Nazarene Harmon-Brewer, for example, described her as the widow of former senator George T. Brewer as well as "a loyal member of the National True Whig Party."[63] Speaking to a notion of aspiration, Burrowes has put forward that in Liberia, "Although valor and patriotism were associated with manhood, those virtues were particularly celebrated when displayed by women."[64] Still, during

---

59 Lee and Vaughan, "Death and Dying," 342.
60 Barber, "Popular Arts in Africa," 9.
61 Lawuyi, *Story about Life*, 109.
62 "Obituary of Julius Cecil Jones," *The Liberia Official Gazette: EXTRAORDINARY*, vol. XLVIII, no. 7, 18 July 1963.
63 The National True Whig Party was the dominant political organisation in the country at the time "Obituary of Malvenia Nazarene Harmon-Brewer," *The Liberia Official Gazette: EXTRAORDINARY*, XLVII, no. 8, 22 August 1960.
64 Burrowes, *Power and Press Freedom in Liberia*, 138.

the period under investigation, in contrast to the Nigerian case where women were frequently represented in the privately commissioned obituaries, by far most state-sponsored obituaries featured stories of successful men. These were typically members of the educated urban elite, in particular those with roots in the United States, the Caribbean, or in the original settlements.

Another key difference to the Nigerian examples was the celebration of business acumen. When compared with political and public service, this characteristic was decidedly devalued in the Liberian advertisements of death. Career-paths associated with the independent state, especially legal careers, received most prominent mention. After having received a bachelor's degree, Edwin Alford Morgan went on to study law and began a career as County Attorney for the County of Grand Bassa.[65] Eugene Himie Shannon also studied law "under the late Chief Justice Louis A. Grimes" and later "he continued his study of law under the tutorship of former Chief Justice M. Nemle Russell of Grand Bassa County."[66] In 1926, he was admitted to the Bar of Bassa County. Born in the former settlement of Brewersville in Montserrado county, Emmanuel Wilmot Williams was a former circuit judge of the Sixth Judicial Circuit in Montserrado County.[67] Unsurprisingly, a social identification with the state in Liberia was predicated on coming from the "right" background.

As in the Nigerian examples, the Liberian obituaries also reveal insights into the correlation between genealogies (both social and political identities) and access to power and wealth. By analysing the obituaries it becomes evident that in contrast to rural Liberians, those with roots in the original settlements experienced their elementary education in a familial setting. Take for example Edwin Alford Morgan, former Senior Senator for Grand Bassa County and President *pro tempore* of the Liberian Senate, who died at the Presbyterian Hospital in New York City in the United States. He was born in Hartford, Connecticut, on the St. John River and received his elementary education "under the tutorship of his parents," who were clearly well-trained enough to competently provide such an education. Eugene Himie Shannon, former chief justice of the supreme court of Liberia, born on 6 December 1893, died at his own farm in Barrake, Maryland County. He also began his education under a family member, his grandfather Reverend O.E.A. Hime Shannon, former Rector of the Protestant

---

[65] "Obituary of Edwin Alford Morgan," *The Liberia Official Gazette: EXTRAORDINARY*, vol. XLVII, no. 10, 8 October 1959.
[66] "Obituary of Reverend O.E.A. Hime Shannon," *The Liberia Official Gazette: EXTRAORDINARY*, vol. XLVII, no. 5, 30 May 1959.
[67] "Obituary of Emmanuel Wilmot Williams," *The Liberia Official Gazette: EXTRAORDINARY*, vol. XLVII, no. 12, 17 October 1959.

Episcopal Church of Harper, Maryland County.[68] A person's manner and place of acquiring early and secondary education implicitly informed the public about the belonging of the deceased to a distinguished social group.

The period after the Second World War reignited the official policy of rural integration for the sake of nation-building, and nation-building for the sake of global integration.[69] Obituaries from the 1950s and 1960s decisively included indigenous elites in this past, present, and future narration of the state. A close examination of these documents makes visible the narrow pathways of social and professional mobility that existed for the indigenous population. As discussed below, the obituaries of Edward Seku King, Counsellor of the Department of State, who died at the age of 41 in 1959; Kolli Selleh Tamba, also a former Counsellor of the Department of State, who passed away at the age of 53 in 1959; Boima Zinnah, former Member of the House of Representative (Western Province), who reached his end at the age of 80 in 1961; and Momo Passawe, former paramount chief of the Teewo (or Tawoh) Chiefdom, and member of the House of Representatives (Grand Cape Mount), who died at 83 in 1963, demonstrate a slightly more precarious path of migration and familial disruption as being necessary to climb social and occupational ladders.

As in other parts of West Africa, some local chiefs showed interest in at least one of their children receiving a missionary education, a path generally encouraged by the state. Edward Seku King, the son of late Clan Chief Boima Kartumu and Madam Karnor had been sent to a mission school as a child and eventually completed a Bachelor of Arts from Liberia College (later, the University of Liberia) in 1942. Following a decade of high school teaching, he was hired as Chief of the Bureau of Archives for the Department of State.[70] Boima Zinnah's obituary celebrated him as a scholar of indigenous Vai ethnic origin. This marked the rare occasion where ethnic identity explicitly featured in an obituary. Furthermore, he was the son of the paramount chief, Bamu Kolli Kamara, and the great-grandson of King Sao Boso Kamara (King Boatswain). Zinnah had received a religious education, having been educated by Reverend and Mrs. John Ricks in the township of Clay-Ashland, about a day's walk from his home in Bo-

---

68 "Obituary of Reverend O.E.A. Hime Shannon," *The Liberia Official Gazette: EXTRAORDINARY*, vol. XLVII, no. 5, 30 May 1959.
69 See, for example, Cassandra Mark-Thiesen, "Of Vagrants and Volunteers During Liberia's Operation Production, 1963–1969," *African Economic History* 46, no. 2 (2018): 147–172.
70 "Obituary of Edward Seku King," *The Liberia Official Gazette: EXTRAORDINARY*, vol. XLVI, no. 9, 19 August 1959.

polu District.⁷¹ Tamba attended St. John's Mission School at Robertsport, Grand Cape Mount County, moving from his home in Gawular district to do so.⁷² For individuals with deep indigenous roots, signalling the experience of a mission education and related internal migration was a way to emphasise one's proximity to official nationalist power, while demonstrating a linkage to a chiefly family indicated the adherence to an alternative nationalist system nonetheless.⁷³

In the Liberian historiography, the year 1944 is also often referred to as a watershed moment for women, with their gaining unprecedented voting rights. However, the *Gazette* promoted a very specific image of Liberian womanhood. Commemorated Liberian women were either the politically notable wives of prominent public figures or female educators, affirming a role of women as nurturers of the body politic and mind. For instance, in the case of Augusta Beatrice Padmore, the deceased wife of Honourable Jerome Padmore, it was her religious activities that "singled her out as an outstanding devoted Christian and Civic worker."⁷⁴ Bertha Ninga Bishop, who died at 88, was engaged in "home missionary work and reared many young men and women." In addition, she had been a "faithful member" of Trinity Cathedral in Monrovia.⁷⁵ Fragments of the female identity that did not fit this mould received no mention in these death announcements.

Conclusion

Obituaries and in-memoriams stand out as fragments of a local mediascape in which past, present, and future converge to shape the identities of the deceased and the bereaved. In terms of ritualistic practice, these commemorations put death either descriptively or figuratively into the printed public sphere.⁷⁶ Practices

---

71 "Obituary of Bioma Zinnah," *The Liberia Official Gazette: EXTRAORDINARY*, vol. XLVIII, no. 1, 4 January 1961.
72 "Obituary of Kolli Selleh Tamba," *The Liberia Official Gazette: EXTRAORDINARY*, vol. XLVII, no. 5, 6 May 1959.
73 Momo Passawe was an exception in that he attended an "Arabic School," or Koranic school, in Sierra Leone, and later returned to his hometown of Mambo in Liberia where he educated local students in a similar manner. "Obituary of Momo Passawe," *The Liberia Official Gazette: EXTRAORDINARY*, vol. XLIX, no. 1, 23 January 1962.
74 "Obituary of Augusta Beatrice Padmore," *The Liberia Official Gazette: EXTRAORDINARY*, vol. XLVII, no. 10, 9 October 1959.
75 "Obituary of Bertha Ninga Bishop," *The Liberia Official Gazette: EXTRAORDINARY*, vol. XLVIII, no. 12, 26 December 1963.
76 Newell, "From Corpse to Corpus," 389–424.

of revealing, hiding, masking, displaying, and concealing mediated the eternalisation of the deceased for multiple purposes. Registering death consoled the bereaved and gave them a platform to solidify and shape the public identity of their loved ones and his or her social group; initially before reading publics, later in front of listening ones. Obituaries and death notices also demonstrated how distinctions between state, individual, and society could conflate when printing the life of the deceased. In both the state-owned Liberian newspapers and in the privately-owned Nigerian newspapers, death announcements highlighted specific achievements of the deceased that elite communities perceived as being worthy of replication in the future. These more figurative commemorations in fact illustrate how not just industry, but also the state functioned as a source of authority; this, even in the late colonial period in Nigeria where political tensions were growing. Hence, through the relationship between society and the individual shone the subliminal prominence of the relationship between the bereaved and the state, in most cases as a provider of social security and professional stability, and not as an object of contestation for members of the elite. This observation situates in-memoriams and obituaries outside of a framework of contemporary newspapers being strictly attentive to the level of official politics. While many editorials and feature articles widely articulated anticolonialism, in obituaries the colonial past simmered to create group identity defined by profession and class. In that sense, both cases show how the shaping and reconfiguring of memory concentrated and fixed the flow of imaginations and social representations at various levels of society and politics in the printed public sphere. In this vortex, time – past, present, future – , (communication) space – textual, visual, acoustic –, as well the aspirations and achievements of individuals, groups, and society converged.

Bibliography

Adebanwi, Wale. "Colonial Modernity and Tradition: Herbert Macaulay, the Newspaper Press, and the (Re)Production of Engaged Publics in Colonial Lagos." In *African Print Cultures: Newspapers and Their Publics in the Twentieth Century*, edited by Derek R. Peterson, Stephanie Newell, and Emma Hunter, 125–150. Ann Arbor: University of Michigan Press, 2016.

Ainslie, Rosalynde. *The Press in Africa: Communications Past and Present*. London: Gollancz, 1966.

Arhin, Kwame. "The Economic Implications of Transformations in Akan Funeral Rites." *Africa International African* 64, no. 3 (1994): 307–322.

Assmann, Aleida. "Memory, Individual, and Collective." In *The Oxford Handbook of Contextual Political Analysis*, edited by Robert Goodin and Charles Tilly, 210–226. Oxford: Oxford University Press, 2006.
Azikiwe, Nnamdi. *My Odyssey:* An Autobiography. London: Hurst, 1970.
Barber, Karin. "Popular Arts in Africa." *African Studies Review* 30, no. 3 (1987): 1–78.
Barber, Karin. *The Anthropology of Texts, Persons, and Publics*. Cambridge: Cambridge University Press, 2008.
Barber, Karin. *Print Culture and the First Yoruba Novel: I.B. Thomas's 'Life Story of Me, Segilola' and Other Texts*. Leiden: Brill, 2012.
Blustein, Jeffrey. *The Moral Demands of Memory*. Cambridge: Cambridge University Press, 2008.
Burrowes, Carl Patrick. *Power and Press Freedom in Liberia, 1830–1970: The Impact of Globalization and Civil Society on Media-Government Relations*. Trenton: Africa World Press, 2004.
Burrowes, Carl Patrick. *Between the Kola Forest and the Salty Sea: A History of the Liberian People before 1800*. Monrovia: Know Yourself Press, 2016.
Coleman, James S. *Nigeria: Background to Nationalism*. Berkeley: University of California Press, 1960.
Diawara, Mamadou, Bernard C. Lategan, and Jörn Rüsen, eds. *Historical Memory in Africa: Dealing with the Past, Reaching for the Future in an Intercultural Context*. New York: Berghahn Books, 2010.
Gore, Charles. "Commemoration, Memory, and Ownership: Some Social Contexts of Contemporary Photography in Benin City, Nigeria." *Visual Anthropology* 14, no. 3 (2001): 321–342.
Gore, Charles. "African Photography." *African Arts* 48, no. 3 (2015): 1–5.
Harding, Leonhard. *Geschichte Afrikas im 19. und 20. Jahrhundert*. München: De Gruyter Oldenbourg, 2013.
Hume, Janice. *Obituaries in American Culture*. Jackson: University Press of Mississippi, 2000.
Larmer, Miles, and Baz Lecocq. "Historicising Nationalism in Africa." *Nations and Nationalism* 24, no. 4 (October 2018): 893–917.
Lawuyi, Olatunde Bayo. "The Story about Life: Biography in the Yoruba Obituaries," *Diogenes*, 37, no. 148 (1989): 92–111.
Lawuyi, Olatunde Bayo. "The Social Marketing of Elites: The Advertised Self in Obituaries and Congratulations in Some Nigerian Dailies." *Africa* 61, no. 2 (April 1991): 247–263.
Lee, Rebekah, and Megan Vaughan. "Death and Dying in the History of Africa Since 1800." *The Journal of African History* 49, no. 3 (2008): 341–359.
Margalit, Avishai. *Ethics of Memory*. Cambridge: Harvard University Press, 2009.
Mark-Thiesen, Cassandra. "Of Vagrants and Volunteers During Liberia's Operation Production, 1963–1969." *African Economic History* 46, no. 2 (2018): 147–172.
McCaskie, Thomas C. "Death and the Asantehene: A Historical Meditation." *The Journal of African History* 30, no. 3 (1989): 417–444.
McCaskie, Thomas C. "Writing, Reading, and Printing Death: Obituaries and Commemoration in Asante." In *Africa's Hidden Histories: Everyday Literacy and Making the Self*, edited by Karin Barber, 341–384. Bloomington: Indiana University Press, 2006.
Newell, Stephanie. "'Paracolonial' Networks: Some Speculations on Local Readerships in Colonial West Africa." *Interventions* 3, no. 3 (2001): 336–354.

Newell, Stephanie. "From Corpse to Corpus: The Printing of Death in Colonial West Africa." In *African Print Cultures: Newspapers and Their Publics in the Twentieth Century*, edited by Derek R. Peterson, Emma Hunter, and Stephanie Newell, 389–424. Ann Arbor: Michigan University Press, 2016.

Oduntan, Oluwatoyin B. "Iwe Irohin and the Representation of the Universal in Nineteenth-Century Egbaland 1." *History in Africa* 32 (2005): 295–305.

Omu, Fred I.A. "The 'Iwe Irohin', 1859–1867." *Journal of the Historical Society of Nigeria* 4, no. 1 (1967): 35–44.

Parker, John. *In My Time of Dying: A History of Death and the Dead in West Africa*. Princeton: Princeton University Press, 2021.

Parker, John. "The Cultural Politics of Death & Burial in Early Colonial Africa." In *Africa's Urban Past*, edited by David Anderson and Richard Rathbone, 205–221. Oxford: James Currey, 2000.

Peterson, Derek R., Stephanie Newell, and Emma Hunter, eds. *African Print Cultures: Newspapers and Their Publics in the Twentieth Century*. Ann Arbor: University of Michigan Press, 2016.

Pratten, David. "Creole Pioneers in the Nigerian Provincial Press." In *African Print Cultures: Newspapers and Their Publics in the Twentieth Century*, edited by Derek R. Peterson, Stephanie Newell, and Emma Hunter, 75–101. Ann Arbor: University of Michigan Press, 2016.

Sawada, Nozomi. "Selecting Those 'Worthy' of Remembering: Memorialization in Early Lagos Newspapers." *Journal of West African History* 2, no. 2 (2016): 79–108.

Sprague, Stephen F., "Yoruba Photography: How the Yoruba See Themselves." *African Arts* 12, no. 1 (1978): 52–59.

Nina S. Studer
Remembrance of Drinks Past: Wine and Absinthe in Nineteenth-century French Algeria

Abstract: This chapter draws links between the colonisation of French Algeria in the nineteenth century and the production, and especially the consumption, of alcohol. The military confrontation with abstentious Muslims prompted many nineteenth century French authors to highlight the correlation between French identity and certain alcoholic drinks. In France's collective memory, wine and absinthe were linked with the conquest of Algeria, with drinks both serving as an *aide-de-mémoire* for settlers returned to France and, more importantly, as an emblematic symbol for Algeria itself. Whether a person consumed or abstained from alcohol became one of the principal dichotomies in the settler worldview, encapsulating perceived cultural differences, with those Muslim men who began to drink alcohol after France's brutal conquest of Algeria often framed as embracing French civilisation or as mimicking French culture. Even French authors who feared the overconsumption of alcohol amongst French settlers and the spread of alcoholism amongst local communities agreed that alcohol played a positive role in the colonisation of Algeria, as settlers both relied on it for comfort and used it to reinforce social contacts. This chapter shows how descriptions of the drinking habits of the French in colonial Algeria helped to define the group identity of a dominant minority surrounded by an oppressed majority, while also examining why later French colonisers so often chose to recall with nostalgia the early colonisation of Algeria (i.e. the 1830s to 1850s) through metaphors connected to alcohol, with French culture likened to vines taking root on North African soil, fortifying conquered territory.

Drinking alcohol, especially wine and to a lesser degree absinthe, was seen as quintessentially French in the nineteenth century. French people produced and consumed these beverages, while the drinks themselves were seen as symbols of their homeland.[1] Since Roland Barthes' pioneering work in the 1950s,

---

[1] See, for example: Patricia Prestwich, *Drink and the Politics of Social Reform: Anti-Alcoholism in France since 1870* (Palo Alto: Society for the Promotion of Science and Scholarship, 1988), 1. It should be added here that this Frenchness was clearly gendered, class-based and urban-centred, and that not all drinks were understood to impart Frenchness to women, the lower classes and

scholars have analysed the proclivity to equate France with particular drinks and the role that alcohol played in the formation of French identity.[2] Barthes stated in his 1957 monograph *Mythologies* that France understood wine to be first and foremost French, comparable to how tea was framed in Britain.[3] More broadly, a scholarly consensus has emerged that what people eat and drink informs how they see both themselves and others.[4]

In France's collective memory, a handful of alcoholic drinks were linked with Algeria in the nineteenth century. These beverages served as both an *aide-de-mémoire* for settlers returned to France – i.e. Proustian madeleines[5] – and, more importantly, as an emblematic symbol for Algeria itself. After a prolonged and deadly conflict that began in 1830 when the French army arrived on the North African coast, Algeria legally became a part of France in 1848. The indigenous population suffered considerable losses of property, land, and life, and Muslims remained marginalised in terms of citizenship and full civil rights. The colonisation of Algeria included the establishment of Algerian vineyards, physical proof of French civilisation occupying the region. Algerian Muslims identified vine-

---

those living in the countryside. Detailed analysis of this important distinction falls beyond the scope of this chapter, but forms part of the author's broader research into the drinking habits of people in the colonial Maghreb. The sources consulted for this chapter focus on French settlers who were male and, if not otherwise indicated, middle class.

2 There is an existing literature on the role that alcohol played in France's self-image, focusing mainly on the importance of wine for the French national identity. Kolleen M. Guy, *When Champagne Became French: Wine and the Making of a National Identity* (Baltimore: John Hopkins University Press, 2003); Kolleen M. Guy, "Rituals of Pleasure in the Land of Treasures: Wine Consumption and the Making of French Identity in the Late Nineteenth Century," in *Food Nations: Selling Taste in Consumer Societies*, ed. Warren Belasco and Philip Scranton (New York: Routledge, 2002), 34–47; Marion Demossier, *Wine Drinking Culture in France: A National Myth or a Modern Passion* (Cardiff: University of Wales Press, 2010).

3 Roland Barthes, *Mythologies* (Paris: Editions du Seuil, 1957), 69. Barthes, however, also criticised wine production in Algeria as forcing Muslims to produce grapes for wine, rather than wheat for their own consumption. Ibid., 70.

4 Thomas M. Wilson, "Food, Drink and Identity in Europe: Consumption and the Construction of Local, National and Cosmopolitan Culture," in *Food, Drink and Identity in Europe*, ed. Thomas M. Wilson (Amsterdam/New York: Rodopi, 2006), 25–26. On the interconnections between identity and drinking, see also Thomas M. Wilson, "Drinking Cultures: Sites and Practices in the Production and Expression of Identity," in *Drinking Cultures: Alcohol and Identity*, ed. Thomas M. Wilson (Oxford: Berg Publishers, 2005), 1–24.

5 The term "Proust's madeleine," which refers to a sensory trigger that evokes memory, comes from Marcel Proust's 1907 *In Search of Lost Time* and his famous passage about madeleine cakes that unlocked childhood memories.

yards, as did the French, as symbols of colonialism.[6] After independence, Algerian Muslims uprooted most of the vineyards in an active undertaking of decolonisation, turning them into wheat fields, thus actively and pre-emptively undoing some potential *lieu de mémoires* of French colonialism on Algerian soil.[7]

Absinthe also held particular associations with Algeria that can be traced to rations of the beverage issued to French soldiers during the initial conquest of Algeria in the 1830s and 1840s. Officials believed the beverage could clean unpotable water and thus protect from disease. French soldiers, who generally had not encountered absinthe before their military service in Algeria, came to like the strong, sweet, cold drink and took their newfound beverage of choice – imbued with symbolism – back to the mainland with them. As Jad Adams stated in his history of absinthe: "Absinthe therefore emerged as a tonic that was patriotic, associated with vigour, the army and the overseas empire."[8] An example of this almost wistful remembrance can be found in a highly Orientalist travel account written by the Belgian author Léon Souguenet, describing Algeria:

> It's the holy hour of the apéritif. The small town exudes the subtle aroma of absinthe, social liquor if there ever was one; the terraces of the cafés flow over onto the roads. One speaks as in France; there is a light brouhaha [a noisy uproar]; there is a motley crowd of bourgeois, soldiers, officers. One watches the magnificently lazy natives pass by, sitting on unfortunate donkeys, whose wounds they never bandage, and women bundled in their white veils.[9]

Many such travel accounts explicitly connect alcoholic drinks with French Algeria and were written to evoke a certain feeling of nostalgic *fernweh* or colonial grandeur in their French readers in the *Métropole* and in the colonies. From the 1880s onwards, these accounts had started to reframe the initial period of

---

6 On the decline of vineyards in Algeria after 1962, see Kolleen M. Guy, "Culinary Connections and Colonial Memories in France and Algeria," *Food and History* 8, no. 1 (2010): 227; Willy Jansen, "French Bread and Algerian Wine: Conflicting Identities in French Algeria," in *Food, Drink and Identity. Cooking, Eating and Drinking in Europe since the Middle Ages*, ed. Scholliers Peter (Oxford: Bloomsbury Publishing, 2001), 202; Giulia Meloni and Johan Swinnen, "The Rise and Fall of the World's Largest Wine Exporter – and its Institutional Legacy," *Journal of Wine Economics* 9, no. 1 (2014): 4.
7 Guy, "Culinary Connections," 229. See also: Owen White, *The Blood of the Colony: Wine and the Rise and Fall of French Algeria* (Cambridge/London: Harvard University Press, 2021), 215, 220.
8 Jad Adams, *Hideous Absinthe: A History of the Devil in a Bottle* (London: I. B. Tauris, 2008), 4.
9 Despite their geography, Tunisia, Algeria and Morocco were framed as part of "the Orient" in nineteenth century France. The quoted passage comes from Léon Souguenet, *Route de Timimoun: Heures religieuses* (Brussels: Oscar Lamberty, 1914), 103. All English translations by the author.

the military conquest and occupation, from 1830 to the 1870s, as a transfer of civilisation, symbolised by the introduction of alcohol, which "oiled" the colonial machinery, so to speak. In France, people nostalgically recalled stays in Algeria through accounts of shared glasses of absinthe consumed on terraces of French bars in the coastal cities and in the houses of family members, friends and acquaintances. Thanks to these accounts, a metropolitan reader might have felt that he was able to experience French Algeria with his daily glass of absinthe: Drinking absinthe, in this context, could be construed as indicative of both imperialism and patriotism.

This chapter addresses the following questions: Did French settlers' production and consumption of alcohol help the French to establish and maintain colonial rule in Algeria? Or did the spread of alcohol – among the colonisers as well as among the colonised Algerian Muslims – obstruct the French from maintaining colonial rule? Building from this, how did European authors remember and judge the role of alcohol during the time of the military conquest of Algeria and the subsequent establishment of a French settler society? This chapter will show that French attitudes toward different groups' consumption of alcohol in the *situation coloniale* can shed light on how the French saw colonisation in Algeria more broadly. French self-identification with certain forms of alcohol expressed itself as a useful tool to reinforce and maintain colonial rule.[10] French colonisers often chose to remember the early colonisation of Algeria through metaphors connected to alcohol, and recollections of French drinking habits in Algeria were used to define the group identity of a dominant minority surrounded by an oppressed minority. From the 1880s onwards, the presence of locally produced, French-owned alcohol in Algeria was remembered as a vindication of colonialism itself; a sentiment that only increased in the first half of the 20th century.

This chapter is based on nineteenth century French settler memoirs, travel accounts and medical publications that mention the consumption of alcohol in the context of the colonisation of Algeria. These sources often represented French Algeria through accounts of drinking, of watching others drink, of how drinks were prepared and of their offering and being offered drinks. Settler memoirs and travel accounts were written by both professional authors and amateurs for a wide audience in the motherland, hungry for the exoticism and adventures

---

[10] These questions have been studied in other colonial contexts. See, for example: Harald Fischer-Tiné, "Liquid Boundaries: Race, Class and Alcohol in Colonial India," in *A History of Alcohol and Drugs in Modern South Asia: Intoxicating Affairs*, ed. Harald Fischer-Tiné and Jana Tschurenev (Abingdon: Routledge, 2014), 89–115; Deborah Toner, "Maize, Alcohol, and Cultural Identity in Colonial Mexico" (MA Thesis, University of Warwick, 2006).

that journeying outside of France allegedly brought.[11] A large segment of this audience saw the colonies as direct proof of France's glory and read these settler memoirs and travel accounts with this assumption in mind. Equally, a wide range of French authors interpreted the consumption of alcohol as a sign of civilisation, of whiteness and of a very specific French identity. They pointed to differences between their own eating and drinking habits and those of colonised Algerians as shorthand to describe perceived cultural differences. Many interpreted the dissemination of their own habits as a victory over the customs of the colonised. Authors of these sources – those who could afford to travel and who chose to document their experiences living in Algeria – were in general both educated and middle- to upper-class.[12] The settler memoirs and travel accounts used for this chapter reached a relatively small audience, yet these metropolitan readers accepted the emphasis that these authors placed on the importance of alcohol in the colonisation of this foreign soil and adapted this idea into a wider discourse pertaining to how the establishment of a French settler colony in Algeria was remembered in France.

Muslim religious and legal tractates that discuss the illegality of alcohol span centuries – far beyond what can be discussed in this chapter.[13] Nonetheless, it can be said that a consensus existed among most nineteenth century Algerian Muslims, based on an interpretation of Suras 5:90 and 5:91, that the Qur'an forbade alcohol. They therefore objected to the introduction and glorification of alcohol and vineyards by the French. On the other hand, despite this prohibition, some Muslims consumed alcohol in Algeria before the French conquest in the region, and not all Muslims rejected the alcohol made available to

---

11 On the long history of French travel accounts, see Elisabeth A. Fraser, "Books, Prints, and Travel: Reading in the Gaps of the Orientalist Archive," *Art History* 31, no. 3 (2008): 342–367.
12 Jacques Boucher de Perthes, for example, was already a famous archaeologist by the time he wrote his travel account in 1859, while Amédée Hennequin was a well-established lawyer at the date of the publication of his report in 1857. Other travel accounts were written by people affiliated with academic and scientific institutions, for example Étienne Bailly in 1868, who was a Corresponding Member of the Imperial and Agricultural Society for Agriculture of France, or Ernest Fallot in 1887, who was the Secretary for the Society for Geography in Marseille. Étienne Bailly, *Études sur l'Algérie en 1855 pendant un voyage exécuté par M. Bailly* (Paris: Imprimerie de F. Malteste, 1868), title page; Ernest Fallot, *Par-delà la Méditerranée: Kabylie, Aurès, Kroumirie* (Paris: E. Plon, Nourrit et Cie, 1887), title page.
13 Due to the limitations that these sources impose as well as space constraints, discussion of how Algerian Muslims depicted and evaluated alcohol during the nineteenth century is absent from this chapter.

them by colonisation, as will be discussed further in this chapter.[14] Additionally, some tried to obtain an economic advantage by producing or trading in alcohol.

French medical experts wrote for two very different audiences – either for other medical experts or for the settlers themselves. The authors, doctors travelling through or living in Algeria, wrote scientific papers about their professional experiences in Algeria and handbooks specifically focused on the climate and circumstances of that colony. They hoped that, with the help of these manuals, the settlers would remain healthy and avoid illness, especially those with limited access to medical institutions. These doctors intended to write recommendations suited to every European living in Algeria. Their advice about what to drink and how much to drink was usually gendered and class-based, but rarely differentiated between the cities and the countryside or between the coast and the desert. Despite intending their publications to reach settlers in remote areas, the descriptions of drinking habits in these medical manuals often assumed easy access to shops, cafés and bars. In addition, these doctors played an important role in settler communities. In her 2016 article, historian Charlotte Ann Chopin described French doctors in Algeria as both the prime representatives of French whiteness on Algerian soil and as individuals who embodied the "emergent values of local settler culture."[15] Their mentions of alcohol should therefore be interpreted as a direct recommendation of healthy living from people cast as role models in these colonial contexts to other potentially less "civilised" white people. The medical descriptions of alcohol consumption in Algeria were generally seen as settler guidelines for successful "white" living in the colony.

This chapter comprises two parts. The first, *Frenchness in a Bottle*, analyses how colonial accounts linked alcohol to nostalgia for the early colonial period – a time of French soldiers and civilians allegedly making the land "habitable" for Europeans. It examines colonial source material that portrays beverages like wine and absinthe favourably, i.e. authors who interpreted alcohol as a vaunted symbol of Frenchness in general or French imperialism in particular. In the second part, *Beyond "All Limits of Plausibility,"* contrasting opinions will be analysed, namely the fear that alcohol would be detrimental to the colonisation

---

14 On Algerian Muslims' consumption of alcohol prior to French conquest in the region, see, for example: Rudi Matthee, "Alcohol in the Islamic Middle East: Ambivalence and Ambiguity," *Past and Present* 9 (2014): 106. Other authors disagree and claim that pre-colonial Algeria had been alcohol free. See, for example: Christopher Cumo, "Algeria," in *The Sage Encyclopedia of Alcohol: Social, Cultural, and Historical Perspectives*, ed. Scott C. Martin (New York: Sage Publishing, 2015), 117–118.
15 Charlotte Anne Chopin, "Embodying 'the New White Race': Colonial Doctors and Settler Society in Algeria, 1878–1911," *Social History of Medicine* 29, no. 1 (2016): 20.

of Algeria in light of the fact that many people, colonisers and colonised alike, consumed it without moderation.

Frenchness in a Bottle

French qualities were often understood to be mirrored in certain drinks, foremost among them wine. The association of wine with Frenchness became even more pronounced in French Algeria than in France itself following the occupation of the African territory in the 1830s, as the newcomers were confronted with groups who had traditionally chosen to not consume wine.[16] This interlinking of metropolitan identity with wine manifested through behaviour such as making the beverage one's daily drink of choice in a predominantly Muslim territory.[17] This not only continued a drinking habit to which many settlers had been accustomed since childhood in France, but also, in the Algerian context, drinking wine was a way to proudly display one's Frenchness.[18]

Consequently, the production and consumption of wine significantly shaped the identity of French settlers in Algeria.[19] Anthropologist Willy Jansen, for example, explained in a chapter on "French Bread and Algerian Wine" that particular foods and drinks helped to establish and construct social identities in colonial contexts and that the preparation and consumption of food and drink delineated boundaries between people. In colonial Algeria, this meant that both the consumption of and abstinence from certain foods and drinks were variously classed as Muslim, Jewish or French. In Jansen's view, wine was the product that most clearly defined the French in Algeria. She further justified this as-

---

16 Michalak and Trocki describe in their article on "Alcohol and Islam" that the abstinence from a product can be as identity-building as its consumption. Laurence Michalak and Karen Trocki, "Alcohol and Islam: An Overview," *Contemporary Drug Problems* 33 (2006): 555–556.
17 American historian Kolleen M. Guy in her 2003 book *When Champagne Became French* has examined the importance of champagne as a "symbol of France" in the French national identity. See Guy, *When Champagne Became French*, 5, 33–34.
18 On the issue of French people accustomed to drinking wine from childhood, see, for example, Octave Saint-Vel, *Hygiène des Européens dans les climats tropicaux, des créoles et des races colorées dans les pays tempérés* (Paris: Adrien Delahaye, 1872), 43–44; Adolphe Bonain, *L'Européen sous les tropiques: Causeries d'hygiène coloniale pratique* (Paris: Henri Charles-Lavauzelle, 1907), 238–239.
19 The geographer Hildebert Isnard, for example, highlighted this phenomenon in his 1947 study of wine in Algeria. He stated: "The culture of the vine has shaped, in this way, the mentality of the Algerian colonist." Hildebert Isnard, "Vigne et colonisation en Algérie (1880–1947)," *Annales. Économies, Sociétés, Civilisations* 2, no. 3 (July-Sept. 1947): 295.

sociation by stating that the overt consumption of wine was almost exclusively a French habit in the colonial context: "The political and economic elite [among the colonised Algerians] would privately enjoy the '*cuvée du president*,' but this did not make wine acceptable as a marker of ascendancy. For the majority of Algerian Muslims, it is not worthy of emulation, as it is a symbol of lewdness and lack of self-control."[20]

In the French understanding of Islam, Muslims simply did not drink alcohol. They therefore could not profit from the positive consequences of wine drinking like the French. Most French authors ignored local alcohol production, such as fig or date liquors and palm wine, which existed both before and during the colonisation of the region, and interpreted alcohol solely as an import from France.[21] As such, alcohol symbolised not only France but specifically their colonising power on hostile Algerian soil. In this narrative, alcohol arrived with the French army and flourished on the North African coast. The spread of alcohol in Algeria therefore served as a triumphant narrative of colonisation and was often remembered as such. Inspired by the presence of Algeria at the *Universal Exhibition in Paris* of 1889 and impressed above all by the array of wines on display from the region, Raoul Bergot wrote a book about the colony that attributed cultural ascent to the intoxicant: "In the three rooms of wine samples, there was a magnificent proof of the modern conquest by French civilisation of this barbarian land. Each bottle of wine represented a small vineyard and often a domain of one hundred hectares." Bergot went on to say that other, more colourful rooms, full of Orientalist fantasies, were more spectacular than those containing the wine samples, so that many visitors had, to his regret, neglected to take in the importance of Algerian wines. He then explained "that the three rooms of this bare exposition, expressed in their simplicity a giant leap made by progress, thanks to the French race, on the other side of the Mediterranean."[22]

Bergot thus measured the "progress" of French colonisation by the spread of wine and vineyards in Algeria – and he was not alone in this regard. By claiming vineyards as a symbol of colonialism, the images of the war of conquest and the

---

20 Jansen, "French Bread," 214.
21 Only a few colonial accounts mentioned local forms of alcohol whose basic existence contradicted this narrative of colonisation through alcohol. See, for example, Lucien Raynaud, "Alcool et alcoolisme au Maroc," *Annales d'Hygiène Publique et de Médecine Légale* 497, no. 3 (1902): 211, 214. The idea that alcohol had been unknown in Algeria before the advent of the French was still proposed as late as 1937, for example by the psychiatrist Jean Sutter: Jean Sutter, "L'épilepsie mentale chez l'indigène nord-africain (étude clinique)," (Med. Thesis, University of Algiers, 1937), 75–76.
22 Raoul Bergot, *L'Algérie telle qu'elle est* (Paris: Albert Savine, 1890), 1.

subsequent violent colonisation of the region were supplanted by that of farmers peacefully cultivating fields and growing a culturally significant product. Based on this, many nineteenth century accounts imply that alcohol in general and wine more specifically "colonised" Algeria. This sentiment seems to have been so common among the settlers that it was turned into a humorous piece of conventional wisdom, a shared anecdote, recounted by both settler authors and travellers in their publications. Ernest Fallot, for example, in his 1887 travel account described how the military conquest was the first step in the colonisation of Algeria, followed by settlers who sold liquid "necessities" to both the military and the settlers:

> A few years later, if business is satisfactory, they built a stone house [i.e. a shop in a stone house] in order to be more at ease and to return to civilised life. The combination of several of these canteeners' houses gives birth to a village, and this is what has made [people] jokingly say that absinthe colonised Algeria.[23]

In this jest, shared among French settlers, the military conquest of Algeria and the colonial authority imposed through violent repression, that resulted in famine, displacement and epidemics which decimated the indigenous population, was trivialised as nothing more than the necessary first step in the ecological and economic development of the region.

Even more important than the idea of alcohol having "conquered" Algeria together with the French army was the notion that certain drinks substantially helped France to maintain its colonial presence. Many French settlers and European travellers imagined that both alcoholic and non-alcoholic drinks played an active role in the colonising of Algeria. The renowned French hygienist Apollinaire Bouchardat, for example, wrote in his *Manual of Medical Matters* in 1856: "Without coffee, our Algeria would be uninhabitable."[24] While medical publications often credited coffee with having made Algeria habitable and French soldiers stronger, this bizarre agency was more widely ascribed to certain alcoholic drinks, such as wine, absinthe and mixed drinks like champoreau.[25]

---

23 Fallot, *Par-delà la Méditerranée*, 29. The same expression of "colonising through absinthe" being something deeply problematic can be found in other publications. See, for example, Eugène Poiré, *La Tunisie française* (Paris: E. Plon, Nourrit et Cie, Imprimeurs-Éditeurs, 1892), 133.
24 Apollinaire Bouchardat, *Manuel de matière médicale, de thérapeutique comparée et de pharmacie*, Vol. 1 (Paris: Germer Baillière, 1856), 304. The author is currently working on an article on this issue under the working title *Coffee Drinking as a Military Strategy: The Service Rendered by Coffee in the French Conquest of Algeria*.
25 Champoreau, a mix of coffee, milk and various forms of alcohol, shared the title of most popular alcoholic beverage in Algeria with wine and absinthe. On the popularity of champoreau,

In the context of wine specifically, vineyards were thought to safeguard both the livelihoods of the settlers and the economic interests of France. By the 1890s, experts declared that the coasts of Algeria, Tunisia and Morocco offered the perfect economic investment for vintners.[26] Kathleen Guy argued in 2003 that proponents of colonialism in France claimed that viticulture proved the economic utility of colonies.[27] French colonists in Algeria succeeded in making wine one of the colony's major exports, even as the proportion of Muslim vineyard owners declined. Historian Susanna Barrows analysed the distribution of vineyards in colonial Algeria and found that while in 1864 "indigenous vineyards accounted for nearly a third of the vines," this figure "fell below 10% in the first years of the twentieth century."[28]

French-owned vineyards in Algeria demonstrated that French settlement had metaphorically and literally taken root in the country. This idea that vineyards and wine helped to make the colony of Algeria more stable and inhabitable for French settlers only solidified over the years. In the early twentieth century, for example, French authors looked back nostalgically to the period of the planting of the vineyards in Algeria and framed these acts as an essential part of the establishment of the settler colony. This can be seen, for example, in Pierre Pinaud's 1933 doctoral dissertation on *Alcoholism among the Arabs in Algeria*, in which he stated that "Wine is, at present, one of the great riches of Algeria. [...] In many parts of Algeria, vines were only planted to ensure the safety of the French settlers."[29] This interpretation of wine as an important agent in the French colonial occupation of Algeria was germane to the Orientalist assumption that prior to French settlement, the region had been in a state of decay under Muslim rule. Such accounts often referred to the fact that the Maghreb had once been known as the breadbasket of Rome with vineyards flourishing in the region. This richness had been destroyed, in this narrative, by devotedly abstinent Muslims.[30]

---

see, for example Jacques Boucher de Perthes, *Voyage en Espagne et en Algérie, en 1855* (Paris: Treuttel et Würtz, 1859), 508. Bailly, *Études*, 158–159.
26 See, for example, Sylvère Leroux, *Traité de la vigne et le vin en Algérie et en Tunisie*, Vol. 2 (Blida: A. Maugin, 1894), 7.
27 Guy, "Culinary Connections," 231.
28 Susanna Barrows, "Alcohol, France and Algeria: A Case Study in the International Liquor Trade," *Contemporary Drug Problems* 11 (1982): 536. See also Keith Sutton, "Algeria's Vineyards: A Problem of Decolonisation," *Méditerranée* 65 (1988): 55.
29 Pierre-Alfred-Hippolyte-André-René Pinaud, "L'alcoolisme chez les Arabes en Algérie" (Med. Thesis, University of Bordeaux, 1933), 17.
30 See, for example, Albin Lafont, *Les dangers de l'alcoolisme* (Lyon: Bureau de la Société de Tempérance, 1893), 5; Guy, "Culinary Connections," 231–232.

Yet prior to the military conquest of the region, Muslims had used much of the land that the French subsequently converted into vineyards to produce wheat. This neglect of the cultivation of a necessity (wheat) for the colonised in favour of the cultivation for a luxury product (wine) for the coloniser, drew criticism from many mid-twentieth century commentators, among them Jean-Paul Sartre in 1964, who stated:

> Between 1927 and 1932, wine-growing increased by 173,000 hectares, more than half of which was taken from the Muslims. However, Muslims do not drink wine. On this land that was stolen from them they grew cereals for the Algerian market. This time it was not only the land that was taken from them; by planting vines there, the Algerian population was deprived of its staple food. Half a million hectares, taken from the best land and entirely devoted to wine-growing, were reduced to unproductiveness and as good as wiped out for the Muslim masses.[31]

Contrary to Sartre's claims about Muslim abstinence, after the conquest of Algeria, with the increased availability of cheap imported and locally produced alcohol, the majority of French authors reported that some Algerian Muslims had started to drink.[32] Colonial publications framed Algerian Muslims developing a taste for alcohol as an ideological decision with far-reaching political and social consequences. French authors suggested that Muslims who chose to drink alcohol must necessarily be on France's side, while those who refused to drink alcohol opposed France, thus conflating alcohol consumption and political and religious identity. Most observers agreed that when Algerian Muslims chose to drink French alcohol, it meant much more than them simply choosing a drink, which can only be truly understood when one considers the notion of alcohol as a symbol of Frenchness. French judge Jean Le Roy explicitly mentioned this connection between Muslim alcohol consumption and an assumed assimilation of Frenchness in his 1911 travel account. He described encounters with Muslims who had allegedly reframed the prohibition of alcohol in the Qur'an to permit their own moderate consumption. Le Roy saw advantages to this

---

31 Jean-Paul Sartre, *Colonialism and Neocolonialism*, trans. Terry McWilliams (London/New York: Routledge, 2001), 37.
32 As there are no numbers for the precolonial consumption of palm wine, wine, fig and date liquor in Algeria, it is not possible to reconstruct if there was an actual increase in alcohol consumption or if that was just the perception of the French authors or if this was a French construction of Muslim alcohol consumption rooted in stereotype rather than evidence. On the history of these precolonial drinks in Tunisia, see Nessim Znaien, "Les raisins de la domination: Histoire sociale de l'alcool en Tunisie à l'époque du Protectorat (1881–1956)" (Doctoral Thesis, Sorbonne University, 2017), 108–111.

way of thinking: "Mahomet outlawed the abuse of wine, but not the moderate use of this liquor. This view is particularly favourable to the societal rapprochement between natives and Europeans, and in fact, when the native Muslims are in the company of Frenchmen, I have always seen them drink wine and liquors without any appearance of scruples."[33]

Some colonial authors reported their attempts to encourage Algerian Muslims to drink as part of the colonial effort to transform them into Frenchmen. A psychiatrist, Dr. Pierre Rouby, claimed in a paper presented at the 1895 *Congress of Psychiatrists and Neurologists of France and of Francophone Countries* that he had initially supported the idea of converting water-drinking Algerian Muslims to wine in order to bring them closer to French civilisation: "I have offered them [his field workers] from it [alcohol], asking them to drink from it, to please me, to not be rude to me; they always refused, a categorical refusal, coming from a deep conviction: 'God forbids it.'"[34] Rouby thus admitted at a prestigious academic conference that he had encouraged Muslims to drink alcohol, despite knowing that their religion prohibited it. The motivation behind his attempt becomes clear if the reader assumes that Rouby considered alcohol a symbol of France. Field labourers' alcohol consumption would have suggested their acceptance of French customs. By drinking the wine or liquor that Rouby offered, they would have demonstrated their gradual assimilation to French culture – but they "rudely" refused and thus chose to remain true to their faith. His personal attempt at colonising through alcohol had, in this instance, failed.

After the war of independence and the decolonisation of Algeria, many nostalgic memoirs connected settler experiences in Algeria to the planting of and caring for vineyards, as well as to the daily "holy hour of absinthe," as mentioned by Souguenet above.[35] Before the prohibition of absinthe in 1914, the French in Algeria would regularly consume it each day at roughly five o'clock, which they called the "hour of absinthe" or "green hour." This was either

---

33 Jean Le Roy, *Deux ans de séjour en petite Kabilie: Un peuple de barbares en territoire français* (Paris: Augustin Challamel, 1911), 57–58.

34 Pierre Rouby, "De l'alcoolisme en France et en Algérie," in *Congrès des Médecins Aliénistes et Neurologistes de France et des Pays de Langue Française*, ed. F. Devay (Paris: G. Masson, 1895), 240.

35 Souguenet, *Route de Timmimoun*, 103. See also A. Villacrose, *Vingt ans en Algérie: Ou tribulations d'un colon racontées par lui-même: la colonisation en 1874, le régime militaire et l'administration civile, mœurs, coutumes, institutions des indigènes, ce qui est fait, ce qui est à faire* (Paris: Challamel aîné, 1875), 150–151; Camille Viré, *En Algérie: Une excursion dans le département d'Alger* (Paris: C. Bayle, 1888), 91–92. Authors who strongly argued against the consumption of absinthe also used the vocabulary of the "hour of absinthe." See, for example, Victor Anselmier, *De l'empoisonnement par l'absinthe* (Paris: Imprimerie de J. Claye, 1862), 11.

done in public spaces, such as cafés or bars, or in private spaces, i.e. the houses of settlers. After the prohibition of absinthe, this habit was transferred to the consumption of different anisettes. The pleasant company, the relaxation, the jokes and stories told by friends and neighbours, the relief this minority felt in company with each other, the ritual of letting the cold water slowly drip into the alcohol, and the drink itself, were all combined into a wistful image of everything that was "good" in French Algeria. This evocative image very often made it into the travel accounts and settler memoirs and shaped how life in French Algeria was seen and remembered back home.

Beyond "All Limits of Plausibility"

Not all European observers interpreted "colonisation through alcohol" as a positive development. Criticism of the interconnections between colonialism and alcohol largely focused on the fact that people in mainland France perceived settlers in most colonies as inveterate drinkers.[36] While overconsumption of alcohol was considered a problem across France's colonial empire, the settlers in Algeria were regularly singled out as the biggest culprits, akin to the infamy in Britain of Kenya's "Happy Valley" set. An anonymous account published in 1907, for example, lamented that "absinthe played, in [Algeria's] colonisation, a malevolent role, and its consumption [among settlers] exceeds all limits of plausibility."[37] People in the metropole generally assumed that overconsumption by French settlers in Algeria negated the positive effects associated with alcohol. One concern stemmed from how they imbibed the beverages that symbolised France "wrongly." Settlers drank immoderately, at the wrong times, and were especially fond of strong liquors instead of alcohol deemed "hygienic," such as wine, beer and cider. Absinthe drinkers were especially deplored as wasting

---

[36] It should be added, however, that it is entirely questionable whether the alcohol consumption of the European settlers in French Algeria actually exceeded consumption levels in mainland France, as alcoholism also presented a very significant – if often neglected – problem in the *Métropole* in the nineteenth century. On the issue of alcoholism in nineteenth century France, see, for example: Guy, "Rituals of Pleasure," 38–39; Patricia E. Prestwich, "Female Alcoholism in Paris, 1870–1920: The Response of Psychiatrists and of Families," *History of Psychiatry* 14, no. 3 (2003): 324; Patricia E. Prestwich, "Temperance in France: The Curious Case of Absinth," *Historical Reflections/Réflexions Historiques* 6, no. 2 (1979): 301.
[37] Anonymous, *Un soldat d'Afrique: l'Algérie* (Limoges: Librairie du XXe siècle, 1907), 200. See also Victor Demontès, "La grande, la moyenne et la petite colonisation en Algérie," in *Congrès de l'Afrique du Nord tenu à Paris du 6 au 10 Octobre 1908: Compte rendu des travaux*, ed. Charles Depincé, Vol 1 (Paris: Augustin Challamel, 1909), 172.

their time drinking instead of working the fields to advance and strengthen French colonial presence. In 1875, A. Villacrose, a French settler in Algeria, described settlers "who are more often playing boules and drinking absinthe than working their field" as one of the major obstacles to extending French power in the region.[38] Botanist Jules Rémy in an 1858 travel account summarised his impressions of the settlers in Algeria: "Algeria needs fewer publicans and small shopkeepers; fewer idlers and absinthe drinkers; fewer disreputable people, and more real workers. I say this with a deep sense of shame: there are in Algeria, with regards to the proportion of its population, more scoundrels than in California."[39]

It was believed that the *pieds-noirs*' overconsumption directly affected the power of French colonisation of the region, as drunken settlers were thought unable to fulfil their role in France's *mission civilisatrice*. Their behaviour set a poor example for the colonised and additionally rendered them physically more likely to succumb to the fevers of the region. Inebriation inhibited the cultivation of fields and thus limited the push to extend France's control inland. In the *Métropole*, it was feared that the settlers might not even be able to defend themselves against attacks from the colonised. Amédée Hennequin in his 1857 *Conquest of Algeria* described the situation around Algiers in 1841. In some villages, settlers were so scared of attack by the colonised that they "dared not even go a few steps from their homes to cultivate the earth, and that colonisation, thus paralysed by terror, had hardly any other representatives than feverish publicans, selling absinthe to the soldiers."[40] For many French authors in the *Métropole*, the absinthe drinkers – both military and civilian – and the publicans selling absinthe and other alcoholic beverages became shameful symbols of French colonialism in Algeria. The European settlers in Algeria, it was feared in France, "succumbed to fever, laziness, absinthe and debts."[41] Many authors even claimed that the settler society in Algeria was so dependent on alcohol that it could not function abstemiously.[42] Villacrose, for example, wrote in his 1875 travel ac-

---

[38] Villacrose, *Vingt ans*, 362.
[39] Jules Rémy, *Lettres d'un voyageur à M. L.G.-G.* (Châlons: Imprimerie de T. Martin, 1858), 5.
[40] Amédée Hennequin, *La conquête de l'Algérie* (Paris: Charles Douniol, 1857), 47.
[41] This quote regarding *pieds-noirs* neglecting their duties can be found in the 1895 account of the famous French author and journalist Robert Charles Henri Le Roux, who wrote under the name Hugues Le Roux about his experiences as a French settler in Algeria. Hugues Le Roux, *Je deviens colon: Mœurs algériennes* (Paris: Calmann Lévy, 1895), 155.
[42] It should be noted that not all commentators expressed such vehement criticism. Some criticised this notion of French settlers in Algeria being inveterate absinthe drinkers and defended the drinking habits of the *pieds-noirs* as suitable to the hard work and harsh climate in Algeria.

count that both trade agreements and social visits in Algeria were fuelled by alcohol: "The settlers in Algeria are unfortunately, for the vast majority, people who only visit each other and talk to each other with a glass in hand."[43]

Dire consequences for French settlers in the region would ensue from their unvarnished dependence on alcohol, warned many in the medical community. Presenting the grave consequences of maintaining two communities with very different levels of alcohol consumption – "sober Arabs" and "alcoholic settlers" – in a paper on *Alcoholism in France and in Algeria*, given in 1895 in Paris, Pierre Rouby connected these fears of French settlers failing in their duties to the question of alcohol:

> From the observation of this fact [i.e. the existence of the following two distinct groups], sober Arabs, alcoholic settlers, we can draw, gentlemen, social and political conclusions, and show that danger threatens our Algerian colony, if no strong medicine comes to cure the disease. When you have lived for some time in Algeria, even when you have arrived there [as an] Arabophile, if you look around you, if you talk with various inhabitants, if you study things closely, it is not long before you notice that from the point of view of French colonisation, you must support the settler, fortify him, help him, because in him lies the future of French Algeria. For the Arab, on the other hand, it is not long before you recognise that he will never be French, he would need to convert; but not one Arab since the conquest has changed religion. [...] Mahomet has told them to treat as an enemy all that that is not Muslim; [...] they wait for a favourable opportunity to take their country back; they would do it tomorrow, as they tried in 1870, if they had any chance of winning. They are enemies, and, additionally, they are six times more numerous than the settlers.[44]

Rouby thus framed the overconsumption of alcohol by French settlers, which he saw as deeply problematic, as one front in the perpetual war of coloniser against colonised in North Africa. He argued that the colonised already possessed the numerical advantage and that because they refused to drink French alcohol, whereas the French settlers were often drunk, Muslim Algerians gained a further advantage – they were sober and strong, while the settlers were weakened by their excesses.

Yet this narrative was complicated by the spread of alcoholism among the Algerian Muslims after the conquest. Despite Rouby's categorical claim of their general abstinence, many were described as enthusiastically adapting the French custom of the "hour of absinthe." French observers frequently deplored the perceived rising levels of alcohol consumption among the Algerian Muslims

---

See, for example, Anonymous, *La fin d'une légende, ou la vérité sur l'arabe, par un vieil Algérien* (Bel-Abbès: Imprimerie de Lavenue, 1892), 166.
43 Villacrose, *Vingt ans*, 353.
44 Rouby, "De l'alcoolisme," 241.

for similar reasons that commentators criticised settlers' drinking habits: alcoholism caused medical problems and diminished the labour force. Ironically, it was also believed that alcohol rendered Algerian Muslims potentially dangerous towards the colonisers – precisely what Rouby feared "sober Arabs" would become. This discourse about "colonisation by alcohol" having a negative influence on the colonised – and consequently on the economic and security interests of the colonisers – was also voiced in other colonial contexts. In 1909, A. Kermorgant, for example, wrote an article for the *Bulletin of the Society of Exotic Pathology* about the situation of *Alcoholism in French Colonies*, in which he proclaimed that: "Nothing is more disastrous than this system of colonisation by alcohol [...]."[45]

Fears of alcoholism spreading among the colonised would seem to directly contradict the positive associations of alcohol for French Algeria discussed above. Yet this can be explained through the difference between drinking alcohol and drinking alcohol excessively. Many authors who feared the rising number of Muslim alcoholics nonetheless accepted alcohol as a positive symbol of France – when consumed in moderation. Crucially, only the French possessed this latter capacity, according to many French authors. This group of commentators believed that Algerian Muslims lacked self-control and thus drank immoderate amounts of strong liquors instead of moderate amounts of "hygienic" alcoholic beverages such as wine, cider and beer.[46] Assuming that all Muslim alcohol consumption led to alcoholism, they therefore strongly disagreed with those who welcomed the rising alcohol consumption of Algerian Muslims as a sign of assimilation into French culture.

---

45 A. Kermorgant, "L'alcoolisme dans les colonies françaises," *Bulletin de la Société de Pathologie Exotique* 2, no. 6 (1909): 331.
46 On the alleged affinity of Algerian Muslims for strong liquors such as absinthe, see, for example, Louis Vignon, *La France en Algérie* (Paris: Hachette et Cie, 1893), 410; Auguste Voisin, "Souvenirs d'un voyage en Tunisie (1896)," *Annales Médico-Psychologiques* 4 (1896): 90. This differentiation between liquors and good, "hygienic" alcohol had far-reaching consequences. Later during the colonisation of the region, there were attempts to limit and control the alcohol consumption of Muslim Algerians. Dr H. Foley of the Pasteur Institute of Algeria, for example, described such measures in a 1938 article on medical issues in Southern Algeria, in which he described a 1917 decree on the suppression of public drunkenness and on the control of places selling alcohol. He added, however, that the Muslim consumption of "hygienic beverages" such as beer and wine could not be controlled as "hygienic beverages" could not be limited. Henry Foley, "Aperçu de la pathologie indigène dans les territoires du Sud algérien," In *La vie dans la région désertique Nord-tropicale de l'ancien monde*, ed. L. Aufrère et al. (Paris: P. Lechevalier, 1938), 302.

Other colonial sources ridiculed even moderate consumption of alcohol among Muslim Algerians. Indeed, very few colonial publications described Muslims in Algeria drinking alcohol in a positive light.[47] Many accounts openly mocked the colonised Muslims who allegedly sought to appear assimilated and civilised through their alcohol consumption, but whose behaviour was invariably portrayed as a clownish imitation by European observers. The English writer W.G. Windham, for example, wrote a book about his travels through Spain and North Africa published in 1862, in which he described the results of civilisation in Algeria:

> From the general prosperity, I, of course, except the Moors and Arabs, who will never, I believe, adopt European civilisation; they seem to recoil before it, like the wild beasts of their native deserts. The French people certainly pointed out to me in the towns one or two *Europeanised* Arabs, and laughed at the idea of their ever becoming '*Français*'. From what I saw, the natives merely adopted the vices without the good qualities of the dominant race. If to be civilised consists in sitting in the cafés, drinking absinthe, playing cards, and speaking bad French, I certainly saw one or two most unquestionable specimens of the Arab adaptability to Gallic impressions; but, with the exception of these brilliant results, I never saw the least token of intercourse between the Moors and their conquerors; indeed, each nation may be said entirely to ignore the existence of the other.[48]

It appears that from Windham's specific perspective – as a non-Muslim, non-French writer – both imitator and imitated were to blame for the lack of "progress" in Algeria: the colonisers set a bad example and sections of the local population copied them badly. As a consequence, alcohol-drinking Muslims, proof of the "Arab adaptability to Gallic impressions," seem to have been the only signs of assimilation observable to Windham. In this case, the alcohol consumption of the Algerian Muslims Wyndham observed demonstrated the failure of French colonisation through alcohol. Drinking corrupted and debased these Algerian Muslims instead of turning them into Frenchmen and thus furthering the French colonisation of the region.

The aforementioned immoderation, which the colonised Muslim Algerians allegedly shared with the French settlers, the so called *pieds-noirs,* in both choice of drink and amount consumed had the consequence that any conjectured assimilation that might result was always flawed. This whole discourse surround-

---

47 In fact, most European observers lamented and ridiculed the idea expressed by a few people like Le Roy that giving Muslims alcohol could be a means of fraternisation between colonisers and colonised. See, for example: Vignon, *La France en Algérie,* 481.
48 W.G. Windham, *Notes in North Africa: Being a Guide to the Sportsman and Tourist in Algeria and Tunisia* (London: Ward and Lock, 1862), 47. Emphasis in the original.

ing assimilation through the consumption of French drinks left the Algerian Muslims with a distinct lack of agency, as many colonial writers agreed with Wyndham and thought that the colonised Muslims had only taken to drinking alcohol to imitate the poor example set by the *pieds-noirs*. Indeed, the settlers were often more directly blamed for the rising alcohol levels among Muslims than the Muslims who actually consumed alcohol.

Conclusion

This chapter examined how French colonial settlers and travellers in Algeria thought about alcohol in the nineteenth century, with a specific focus on what influence they believed intoxicants had on the colonisation of the region. Even though many of the authors covered in this chapter spent very limited time as travellers in Algeria, their *fernweh*-soaked accounts had an enormous influence on how life in Algeria was understood back in France. The spread of different kinds of alcohol and the planting of vineyards in Algeria were proudly glorified as symbols of colonisation by many French authors covering the early colonial period from the 1830s to the 1870s, the time during which a European settler society was established in Algeria through a brutal war of conquest. Later authors were able to look back on this early period as the successful foundation of the French colonisation of Algeria.

The discourse around alcohol in nineteenth-century Algeria was deeply influenced by nostalgia for the "glory" of the conquest of Algeria in France and for French ideals and civilisation in Algeria. Yet the role that drinks were perceived to play in the many recollections of French Algeria was much more complex than that of simply the Proustian madeleines evoking a wide range of emotions and memories. Even those French commentators who saw in the spread of alcoholism a tangible danger to the continuation of the colony agreed that wine, beer, absinthe and other beverages had played a significant role in the colonisation of Algeria, as settlers had relied heavily on them for comfort and to cultivate social contacts.

While there was a high degree of ambivalence in the French colonial publications around the question of whether alcohol assisted or hindered French colonial rule in Algeria, this lack of consensus was always linked to the issue of overconsumption. Excessive drinking turned alcohol from an allegedly useful tool of colonialism into a danger that threatened its very foundation and was linked to questions of identity in the colonial discourse. To those in the motherland, French settlers who drank too much were no longer considered French but rather *pieds-noirs*, with all the connotations of laziness and immoderation that this sobriquet entailed. They had lost touch with their French identity, which, it was argued, would have given them the moderation necessary to refrain from consuming excessive amounts of alcohol. They had to be retaught by French doctors how to be French and how to drink alcohol in a civilised, sensible French way in order to be successful white colonists. Only if they reconnected with their "true" French identity could they be expected to further the colonial mission. Algerian Muslims, on the other hand, tried, in the eyes of French observers, to become French through their alcohol consumption. The fact that they drank too much, and, at times, the wrong drinks demonstrated their failure in that endeavour.

Much of the discussion concerning alcohol in Algeria concerned the extent of its influence and the moral questions connected with identity-linked moderation. However, this discussion did not address the basic question of whether alcohol could, in fact, impact the colonial project. Alcohol in general and wine in particular were seen as symbols of a particularly French identity. In the context of Algeria, certain drinks were portrayed as valiant "fighters" for France's colonial interests, conquering North African soil with vineyards that pushed settlers deeper into a landscape "pacified" by the military. There is, of course, no actual agency in the substance of alcohol but it is telling to contrast these surprising claims regularly attributed to alcoholic drinks with descriptions of North Africans – even if it is only in a jocular way. In publications by French settlers and travellers who waxed nostalgic about their memories of Algeria, the agency of the European drinkers was transferred to the drink. Meanwhile, no matter what they consumed, Muslims' drinking habits drew criticism: to drink water implied a stubborn refusal of France and unwillingness to change, adapt or progress. Yet the actual consumption of alcohol by Muslims yielded no plaudits for assimilating, adapting or developing new tastes but only condemnation for badly imitating the worst behaviour of the French. Such descriptions highlight the power imbalance of the colonial situation. The question of agency was turned on its head, however, when it came to alcoholism. Negative issues surrounding alcohol drinking were also connected to overconsumption, a character trait that both *pieds-noirs* and Algerian Muslims allegedly shared. Consequently, the blame for all the negative consequences of alcoholism was not ascribed to the drinks – and thus not to the country that they symbolised – but to the individual drinkers. This dual view allowed people across the Mediterranean to remember French Algeria longingly when they drank a glass of wine or absinthe, without blemish to the drinks, to French Algeria, or to France.

Representing French colonisation of Algeria through metaphors connected to wine and absinthe – instead of the military or colonial medicine, for example – helped colonialism seem beneficial in the eyes of the French readers in the

Métropole, some of whom were very critical of France's colonialism, and in the eyes of French settlers, whose fears were assuaged by either the jolliness or the grandeur of these narratives. To French settlers in Algeria, confronted with the reality of being among the minority that suppressed the colonised majority, alcohol consumption helped to create a system of sociability and engender a feeling of safety. Drinking hours dictated when and where one could meet other settlers – wine during meals and coffee after meals in the houses of friends and relatives; apéritifs in the afternoons and early evenings in the bars and cafés. The existence of these French drinks further created a feeling of familiarity in a land far from home in which they often felt threatened and beset.[49] Drinking alcohol not only defined the French identity of the settlers in a foreign context, it also allowed them to unwind and to remember and celebrate their French way of living, absent friends, neighbours and family members across the Mediterranean. Each glass of wine directly connected them to their memories of a distinctly French way of life; one that most of them had been part of in their recent past, and that they still felt they belonged to despite the physical distance.

To the French in the *Métropole*, on the other hand, accounts of settlers sipping absinthe on the terraces of the cafés in the middle of an Orientalist tableau – obviously based more on the expectations of the writers than on reality – painted a picture of Algeria that was both excitingly foreign yet reassuringly French. Statistics about the spread of French vineyards and numbers of the production of Algerian wines were evidence of the success of France's colonising mission. What better proof of harmlessness and success could there be than the spread of French vineyards on the other side of the sunny Mediterranean?

Bibliography

Adams, Jad. *Hideous Absinthe: A History of the Devil in a Bottle*. London: I. B. Tauris & Co. Ltd., 2008.
Anonymous. *La fin d'une légende, ou la vérité sur l'arabe, par un vieil Algérien*. Bel-Abbès: Imprimerie de Lavenue, 1892.
Anonymous. *Un soldat d'Afrique: l'Algérie*. Limoges: Librairie du XXe siècle, 1907.
Anselmier, Victor. *De l'empoisonnement par l'absinthe*. Paris: Imprimerie de J. Claye, 1862.
Bailly, Étienne. *Études sur l'Algérie en 1855 pendant un voyage exécuté par M. Bailly*. Paris: Imprimerie de F. Malteste, 1868.
Barthes, Roland. *Mythologies*. Paris: Editions du Seuil, 1957.
Barrows, Susanna. "Alcohol, France and Algeria: A Case Study in the International Liquor Trade." *Contemporary Drug Problems* 11 (1982): 525–543.

---

[49] See: Rouby, "De l'alcoolisme," 241.

Bergot, Raoul. *L'Algérie telle qu'elle est*. Paris: Albert Savine, 1890.
Bouchardat, Apollinaire. *Manuel de matière médicale, de thérapeutique comparée et de pharmacie*. Vol. 1. Paris: Germer Baillière, 1856.
Boucher de Perthes, Jacques. *Voyage en Espagne et en Algérie, en 1855*. Paris: Treuttel et Würtz, 1859.
Bonain, Adolphe. *L'Européen sous les tropiques: Causeries d'hygiène coloniale pratique*. Paris: Henri Charles-Lavauzelle, 1907.
Braudel, Fernand. *Civilisation matérielle, économie et capitalisme, XVe-XVIIIe siècle: Les structures du quotidien*. Paris: Armand Colin, 1979.
Chopin, Charlotte Anne. "Embodying 'the New White Race': Colonial Doctors and Settler Society in Algeria, 1878–1911." *Social History of Medicine* 29, no. 1 (2016): 1–20.
Cumo, Christopher. "Algeria." In *The Sage Encyclopedia of Alcohol: Social, Cultural, and Historical Perspectives*, edited by Scott C. Martin, 117 ff. New York: Sage Publishing, 2015.
Demontès, Victor. "La grande, la moyenne et la petite colonisation en Algérie." In *Congrès de l'Afrique du Nord tenu à Paris du 6 au 10 Octobre 1908: Compte rendu des travaux*, edited by Charles Depincé, Vol 1, 150–174. Paris: Augustin Challamel, 1909.
Demossier, Marion. "The Quest for Identities: Consumption of Wine in France." *Anthropology of Food* (2001). Accessed 18 December 2020, http://journals.openedition.org/aof/1571.
Demossier, Marion. *Wine Drinking Culture in France: A National Myth or a Modern Passion*. Cardiff: University of Wales Press, 2010.
Fallot, Ernest. *Par-delà la Méditerranée: Kabylie, Aurès, Kroumirie*. Paris: E. Plon, Nourrit et Cie, 1887.
Fischer-Tiné, Harald. "Liquid Boundaries: Race, Class and Alcohol in Colonial India." In *A History of Alcohol and Drugs in Modern South Asia: Intoxicating Affairs*, edited by Harald Fischer-Tiné and Jana Tschurenev, 89–115. Abingdon: Routledge, 2014.
Foley, Henry. "Aperçu de la pathologie indigène dans les territoires du Sud algérien." In *La vie dans la région désertique Nord-tropicale de l'ancien monde*, edited by Léon Aufrère et al., 275–305. Paris: P. Lechevalier, 1938.
Fraser, Elisabeth A. "Books, Prints, and Travel: Reading in the Gaps of the Orientalist Archive." *Art History* 31, no. 3 (2008): 342–367.
Guy, Kolleen M. "Rituals of Pleasure in the Land of Treasures: Wine Consumption and the Making of French Identity in the Late Nineteenth Century." In *Food Nations: Selling Taste in Consumer Societies*, edited by Warren Belasco and Philip Scranton, 34–47. New York: Routledge, 2002.
Guy, Kolleen M. *When Champagne Became French. Wine and the Making of a National Identity*. Baltimore: John Hopkins University Press, 2003.
Guy, Kolleen M. "Culinary Connections and Colonial Memories in France and Algeria." *Food and History* 8, no. 1 (2010): 219–236.
Hennequin, Amédée. *La conquête de l'Algérie*. Paris: Charles Douniol, 1857.
Isnard, Hildebert. "Vigne et colonisation en Algérie (1880–1947)." *Annales. Économies, Sociétés, Civilisations* 2nd Year, no. 3 (July-Sept. 1947): 288–300.
Jansen, Willy. "French Bread and Algerian Wine: Conflicting Identities in French Algeria." In *Food, Drink and Identity. Cooking, Eating and Drinking in Europe since the Middle Ages*, edited by Peter Scholliers, 195–218. Oxford: Bloomsbury Publishing, 2001.

Kermorgant, A. "L'alcoolisme dans les colonies françaises." *Bulletin de la Société de Pathologie Exotique* 2, no. 6 (1909): 330–340.
Lafont, Albin. *Les dangers de l'alcoolisme*. Lyon: Bureau de la Société de Tempérance, 1893.
Le Roy, Jean. *Deux ans de séjour en petite Kabilie: Un peuple de barbares en territoire français*. Paris: Augustin Challamel, 1911.
Le Roux, Hugues. *Je deviens colon: Mœurs algériennes*. Paris: Calmann Lévy, 1895.
Leroux, Sylvère. *Traité de la vigne et le vin en Algérie et en Tunisie*. Vol. 2. Blida: A. Maugin, 1894.
Matthee, Rudi. "Alcohol in the Islamic Middle East: Ambivalence and Ambiguity." *Past and Present* (2014): 100–25.
Meloni, Giulia, and Johan Swinnen. "The Rise and Fall of the World's Largest Wine Exporter – and its Institutional Legacy." *Journal of Wine Economics* 9, no. 1 (2014): 3–33.
Michalak, Laurence, and Karen Trocki. "Alcohol and Islam: An Overview." *Contemporary Drug Problems* 33 (2006): 523–562.
Pinaud, Pierre-Alfred-Hippolyte-André-René. "L'alcoolisme chez les Arabes en Algérie." Med. Thesis, University of Bordeaux, 1933.
Poiré, Eugène. *La Tunisie française*. Paris: E. Plon, Nourrit et Cie, Imprimeurs-Éditeurs, 1892.
Prestwich, Patricia E. "Temperance in France: The Curious Case of Absinth." *Historical Reflections/Réflexions Historiques* 6, no. 2 (1979): 301–319.
Prestwich, Patricia E. *Drink and the Politics of Social Reform: Anti-Alcoholism in France since 1870*. Palo Alto: Society for the Promotion of Science and Scholarship, 1988.
Prestwich, Patricia E. "Female Alcoholism in Paris, 1870–1920: The Response of Psychiatrists and of Families." *History of Psychiatry* 14, no. 3 (2003): 321–336.
Raynaud, Lucien. "Alcool et alcoolisme au Maroc." *Annales d'Hygiène Publique et de Médecine Légale* 497, no. 3 (1902): 211–223.
Rémy, Jules. *Lettres d'un voyageur à M. L.G.-G*. Châlons: Imprimerie de T. Martin, 1858.
Rouby, Pierre. "De l'alcoolisme en France et en Algérie." *Congrès des Médecins Aliénistes et Neurologistes de France et des Pays de Langue Française*. Paris: G. Masson, 1895: 237–250.
Saint-Vel, Octave. *Hygiène des Européens dans les climats tropicaux, des créoles et des races colorées dans les pays tempérés*. Paris: Adrien Delahaye, 1872.
Sartre, Jean-Paul. *Colonialism and Neocolonialism*. London/New York: Routledge, 2001.
Souguenet, Léon. *Route de Timmimoun: Heures religieuses*. Brussels: Oscar Lamberty, 1914.
Sutter, Jean. "L'épilepsie mentale chez l'indigène nord-africain (étude clinique)." Med. Thesis, University of Algiers, 1937.
Sutton, Keith. "Algeria's Vineyards: A Problem of Decolonisation." *Méditerranée* 65 (1988): 55–66.
Thierry, H. "Étude sur les pratiques et superstitions médicales des Marocains et sur l'influence de la médecine française au Maroc." Med. Thesis, University of Paris, 1917.
Toner, Deborah. "Maize, Alcohol, and Cultural Identity in Colonial Mexico." MA Thesis, University of Warwick, 2006.
Vignon, Louis. *La France en Algérie*. Paris: Hachette et Cie, 1893.
Villacrose, A. *Vingt ans en Algérie: Ou tribulations d'un colon racontées par lui-même: la colonisation en 1874, le régime militaire et l'administration civile, mœurs, coutumes, institutions des indigènes, ce qui est fait, ce qui est à faire*. Paris: Challamel aîné, 1875.
Viré, Camille. *En Algérie: Une excursion dans le département d'Alger*. Paris: C. Bayle, 1888.

Voisin, Auguste. "Souvenirs d'un voyage en Tunisie (1896)." *Annales Médico-Psychologiques* 4, 54th Year (1896): 89 f.

White, Owen. *The Blood of the Colony: Wine and the Rise and Fall of French Algeria.* Cambridge/London: Harvard University Press, 2021.

Wilson, Thomas M. "Drinking Cultures: Sites and Practices in the Production and Expression of Identity." In *Drinking Cultures: Alcohol and Identity*, edited by Thomas M. Wilson, 1–24. Oxford: Berg Publishers, 2005.

Wilson, Thomas M. "Food, Drink and Identity in Europe: Consumption and the Construction of Local, National and Cosmopolitan Culture." In *Food, Drink and Identity in Europe*, edited by Thomas M. Wilson, 11–29. Amsterdam/New York: Rodopi, 2006.

Windham, W.G. *Notes in North Africa: Being a Guide to the Sportsman and Tourist in Algeria and Tunisia.* London: Ward and Lock, 1862.

Znaien, Nessim. "Les raisins de la domination: Histoire sociale de l'alcool en Tunisie à l'époque du Protectorat (1881–1956)." Doctoral Thesis, Sorbonne University, 2017.

Epilogue

Ruramisai Charumbira
The Historian as Memory Practitioner

Abstract: Studying Africa without using African languages makes that continent a place most studied by non-Africans who have their own, often noble, agendas. If this sounds parochial or dramatic, imagine any Western European country's or American or Canadian history (and memory) researched and written by Africans in any African languages, such as isiXhosa, isiZulu, chiShona, Igbo, or even Kiswahili? What kind of history do you think those Africans, as historians and scholars of Europe, would produce? Whose interests would that scholarship serve first and foremost? Indeed, how many Europeans would read those African-originated histories and studies written in African languages? This chapter invites a conversation about African languages in the research and narration of African histories and cultures for African ontological and epistemological freedom, and global reconsideration.

Invocation:

Jan-Georg Deutsch: you lived well. You loved well, and are still deeply loved by those who remember your life and work. Look at what your life's work has brought forth, an extraordinary volume of work presented here, and elsewhere among those whose lives you touched.

To the living: Let your sorrow be tempered by the knowledge that you have another intimate ancestor in the winds. We lift your memory, Jan-Georg, to the company of all our personal ancestors, and yours, and to the Source of all that is. Rest in glory.

Reckoning with the Long Cold Shadow of Feigned Racial Innocence

In early April 2015, my beloved dog Chipo and I went for a walk in the northwest hills of Austin, Texas, where we lived at the time. Chipo was an intrepid Portuguese Water Dog in love with life. Every day of her life, she inspected the trails with her nose as though encountering them for the first time. She embodied what one might call the daily practice of engaged and embodied encounters. On that April morning, I followed Chipo as she elegantly and gracefully sniffed and jumped her way up a rock cliff; while I lumbered along, plotting each move based on how much rock or tree stump I could grab without sliding down or disturbing a snoozing snake. When I saw Chipo leap over a tree stump, I reached for it pulling myself up the rock, and as I did so, I felt something supple. Atop the rock, I turned around and was struck by the fact that the stump was both dead and alive. The original tree was gone, yet it was alive with roots deep in the ground still feeding dozens of new shoots that I could not see from the lower end of the rock. It is to that dead-but-alive tree in then drought-stricken central Texas, that I reach for a metaphor for the first two parts of this chapter—the stump as history and its shoots as memory.

The metaphor returned to my conscious mind in early 2017 as Chipo and me walked the woods of our new home in Switzerland, introducing ourselves to the land, its people, the mountains and forests and other beings that call those forests and the landscapes home. That stump and its lush new shoots returned because, I realised, though I had visited and stayed in Switzerland, and Western Europe, for short periods before (a year at most), this time I was staying long-term, and so had beginners' eyes. I was encountering Europe at home, not the colonial or postcolonial Europe of Africa, the continent of my birth, or of North America, my adopted continent. I was encountering a Europe alive to its display of (what it considers) its uniqueness, success, and superiority over all Others landing on its southern and eastern shores, dead or alive. The stump and its fresh signs of revival also came to mind because my very existence, my humanness as a Black person in these parts was, and is, representative of those too often drowning migrants – people who "do not belong" in Europe. My being an Other – and I capitalise the word on purpose here – was something I was going to have to get used to in this place where silent, stony stares, or some other form of passive-aggressive behaviour told (and tells) me in a thousand little humiliating ways – "You do not belong here." To be sure this was not my first experience of racialised encounters, as in the Southern Africa of my birth, conversations about the legacy of colonial and racial histories are still inflected by the unhealed traumas of European imperialism, apartheid, and the psychic introjection of internalised racial inferiority. All this was nurtured by anxious and brutal settler colonialism that, in turn, birthed deeply colonised nationalist leaders many of whom inflicted further harm on their own people once in power.[1]

---

[1] On this psychic introjection, see among others, Frantz Fanon, *Black Skin, White Masks* (New York: Grove Press Inc., 1967), Steve Bantu Biko, *I Write What I Like: Selected Writings* (Chicago: University of Chicago Press, 2002); Mamphela Ramphele, *Across Boundaries: The Journey of a South African Woman Leader* (New York: Feminist Press, 1999).

In the North America of my choice,[2] conversations about the legacy of colonial and racial histories are inflected by many strands, two of which are important in this discussion. First, the continued settler colonialism and subjugation of the First Peoples who, though present in cities and other spaces, are often portrayed as only alive in reservations.[3] In the United States, for example, the whitewashed history of the country glorifies colonial history through tropes of intrepid and resilient European pioneers who tamed a savage land and its savage peoples.[4] This frontier gospel is telegraphed to (naïve?) new immigrants as the American Dream with the cumulative effect of suggesting that Indigenous Peoples prefer to live in reservations, as though they chose it for themselves in the first place.[5] The historian who practices a history focused on the conqueror, even when telling stories of the vanquished, unwittingly practices the memory for the powerful. Second, the cruel history and long cold shadow of enslavement means that African Americans, from 1619 to the present, have had to fight for every inch of freedom that is their birth right, freedom that enshrines their full humanity.[6] All to say, in both Southern Africa and North America, the colonial past and its racialised cruelties are present in vivid ways that have defined continental and diasporic African experiences. A similar experience marks most Indigenous (American) experiences as their histories and cultures have been under assault, including incorporation into mainstream culture as part of the settler-American experience that glorifies the settler and the immigrant at the expense of the indigenous peoples.

By contrast, in Switzerland and in in Western Europe, I encountered a practice of memory steeped in amnesia, an amnesia that postured a Europe innocent

---

[2] By North America, I particularly mean Canada and the United States, my adopted countries. This, however, does not exclude the third North American country, Mexico, or Central and South America from racist colonial histories with Spain, and Portugal.
[3] See among others, Vine Deloria, Jr., *Custer Died for Your Sins: An Indian Manifesto* (Norman: University of Oklahoma Press, 1988); Roxanne Dunbar-Ortiz, *An Indigenous Peoples' History of the United States* (Boston: Beacon Press, 2014).
[4] Paula Gunn Allen, "Introduction," in *Spider Woman's Granddaughters: Traditional and Contemporary Writing by Native American Women*, ed. Paula Gunn Allen (New York: Fawcett Books, 1989), 1–25.
[5] Recent critical engagements with this historical erasure includes, among others: Joy Harjo, *An American Sunrise: Poems* (New York: W.W. Norton & Company, 2019); Layli Long Soldier, *Whereas: Poems* (Minneapolis: Graywolf Press, 2017); Tommy Orange, *There There* (New York: Vintage 2019).
[6] See among others, James Baldwin, *James Baldwin: Collected Essays*, Collected by Toni Morrison (New York: The Library of America, 1998).

of the racial discord that has marked our world for the past five hundred years.[7] For example, I cannot tell you how often some people who style themselves simple Swiss folk habitually invoke their simple-ness (which is not the same as simplicity) with certitude, while clutching at some old irrational ideas about black and brown bodies, like: black people do not burn in the sun because they have dark skin. Or the desire to have a black friend and at the first shared laughter at something funny, there's an assumed intimacy where someone (white) immediately reaches to touch a black person's hair as though one's personhood were a petting zoo. Even in a zoo, touching cannot be cavalierly permitted as it assumes that we, humans, are entitled to other creatures' lives and bodily integrity. These anecdotes may seem trivial compared to the behemoth of white supremacy, but that is my point: white supremacy's foundation is girded and anchored by such wilful (and supposedly simple) ignorance among ordinary European people who, though literate and highly skilled at their trades, are often unwilling to educate themselves in their claim to white inheritance through "first world," now Global North, status. James Baldwin articulated the problem with white innocence and simple-ness in his essay "Stranger in the Village" about his experience in a Swiss village, an essay whose thunder's rumbling I will not steal by summarising it.[8] Toni Morrison deepened Baldwin's articulation with her own revolutionary take on the making of European whiteness in the United States through its literature.[9] These intellectuals' works urge the historian of continental and diasporic Africans to confront the feigned innocence of continental and settler Europeans in the making and telling of racialised histories, at home and abroad. It not only liberates those oppressed by history, but it also liberates those who inherited such an oppressive history.

The urgency of the "The Historian as Memory Practitioner" that is the title of this chapter, then, crystallised in my mind one day while I was going about my normal errands of everyday life in Switzerland without experiencing those overt or subtly racialised dramas. As I drove home without an incident to process or drown out with some soothing music, it occurred to me that I needed to figure out how to change my response in this reserved (or repressed?) society, from one of silent retreat and internalising the pain and humiliations to one of engaged citizenship to those who claim to be "innocent" white people from an Alpine

---

[7] See, for example, essays in Patricia Purtschert and Harald Fischer-Tiné, eds., *Colonial Switzerland: Rethinking Colonialism from the Margins* (London: Palgrave Macmillan, 2015).
[8] Baldwin, *James Baldwin: Collected Essays*, 117–129.
[9] Toni Morrison, *Playing in the Dark: Whiteness and the Literary Imagination* (New York: Vintage Books, 1992).

country, much like Heidi and Alm-Uncle, her grandfather.[10] For my part, I decided that instead of stoically looking on, striking a resistant pose and rejecting the typecasting as just *"eine schwarze/dunkle Frau"* (a black or dark woman), I would turn to history for some answers as it occurred to me that in most encounters many people do not know much history, their own or others'. This is compounded when they see in me, or another person of African descent, a foreigner who does not belong in "their white country," instead of just another human being searching for life's meaning. Remembering that I was also a trained historian meant that I chose not to play the politics of respectability, choosing instead, to find a way to assert my historical knowledge so people can make sense of the dissonance that our racially charged encounters dredge up from our psyches. Afterall, this is the same country (Switzerland) from whence emerged that other godfather of modern psychoanalysis, Carl Gustav Jung, whose views on African minds exercise Jungian scholars and practitioners.[11] And as a student and historian of European encounters with "Others" in their parts of the world, then, I needed to be a scholar who challenges these amnesiac responses to Europe's inheritance by holding up the mirror of history, a racialised history, that contemporary memory would rather forget; a mirror that shows that Europe is neither innocent nor untouched by the making of racialised others in Africa and elsewhere. After all, we are all living in a global capitalist system originally designed in Europe with not much care for the Earth or non-Europeans. This is a hard conversation we all need to have on (and not under) the table, so we subjectively and objectively reckon with our own complicity in maintaining the white supremacist status quo in academia. I see myself in that same mirror of complicity as I am not just holding it up for others with an accusatory finger.

This recognition of my body and my place in everyday life, now that I live in Europe, has had the same awakening effect as that April day when I followed Chipo up the rock face and my hands touched the dead tree stump and its supple shoots. The stump of history seems embodied in black and brown bodies, reminding Europe of its past self, even as contemporary Europe clutches at the new supple shoots of its precious economic prosperity against what it sees as hordes landing on its shores, eager to devour that prosperity. My practice of the discipline of History, more than ever, has to consciously include my skin col-

---

10 Names borrowed from the children's novel, *Heidi*, by Johanna Spyri.
11 Here I am focused on Switzerland, hence my mention of Jung only. Farhad Dalal initiated an examination of Jung's body of work with a focus on race and published a paradigm shifting article, "Jung: A Racist" *British Journal of Psychotherapy*, no. 4 (1988): 263–279. Responses to Dalal's article include, the British Psychotherapy Foundation, "Jung and Racism," accessed 25 February 2021, https://www.britishpsychotherapyfoundation.org.uk/insights/blog/jung-and-racism.

our as the perfect conduit for not only bearing witness to the lives of striving fellow human beings crossing the Mediterranean Sea, or some other physical and psychic geography around the world, but holding space for the awkward conversations that need to be had in countries that imagine racism does not exist in a country like Heidi's alpine country. In this chapter, then, I invite everyone into a spirited conversation about the importance of rigorous scholarship that remembers or commemorates the imagined place we call "the West" and its place in African history and memory.[12] Take, for example, the forgetting of European mass emigration in the nineteenth century, right into the middle of the twentieth, that needs reconsideration. It was a time when millions of ordinary (and often poor) Europeans eagerly boarded both legal and illegal ships destined for distant shores. This is the subject of my second book that I hope will contribute something important in our study of European imperial and colonial histories in Africa. I say this because in African History, the overwhelming narrative of European migration and immigration to parts of the continent are mainly studied through the lens of the colonial project and its civilising mission. What if we asked new questions, because those European emigrants and migrants were not unlike many of the brave young people crossing or drowning in the Mediterranean Sea today. A century or two ago it was mostly young Europeans who crossed the treacherous seas in large numbers to become Americans, Canadians, Australians, New Zealanders, South Africans, or Rhodesians. Then as now, they were in search of a better life for themselves and their families. The critical difference, of course, is that one set of migrants and immigrants had Western European imperialism and whiteness as foundation, anchor, and protection; while the other set, has colonialism and their black or brownness as source of rejection and or inhumane treatment.

Language as the Practice of History

I began this chapter with an anecdote related to a canine and a sprouting tree stump in a rocky forest because it also stirred my thinking about how many of us historians and scholars of Africa have denatured Africans in our bid to show (who?) that Africans are not the gyrating savages of the wild bush in European colonial history. At some level, it seems to me, we continue the ancestor

---

[12] Historian Dipesh Chakrabarty's argument about the importance of other worlds and their ontologies in modern thought informs my own thinking here. See Dipesh Chakrabarty, *Provincializing Europe: Political Thought and Historical Difference* (Princeton: Princeton University Press, 2007).

worship of Georg Hegel, a ritual revived by Hugh Trevor-Roper in the 1960s.[13] To that end, I will not quote these men as the continued repetition of their spiteful words and wilful ignorance continue to feed racist rhetoric toward Africans and people of African descent everywhere.[14] It seems to me we continue this practice of ancestor-worshipping Hegel and his ilk by our willingness to wear the blindfold of whitewashed history, excluding African languages from our practice of historiography, save for those doing historical linguistics.[15] We seem to choose to practice African history primarily in Western languages, and more so in that special dialect called academese in which only a few are fluent and literate. Hegel's views may seem dead at this point because several generations of Africans and Africanist scholars have engaged with those views, yet it would seem, Hegel and his disciples still have us mesmerised unable to break their hypnotic appeal of quoting them as a sign of learning. Hegel's views are the dead treestump of history whose deep roots are nurturing new shoots that hold both barbed and warped views about Africa. They also manifest as the ever-expanding benevolent intentions that send aid to Africa, an Africa that still functions as the world's posterchild for charity. As I understand it, Jan-Georg Deutsch, was on a new scholarly path, studying commemoration with a focus on slave museums around Africa.[16] What this suggests to me is that any serious scholar, at some point in their life, must reckon with the deeper truths of the histories they study, including the uncomfortable truths that show us our own complicity in narrating Africa for audiences that do not include the majority of Africans. For us all, and especially the next generation of scholars, this is a call to recognise African agency so the majority of Africans can see themselves – their individual selves and their collective histories – in the works of historians and scholars of Africa, and global studies, too.[17] I think we all can agree that the majority of

---

13 See, for example, Finn Fuglestad, "The Trevor-Roper Trap or the Imperialism of History: An Essay," *History in Africa* 19 (1992): 309–326.
14 Georg W.F. Hegel, *The Philosophy of History*, trans. J. Sibree (Kitchener, ON: Batoche Books, 2001), 109–112.
15 My earlier critique of this ancestor worship is found in: Ruramisai Charumbira, "Ancestor Worship: Just Who is Worshipping Whom?: Theoretical and Methodological Reflections on Power and Knowledge about Africa." (M.A. Thesis, University of Toronto, 2001), accessed 25 February 2021, https://tspace.library.utoronto.ca/bitstream/1807/15836/1/MQ63231.pdf.
16 Personal communication from the conference organisers, October 2017, and his obituary: "Jan-Georg Deutsch," Faculty of History, University of Oxford, 23 December 2016, accessed 18 December 2020 https://www.history.ox.ac.uk/article/jan-georg-deutsch.
17 See another tribute by Festo Mkenda here: Festo Mkenda, "A Tribute to Jan-Georg Deutsch (1956–2016," Africa Oxford Initiative, University of Oxford, 22 December 2017, accessed 18 December 2020, http://www.afox.ox.ac.uk/news/a-tribute-to-jan-georg-deutsch/.

Africans have a right to read many of those histories in the languages of their intimacies, the languages in which they make love and sing to their children; languages some choose to mash-up with former colonial ones to form new expressions.[18] The majority of Africans deserve histories that open not just their own eyes, but those of Others, too, so everyone can see Africa again, for the first time. This is the practice of daily engaged encounters that I learned from my dog, Chipo; that tenacious and focused scholarship that is inviting like a book of fiction and yet deeply generous like a well-researched monograph, affording readers a revelation of some kind.

This brings me back to the important issue of nature in African histories and African Studies practiced in African languages. The inimitable Ngũgĩ wa Thiong'o is probably one of the most focused and tenacious advocates of African languages in literature and scholarly endeavours. In his many works, especially in *Something Torn and New: An African Renaissance*, he argues for an Africa revitalised and powered by African languages.[19] African languages are the memory bank not fully utilised in the study of the bulk of African histories. African languages (not just a word here and there) are primary sources with potential to not only power the arts as they already do, but also the growth of the natural and social sciences, new technologies, and innovation in imagining climate renewal in this century and beyond. To those who raise an eyebrow to that assertion about African languages' potency, Ngũgĩ, in the aforementioned text, emphasises that it is worth remembering that not too long ago, the powerful contemporary languages of Western Europe were once considered vernaculars, "far inferior," and not sophisticated enough to articulate science, literature, philosophy, technological advancement, and all scholarly learning which was deemed to derive from the Greek and Latin languages – colonial languages to those non-Greek and non-Latin Europeans. Yet, in the last four centuries or so, some of those same European vernaculars – especially English, French, and Portuguese – have had a grip on Africa as the languages of the humanities, sciences, mathematics, engineering and technology in much of Africa's education systems. The argument is that there is no math or science in African cultures and traditions, and therefore no language for those fields of study, which tells me that we, historians, have been far too focused on the racists rather than showing and tell-

---

18 John Mugane's introductory piece, and articles in this issue are all worth reading on what I am discussing here; see: John Mugane, "Contemporary Conversations: Is English an African Language?" *Journal of African Cultural Studies* 30, no. 2 (2017): 121–123.

19 It is important to reiterate that I am not discussing some primordial essentialism when discussing indigenous languages or ways of being in Africa. See, Ngũgĩ wa Thiong'o, *Something Torn and New: An African Renaissance* (New York: Basic Civitas Books, 2009).

ing African narratives that include African languages. Ngũgĩ's critical argument, then, is that as long as Africans (and Africanists) do not write (some of) their works in African languages, with the majority of continental Africans and diasporic Africans in mind, Africa cannot bequeath to its own peoples, and to the world, a renaissance that all deserve.

By not using African languages to write and imagine new African histories and African Studies, Africa remains a place most studied by non-Africans who have their own, often noble, agendas. If this sounds parochial or dramatic, imagine any Western European country's or American or Canadian history (and memory) researched and written by Africans in any African languages, such as isiXhosa, isiZulu, chiShona, Igbo, or even Kiswahili? What kind of history do you think those Africans as historians and scholars of Europe would produce? Whose interests would it serve first and foremost? Indeed, how many Europeans would read those African originated histories written in African languages? This, of course, is not to say no one else but Africans can or should write about Africa; nor is it to choke the creativity and self-expression of those non-Africans passionate about the continent's deep and recent past in any language. If it is any comfort, some of my most cherished teachers of Africa were non-Africans, and some were fluent in the languages of the peoples they studied. What I am insisting on here is that within a language lies the memory bank of a people's culture, their ontological and epistemological freedoms where they can reimagine themselves and innovate anew. Thus, being a memory practitioner of African scholarship means holding up the mirror to oneself before holding it out to others. By holding the mirror up to oneself and one's practices, one examines not just the documents in the archives and libraries, but the full meaning and effect of one's work in the world.

To illustrate my foregoing point, I will also use a non-African example of the philosopher-historian Paul Ricoeur's magisterial work *Memory, History, Forgetting* to illustrate my point about the importance of language in the histories we study and practice, African or otherwise.[20] I designed and taught a graduate course for many years entitled "History and Memory" in which I assigned Ricoeur's book as a core reading requirement that most students found challenging at first. I taught it in sections throughout the semester, and as we slowly read through the text and went over passages together carefully, it won students' applause because it illustrated an important point: valuing the languages of those whose history is under study yields a much richer history. Ricoeur's text takes a

---

[20] Paul Ricoeur, *Memory, History, Forgetting*, trans. Kathleen Blamey and David Pellauer (Chicago, Ill: University of Chicago Press, 2010).

long view of history and memory in the Western philosophic and historical canon, starting with the ancient Greeks through the Romans to modern times. In each chapter he reminds us that he is not writing an intellectual history of all the world's scholarly thought on history, memory, and forgetting, but rather a very European-centred history with assumed resonances in other parts of the world. For Ricoeur, the written text is the central reservoir of deep historical knowledge, and the ability to read and interpret those texts gives his book its Europeanness that invites its readers to the original texts and their interpretations over the ages. My point here is that Ricoeur did what students of African history and African Studies do not do much of these days, immersion in the first languages of the people studied. To my mind, the importance of African languages is that they "re-member" African lives in relation to the past and present.[21] This is much the same that scholars of British, Italian, German, or French histories do, using those languages to re-member those histories, illuminating the past for the insider and outsider, including the contested historical roots of some of those languages and cultures. On the other hand, it is also true that we all write for different publics and audiences, but my point here is that it is striking that there is far more written about Africa and Africans not aimed at the majority of Africans but global (read western) eyes. This raises the question: who needs written history, the powerful or ordinary folk?

Back to Africa and nature, the late political historian, Ali Mazrui, famously said: "Geography is the mother of history."[22] By which he meant that "the most potent indigenous force in Africa's experience is Africa's environment, the combined elements of geophysical features, location and climate."[23] While geography is not the same as nature, I use it here in the idiomatic sense to reiterate the importance of African languages to the study of African people's lives and the importance of knowing not just what names Africans gave to their physical geographies across the continent, but the context of those names and the historical and contemporary meanings embedded in those names. I analysed this issue in my first book, *Imagining a Nation: History and Memory in Making Zimbabwe*, a book that made some of the mistakes I critique here, hence I am not

---

21 For an original inspiration, see Ngũgĩ wa Thiong'o, *Re-membering Africa* (Nairobi: East African Educational Publishers, 2009.)
22 Ali Mazrui, *The Africans: A Triple Heritage* (Boston: Little, Brown and Company, 1986), 41. This book is a companion guide to his nine-part television series of the same name, accessed 18 December 2020, https://www.bbc.co.uk/programmes/p00gq1wn/episodes/player. See also his 1979 *Reith Lectures: The African Condition*.
23 Ibid.

exempt.²⁴ Be that as it may, I refer back to geography and nature to also ask: What use is nature and natural history to the historian, especially the historian of Africa still burdened with proving Hegel wrong? What use is nature when Africa's natural geography and its flora and fauna was (and is) what many people, including young people in the West today, think of when Africa comes to mind? What use is nature when Africa is "rising," yet it is still its natural resources that grease the wheels of international trade at Africa's expense? What use is nature even as Africa is putting the past behind, thanks to new technologies, especially information technology, that allows self-representation that does not need to rely on much else besides the self?

Guild historians,²⁵ like most historians, spend hours and years in "the field," in the archives and in libraries, looking for, and gathering, materials that show a different Africa than the one Immanuel Kant or Georg Hegel declared. This includes the contemporary Africa of the "bleeding heart" television commercials and infomercials. These media representations generally appeal to the Westerners' sense of guilt over their material comforts in contrast to the poor people on the television screen cast as disempowered and demoralised, not just by a material reality that does not include running water, electricity, or even hope, but by their Africanness – or Third Worldness. Westerners are made to feel that their financial contributions will restore hope if only they could send a few euros or dollars or pounds to lift the poor out of their material poverty. The overarching narratives of these commercials and infomercials are that those poor people must battle with nature's elements like the West did during the long nineteenth-century. Now, there's nothing wrong with "lifting people out of poverty" to be sure, but if we remember that this lifting has been going on for generations in Africa's relationships with the West, then I would argue Hegel's assertions, though dead like that tree-stump are is still alive, nourishing new shoots from the same old craggy tree.

I would argue that in our telling African histories aimed at most Africans, we not only need to listen to Africans' narrative, but heed the late Toni Morrison's cautionary wisdom when she said: "No one can blame the conqueror for writing history the way he sees it, […]. [H]istory supports and complements a very grave

---

24 Ruramisai Charumbira, *Imagining a Nation: History and Memory in Making Zimbabwe* (Charlottesville: University of Virginia Press, 2015), 101–103, more broadly, read through 77–137.
25 Here I specifically use guild to highlight the political power and influence academic historians have over the study of history in schools and universities – much more than (other professional) historians outside academia.

and almost pristine ignorance."²⁶ The real problem, Morrison continues, is that the telling of the African and Africanist history has been too focused on trying to prove Africans' humanity, instead of showing African lives in all their complexity for, first and foremost, the Africans themselves; because something that is true and authentic will resonate beyond its particular community. "The function of racism is distraction" Morrison reminds us, "it keeps you explaining over and over again, your reason for being. Somebody says you have no language and so you spend 20 [sic] years proving that you do. Somebody says you don't have [...]."²⁷ All of us, then, are challenged to not prioritise our becoming mere elite scholars; rather, maybe we ought to prioritise writing narratives that ordinary people can read and or take into their lives as a way of knowing and re-knowing themselves as conscious beings. To my mind, histories that illumine different avenues toward self-knowledge and actualisation are the holy grail of liberatory scholarship. It is a scholarship that seeks to break with the academic past that prioritises the elites of society and their epistemological ways in the narration of history, even when telling of ordinary people's histories.²⁸

Language as the Practice of Memory

In this last section, I will conclude with three examples (not all from Africa or about Africans) that show the importance of embedding not only nature in African histories, but also getting history to be of service to the dead and the especially the living. Here, I will use the metaphor of water in a river to highlight the importance of innovation, creativity, and fluidity in the practice of the historian's craft in service of the subject. By insisting on returning nature to human history in Africa, I do not mean it as merely a part of "environmental history" or "environmental humanities," but as part of the human stories that Africans told and tell themselves about themselves and their geographies; stories they pass(ed) on

---

26 Portland State University; Morrison, Toni; St. John, Primus; Callahan, John; Callahan, Judy; and Baker, Lloyd, "Black Studies Center Public Dialogue. Pt. 2" (1975). *Special Collections: Oregon Public Speakers*, 90, accessed 18 December 2020, https://pdxscholar.library.pdx.edu/orspeakers/90; Please note that though the above is the recommended citation from the original audio source, I used a transcript of Toni Morrison's talk done by Keisha E. McKenzie. Morrison's talk was entitled, "A Humanist View," accessed 18 December 2020, https://www.mackenzian.com/wp-content/uploads/2014/07/Transcript_PortlandState_TMorrison.pdf.
27 Ibid.
28 Here, Walter Benjamin's essay "The Author as Producer" is worth reading for its insistence on writing with the regular person in mind – though some might argue that he did not make his own writing accessible.

to their descendants, stories that could be lost in our bid to prove Hegel and his intellectual descendants wrong for the past two hundred or so years. The three women scholars whose lives and work I briefly consider in this section are scholars who rode and ride the currents of the rivers of time, place, and space to bring us to another understanding of what radical scholarship means. Radical here is not so much flame throwing as it is insistence that those who inherited the cruelties of recent history have a right to right the wrongs of history through the writing of memories they carry in their bodies and their communities. The common denominator among these three women is that they all experienced colonialism in some form in Africa (Kenya), east Pacific (New Zealand), and North America (USA.).

I consider these women scholars my mentors, too, for through their work, they continue the work my first mentor, my late mother, taught me to re-member the past and the future through reverence for all of life in the present; from the dust under my feet to the dust of stars in the Milky Way visible in the night sky at her homestead in Gutu. These three women scholars model the courage to make the return journey back to their intuitional intellectual roots without negating their academic disciplines, even as some were first wounded by their disciplines. They are not professional historians by training, but they each found individual ways to return to *indigenous ways of knowing*, which, for some, includes indigenous languages. The new scholarship each created, gave, and gives back to themselves, and to the communities from which they emerged, which include communities of the mind from whence they learned their scholarly and scientific skills. And by indigenous, I do not mean some esoteric and unchanging ways of knowing and being, I mean the return to that primordial spark within each of us, our beingness, no matter into what culture we were born. In other words, I am of the view that all humans are indigenous to this planet and this solar system, and some people, though scarred by the last five hundred years of racist history, still retain that deep love and kinship with the fullness of life on this our planet. Here, then, are the three women who model the historian as memory practitioner, expanding their own disciplines and fields of study through engaged and embodied transdisciplinary scholarship of history and memory.

Wangari Maathai of Kenya

The late Maathai was educated in Kenya (her country of birth), and in the United States and Germany.[29] She majored in biology, and it was that training she leaned on as she awakened to the importance of neglected indigenous knowledge systems of ecological diversity for solving economic development problems in the present. The importance of that indigenous knowledge was symbolised by the death and disappearance of a huge sycamore fig tree that once defined her youth growing up in Kenya. That fig tree, she learned, was in reciprocal relationship with the life forms it supported and was supported by, indirectly inspiring her scholastic trajectory as she spent hours, as a young girl, trying to catch frog eggs strung out like beads along the running water brook.[30] It was not so much nostalgia for that particular tree for Maathai, but the realisation that all other life forms – the shrubs, birds, and the stream – had disappeared along with the fig tree, and the people were now poor waiting on, and hoping for, some international aid. She remembered that when she was a young girl, she was sent out to fetch firewood, she brought back wood from the sycamore fig tree near her home. Maathai's mother then taught her not to collect any firewood from the fig tree because, she said, it was "the Tree of God," requiring respect and care. What Maathai's mother and her community were teaching young Wangari was that the fig tree was both a foundational and dependent creature in an ecosystem sustained by a stream of fresh spring water that bubbled up from deep in the earth.[31] Maathai's and her community's practice of animism, though not named as such, was what sustained a community that had not known what dependency on international aid meant. They passed the stories to their children, including young Wangari.

She went on to study biology and veterinary medicine at home and abroad, earning her doctorate; becoming an accidental environmental and political activist because gender discrimination and an untenable marriage shut her out of

---

29 Wangari Maathai, *Unbowed: A Memoir* (New York: Alfred A. Knopf, 2006).
30 Wangari Maathai, *Replenishing the Earth: Spiritual Values for Healing Ourselves and the World* (New York: Doubleday, 2010), Chs. 1–2; Wangari Maathai, Nobel Lecture, *NobelPrize.org*, accessed 18 December 2020, https://www.nobelprize.org/prizes/peace/2004/maathai/26050-wangari-maathai-nobel-lecture-2004/.
31 For ecological discussion on what some call "keystone species," see, for example, Robert W. Paine, "Food Web Complexity and Species Diversity," *American Naturalist* 100, no. 910 (1966): 65–75; Kevin D. Lafferty and Thomas H. Suchanek, "Revisiting Paine's 1966 Sea Star Removal Experiment, the Most-Cited Empirical Article in the American Naturalist" *American Naturalist* 188, no. 4 (2016): 365–378.

academia. Together with the women and men she worked with, she founded the Green Belt Movement in 1977. That movement was caught in the crossfires of the increasingly oppressive postcolonial government of Daniel arap Moi, which was eager to launder money through dubious real estate developments on some of Kenya's prime real estate, for example, Uhuru Park in Nairobi. Her initial idea to plant trees, she wrote and spoke, was to solve an economic development problem for women who, as mothers and wives, were despairing with limited resources to feed their families. When she convinced a handful of women that one easy and affordable solution with long-term benefits to their economic problems was planting trees, neither she nor they foresaw that such a simple solution would take off and change all of their lives.[32] This novel initiative earned her the 2004 Nobel Peace Prize for her work with the Green Belt Movement whose ideas and methodologies have spread around the world.

Her memoir *Unbowed* explores her journey from consumer of knowledge to technician of knowledge to intuitive inventor and innovator, demonstrating that historians of Africa, in whatever specialty, can make knowledge of the past relevant and meaningful to people's lives. Maathai moved from merely solving an economic development problem to seeking to renew indigenous people's relationship with the land and their now forgotten relationships with nature writ large. Maathai's work with women and communities in Kenya's rural spaces over time, affirmed what fellow Kenyan, Ali Mazrui, had intuited: geography is, indeed, the mother of history. She groped her way back to an engaged practice of ecological diversity she knew in her personal history. To my mind, Maathai practiced an engaged historical memory that participated in the planting of not only fast growing trees, but especially indigenous local species of trees, and in the process, participated in sifting history for usable memory to solve local problems without waiting on someone's charitable hand.[33] Maathai's life history and work suggest that it is important that scholars not become mere practitioners of book learning, but engage as scholar-practitioners who research and write histories of the powerless. Research and writing about the agency of Africans that does not provide opportunities for their self-knowledge and actualisation protects the history and memory of the powerful. To say it another way: Western-attuned research on and in Africa, by Africans and Africanists, whose scholarship primarily serves academic careers more than the lives of the studied

---

[32] Lisa Merton and Alan Dater, *Taking Root: The Vision of Wangari Maathai* (Malboro, VT: Malboro Productions, 2008).
[33] On the reciprocal relationships the sycamore fig tree has with a variety of species, see the documentary film, Mark Deeble and Victoria Stone, *The Queen of Trees*, 2019, accessed December 18, 2020, https://www.youtube.com/watch?v=xy86ak2fQJM.

is practicing history as memory for the powerful and the privileged. It is telling African stories accessible to a few who get the academic jargon, but not those whose lives and stories enrich the academic practitioner's life and career in the first place. I generalise, of course, and yes, giving back does not have to be Oprah-sized; the point is to break with that one-sided fact of academic research that largely benefits the academicians.

Linda Tuhiwai Smith of New Zealand/Aotearoa

In the process of re-reading Ngũgĩ wa Thiong'o's *Decolonizing the Mind* for my graduate work in Canada, I had my first encounter with the work of Linda Tuhiwai Smith of New Zealand/Aotearoa, a social theorist, historian of educational sociology, and indigenous researcher/activist. Her ground-breaking book *Decolonizing Methodologies: Research and Indigenous Peoples* followed in the critical tradition of Frantz Fanon, Edward Said, and especially Ngũgĩ wa Thiong'o whose aforementioned book, she said, inspired her own.[34] Tuhiwai Smith put her finger on the pulse of Western academic production as a form of the continuing colonisation of the non-Western world, a system designed to study indigenous peoples rather than be tools for self- knowledge and actualisation. Reading Ngũgĩ's *Decolonizing the Mind* changed her perspective on Western education of formerly colonised peoples. Her work critiques the power of academic research that often affords even the most ordinary Westerners (and Western-educated indigenous peoples) the wherewithal to create narratives about the studied with often little accruing to those studied. These Western and western-oriented scholars bring their theories and methods, which, if not practiced with care, and critical engagement, vandalise people's sense of self even in the most well-meaning scenarios.

Tuhiwai Smith's major contention is that the conceptualisation, design, implementation, writing, and dissemination of research often empowers the researcher rather than the researched. This has had a knock-on effect on the use of unexamined theories, including runaway deconstruction that has become an end in itself. Her work reminded me, and reminds us all, that it behoves the historian, broadly defined, to practice with care because as far as the formerly colonised are concerned, historical research and the making of the archive often (though not always) are the memory and toolkit of the coloniser or the

---

[34] Linda Tuhiwai Smith, *Decolonizing Methodologies: Research and Indigenous Peoples* (London: Zed Books, 1999).

powerful. "The word 'research'," she writes at the beginning of her pathbreaking book, "is probably the dirtiest word among indigenous people."[35] By this expression, I understand her to mean that academia and the research process often empowers irresponsibility toward the studied, the researcher worries more about the Academic Review Board than the researched. Research also endows the researcher with unearned power over the studied; thus, research methodologies as practice, she reminds us, have to be critically examined as they are a poisoned inheritance from "explorers" and colonizers eager to imagine the savagery of Natives in far flung places, than for mutually beneficial research. To that end, her wisdom is that those of us doing research among the disempowered, and especially the former colonised, have to be alert to complicit recruitment by an academy that continues the implicit debasement of indigenous peoples when research mostly benefits the outsiders more than the insiders. Tuhiwai Smith taught me that doing right by the former colonised or the powerless is not just about deconstructing colonial theories and methodologies to show one's book learning but centring the lives and stories of those who survived the traumas of colonialism and its long legacy evidenced by the continued plague of global racism. Like Maathai, Tuhiwai Smith returned herself to her intellectual home, and the community to itself so they could tell their own histories and stories, including their resilience in finding the salvageable indigenous ways of knowing whose shards remain in the once denigrated and diminished indigenous languages and systems that colonial powers far too often deemed mere savagery.

Robin Wall Kimmerer of the Citizen Potawatomi Nation/USA.

A member of the Citizen Potawatomi Nation, Robin Wall Kimmerer is a mother, scholar, and botanist.[36] A bryologist and plant ecologist, Wall Kimmerer reopened a door I had almost sealed off and deemed unavailable to me in my pursuit of an historian's career that insisted on aloof objectivity. Through her first book, *Gathering Moss*, Wall Kimmerer breached the sound barrier between culture, nature, and history through her loving embrace of oral traditions in the dynamic

---

35 Ibid., 1.
36 Robin Wall Kimmerer, "Two Ways Of Knowing," interview by Leath Tonino, *The Sun Magazine*, April 2016, accessed 18 December 2020, https://www.thesunmagazine.org/issues/484/two-ways-of-knowing.

ways they occurred in their communities of origin.[37] She enlivened the scientific method, whose practitioner had often struck a frozen pose behind the micro-or-telescope, by reimagining the use of scientific instruments to enhance, rather than diminish, indigenous ways of knowing. Wall Kimmerer brings to her work the painful and resilient worlds she inherited – the legacy of Native American dispossession, forced removals and alienation from the land through forced assimilation – histories of surviving and thriving despite it all. In her case, she is descendant from those who, when they were children, were removed from their families and communities to colonial boarding schools or "rehomed" with white families who would "clean" them of their imagined untamed cultures – the civilising mission.

In her book *Braiding Sweetgrass: Indigenous Wisdom, Scientific Knowledge, and the Teachings of Plants*,[38] Wall Kimmerer writes as both poet and scientist, and most importantly for me, as a soul who knows that all of creation is one. Her research and writings about plants and the nature histories of the First Peoples of the Americas is done with great love, care, and rigor, balancing the subjective and objective in the telling of cultural and natural histories of human relations with plants, and plants' own relationships with one another. Her work showed me the importance of tenacity against the publish-or-perish academic treadmill that often forces people to produce works that are accessible to a few for the sake of promotion. Wall Kimmerer, like the other two women in this section, takes much of what academic science discarded as unscientific among Native American peoples and applies a rigorous scientific analysis of that discarded knowledge illumining not only the wisdom in their ways of knowing, but also the power and wisdom of the natural world that bends to entice humans into kinship, rather than relationships of domination and taming through taxonomies and profiteering. My reading of her two books drew me into a deeper curiosity about botany everywhere because she balances the wisdom traditions with "science [which] polishes our way of seeing and knowing" the world.[39] Her research methods, to my mind, extend our senses so we can know what the ancients knew, those who lived in intimate relationships with their physical geographies and natural environments. For her, any research work and expertise

---

37 Robin Wall Kimmerer, *Gathering Moss: A Natural and Cultural History of Mosses* (Corvallis, OR: Oregon State University Press, 2003). I am not negating the work done by historians like Jan Vansina in the 1960s, but what I mean here is that Kimmerer is not into explaining how it works, but just doing it, especially in her second book.
38 Robin Wall Kimmerer, *Braiding Sweetgrass: Indigenous Wisdom, Scientific Knowledge, and the Teachings of Plant* (Minneapolis, MN: Milkweed Editions, 2014).
39 Ibid, 48.

without relationships between plants and people reveals little and tells us more about the researchers whose (colonised) research methods narrow the range of possibilities of what can be known and how.

My reading of Robin Wall Kimmerer, is that the historian, broadly defined, is a memory keeper who is eager to reciprocate the gifts of history with a memory that liberates even history from itself. Her methodology is one that says the past contained in plant life, and in the natural world around us, is for us the living who reinvent traditions to pass them on as seed for the next generation. We, the living are the ones who are searching for meaning and depth, the ones who should challenge and resist unconscious consumption of anything in our world without asking what good can I do in return? How can I reciprocate the abundance before me? In my late mother's chiShona language, this idea is articulated as: "*Katswanda kanoenda kwabva kamwe*" ("When one receives a gift, reciprocity is only natural"). Wall Kimmerer's work as memory practitioner includes retrieving stolen tongues, including her own that she has had to learn in adulthood. By retrieving and salvaging what is possible, she brings forth not only what is possible, but also the importance of intimacy that holds reverence for the animacy of all living beings from moss to blue whales to elephants, ants, and butterflies.[40] Her work is closest to what I learned from my own mother and grandmother, a practice of love, care, reciprocity, and kinship with all beings and my telling of their stories. That knowledge from my mother and her mother moves me to insist that the historian should be a practitioner of memory who returns the human to nature, so history is alive; not in fragments that build an academic historiography alone, but the wholeness of all who encounter the work. Our discipline and its historiography cannot be about piecing fragments together, its future may lie in the telling of the whole anew.

Thanksgiving in Lieu of a Conclusion

If I pinched a nerve too tight, know that I do not place myself above you, I am just as guilty and complicit in this erasure. My intent here is to pull back the veil on those discomforts we are often too polite to talk about in public in African Studies, and academia more generally. These are discomforts, which when named, often free us all from the fear that keep us wedded to the (guild) status quo rather

---

[40] See, or listen to, her 2018 interview with Krista Tippett titled: "The Intelligence of All Kinds of Life", accessed 18 December 2020, https://onbeing.org/programs/robin-wall-kimmerer-the-intelligence-in-all-kinds-of-life-jul2018/.

than to the truth that sets us all free. Thus, in lieu of a formal conclusion, I will circle back to Chipo, and that dead-but-alive tree stump. Sadly, Chipo died suddenly on 7th November 2017, of a sterile brain infection that no one could explain. Nature had her way with a beloved canine. And yet, it is because of that beloved canine that I fully embraced the importance of the historian's engaged practice as deep scholarship. I often think that though the new shoots on that craggy dead stump in central Texas may have rejuvenated some life in its new shoots, considering where it was perched on a rock, it was also obvious to me that those shoots' future would not be long; it would be a struggle to bring back the same old vigour that the old tree once had. In other words, overt and subtle racist ways of relating to Africa, Africans, and people of African descent everywhere (including Switzerland) while still nourished by the dead tree stump of modern European imperialism, slavery, and colonialism, it is now a craggy old stump on the way out. As historians and scholars, we have an opportunity to not just dig up the poison of Hegel's racist pronouncements but do the real important work of prioritising the majority of Africans in our showing and telling of African Studies. That, indeed, maybe our more important task of bearing witness to African lives on the continent and in the diaspora; writing scholarship that rebukes white supremacy's innocence in everyday life whether here in Switzerland, Europe, or elsewhere. When care and reciprocity are central to one's practice of historiography, one elevates the practice of critical history into critical memory for the living.

Bibliography

Allen, Paula Gunn, ed. *Spider Woman's Granddaughters: Traditional and Contemporary Writing by Native American Women*. New York: Fawcett Books, 1989.

Baldwin, James. *James Baldwin: Collected Essays*. Collected by Toni Morrison. New York: The Library of America, 1998.

Biko, Steve. *I Write What I Like: Selected Writings*. Chicago: University of Chicago Press, 2002.

Chakrabarty, Dipesh. *Provincializing Europe: Political Thought and Historical Difference*. Princeton: Princeton University Press, 2007.

Charumbira, Ruramisai. *Imagining a Nation: History and Memory in Making Zimbabwe*. Charlottesville: University of Virginia Press, 2015.

Charumbira, Ruramisai. "Ancestor Worship: Just Who is Worshipping Whom?: Theoretical and Methodological Reflections on Power and Knowledge about Africa," M.A. thesis, University of Toronto, 2001, https://tspace.library.utoronto.ca/bitstream/1807/15836/1/MQ63231.pdf.

Dalal, Farhad. "Jung: A Racist" *British Journal of Psychotherapy*, no. 4 (1988): 263–279.

Deloria, Vine, Jr. *Custer Died for Your Sins: An Indian Manifesto*. Norman: University of Oklahoma Press, 1988.

Dunbar-Ortiz, Roxanne. *An Indigenous Peoples' History of the United States.* Boston: Beacon Press, 2014.
Fanon, Frantz. *Black Skin, White Masks.* New York: Grove Press Inc., 1967.
Fuglestad, Finn. "The Trevor-Roper Trap or the Imperialism of History: An Essay." *History in Africa* 19 (1992): 309–326.
Harjo, Joy. *An American Sunrise: Poems.* New York: W.W. Norton & Company, 2019.
Hegel, Georg W.F. *The Philosophy of History.* Translated by J. Sibree. Kitchener: Batoche Books, 2001.
Kimmerer, Robin Wall. *Gathering Moss: A Natural and Cultural History of Mosses.* Corvallis: Oregon State University Press, 2003.
Kimmerer, Robin Wall. *Braiding Sweetgrass: Indigenous Wisdom, Scientific Knowledge, and the Teachings of Plant.* Minneapolis: Milkweed Editions, 2014.
Lafferty, Kevin D. and Thomas H. Suchanek. "Revisiting Paine's 1966 Sea Star Removal Experiment, the Most-Cited Empirical Article in the American Naturalist." *American Naturalist* 188, no. 4 (2016): 365–378.
Long Soldier, Layli. *Whereas: Poems.* Minneapolis: Graywolf Press, 2017.
Maathai, Wangari. Nobel Prize for Peace Lecture 2004. *NobelPrize.org.* Accessed 18 December 2020, https://www.nobelprize.org/prizes/peace/2004/maathai/26050-wangari-maathai-nobel-lecture-2004/.
Maathai, Wangari. *Unbowed: A Memoir.* New York: Alfred A. Knopf, 2006.
Maathai, Wangari. *Replenishing the Earth: Spiritual Values for Healing Ourselves and the World.* New York: Doubleday, 2010.
Mazrui, Ali. *The Africans: A Triple Heritage.* Boston: Little, Brown and Company, 1986.
Merton, Lisa, and Alan Dater. *Taking Root: The Vision of Wangari Maathai.* 2008.
Morrison, Toni. "A Humanist View." In Portland State University, Public Speakers Collection, "Black Studies Center Public Dialogue. Pt. 2" (May 30, 1975). *Special Collections: Oregon Public Speakers.* 90.
Morrison, Toni. *Playing in the Dark: Whiteness and the Literary Imagination.* New York: Vintage Books, 1992.
Mugane, John. "Contemporary Conversations: Is English an African Language?" *Journal of African Cultural Studies* 30, no. 2 (2017): 121–123.
Orange, Tommy *There There.* New York: Vintage, 2019.
Purtschert, Patricia, and Harald Fischer-Tiné, eds. *Colonial Switzerland: Rethinking Colonialism from the Margins.* London: Palgrave Macmillan, 2015.
Robert W. Paine. "Food Web Complexity and Species Diversity," *American Naturalist* 100, no. 910 (1966): 65–75.
Ricoeur, Paul. *Memory, History, Forgetting.* Translated by Kathleen Blamey and David Pellauer. Chicago: University of Chicago Press, 2010.
Smith, Linda Tuhiwai. *Decolonizing the Mind: Research and Indigenous Peoples.* 2nd edition. London: Zed Books, 2012.
Spyri, Johanna. *Heidi.* New York: Dell Publishing, 1990.
Thiong'o, Ngũgĩ wa. *Decolonizing the Mind.* Oxford: James Currey, 1986.
Thiong'o, Ngũgĩ wa. *Something Torn and New: An African Renaissance.* New York: Basic*Civitas* Books, 2009.
Thiong'o, Ngũgĩ wa. *Re-membering Africa.* Nairobi: East African Educational Publishers, 2009.

Figures

Fig. 1: Jacket for GHA Vol VII (1985). Reproduced courtesy of UNESCO Publishing, Paris. —— 65
Fig 2: West African Pilot, 7 November 1949. —— 154
Fig.3: Nigerian Tribune, 3 March 1953. Reproduced courtesy of the Nigerian Tribune. —— 155
Fig. 4: West African Pilot, 10 September 1965. —— 156
Fig. 5: West African Pilot, 1 October 1965. —— 156
Fig. 6: Daily Times, 6 October 1954. —— 157

List of Contributors

Casper Andersen is an Associate Professor of the History of ideas at Aarhus University. His field of research is history of ideas, science and technology in imperial and global contexts. The main focus of his current research is science, knowledge and decolonisation in Africa with a specific emphasis on the role of UNESCO. Within the Department of Philosophy and History of Ideas at Aarhus University he organises and convenes the History and Philosophy of Science and Technology (HPST) research seminars and in 2015 was elected to T*he Young Academy* of the Royal Danish Academy for Sciences and Letters.

Ruramisai Charumbira is a poet-historian and the author of *Imagining a Nation: History and Memory in Making Zimbabwe* (University of Virginia Press, 2015). She is currently working on Humanities entrepreneurship projects that include the Walter Benjamin Kolleg (University of Bern) hosted Humanities platform: THoR, Taking the Humanities on The Road; and a personal blog at: https://ruramisaicharumbira.com/

Natacha Filippi's research currently focuses on historical ethnobotany, collective memory and local development studies. She works as a researcher and project manager at Els Corremarges and l'Aresta Cooperative in Catalonia. She completed her D.Phil. in History, based on a study of Pollsmoor Prison and Valkenberg Psychiatric Hospital in South Africa (1964–1994), at the University of Oxford in 2014.

Edward Goodman completed his BA, M.St. and D.Phil. at the University of Oxford, the latter as a Peter Storey scholar. His doctoral thesis looked comparatively at ideas about community in Kenya and Tanzania in the (roughly) twenty years between the second world war and independence, tracing the story of how intellectuals in the two countries, confronted by a broadly shared regional crisis, and drawing on shared intellectual models, came to construct distinct visions of the nation. Currently, he is thinking about Kenya's "second liberation," the re-introduction of multi-party politics in 1992, and in particular about democratisation as a popular movement.

Mohamed Haji Ingiriis is pursuing a D.Phil. in History at the University of Oxford. He is also a research associate at the African Leadership Centre, King's College London. He is a book reviews editor for the *Journal of Somali Studies* and the *Journal of Anglo-Somali Society* and author of *The Suicidal State in Somalia: The Rise and Fall of the Siad Barre Regime, 1969–1991* (University Press of America, 2016).

Rouven Kunstmann is a Research Fellow at the University of Erfurt, Germany. Previously, he was a Postdoctoral Research Fellow at the University of London (London Business School) in the ERC-funded project, "The Political Economy of African Development: Ethnicity, Nation, and History." He holds a D.Phil. in History from the University of Oxford. His research focuses on print cultures, decolonisation, ethnicity, nationalism, and visuality in West Africa, also addressing global and local information circulation. His is an editor of *The Global Histories of Books: Methods and Practices* and his work has been published in *Fighting Words: Fifteen*

Books That Shaped the Postcolonial World, *Social Dynamics: A Journal of African Studies*, and the *Journal of West African History*.

Cassandra Mark-Thiesen is Junior Research Group Leader for the interdisciplinary project "African Knowledges and the History *Public*ation" at the Africa Multiple Cluster of Excellence, University of Bayreuth. Before that she lectured at the University of Basel. She is also a former Marie Heim-Vögtlin Research Fellow (Swiss National Science Foundation). She is author of *Mediators, Contract Men and Colonial Capital: Mechanized Gold Mining in the Gold Coast Colony, 1879–1909* published by the University of Rochester Press in 2018.

Moritz A. Mihatsch is a global historian interested in nationalism, self-determination and sovereignty. He wrote his D.Phil. dissertation at the University of Oxford on political parties and the concept of nation in Sudan in the 1950s and 1960s. He taught in Egypt for multiple years (2014–17), then spent two years between Brussels, Vienna, Copenhagen and Madrid (2017–19) before returning to the British University in Egypt in February 2020.

Michelle M. Sikes is an Assistant Professor of Kinesiology, African Studies, and History at Pennsylvania State University. She completed her D.Phil. at the University of Oxford and held faculty positions at the University of Cape Town and Stellenbosch University. Sikes is co-editor with John Bale of *Women's Sport in Africa* and co-editor with Matthew Llewellyn and Toby Rider of *Sport and Apartheid South Africa: Histories of Politics, Power, and Protest*. Her research has appeared in *History in Africa*, *International Journal of the History of Sport*, *Review of African Political Economy*, *Journal of Sport History*, *Sport in Society*, and other venues, including popular outlets such as the *Washington Post* and the BBC.

Nina S. Studer is a historian and Arabist who has studied at the Universities of Zürich and Oxford, and worked at the Universities of Zürich, Bern, Marburg, Heidelberg and Hamburg. Her Ph.D. was published under the title *The Hidden Patients: North African Women in French Colonial Psychiatry* in 2015 by Boehlau Verlag. She has published a series of peer-reviewed articles on gender, medical and psychiatric issues, and the history of drinks in colonial Maghreb. For a broader public, she has also contributed articles to *Gastro Obscura*, *Nursing Clio*, *Geschichte der Gegenwart*, the *Tages-Anzeiger* and *NZZ Geschichte*.

Index of names

Ajayi, Jacob Festus Ade 52, 67
Ali, Yusuf Abdi 'Tukeh' 108
Asantehene 149
Azikiwe, Nnamdi 147

Barre, Mohamed Siad 78, 108, 111, 114–124, 126 f., 130 f., 133 f.
Barthes, Roland 169 f.
Bhabha, Homi 60
Biihi, Muuse 123, 125
Boahen, Albert Adu 52, 63–67
Bouchardat, Apollinaire 177

Deutsch, Jan-Georg 3, 15, 23, 42, 143, 195, 201
Diop, Cheikh Anta 57–59, 67

Egaal, Mohamed Haji Ibrahim 115

Fage, John D. 59 f.
Falola, Toyin 51, 63
Farmaajo, Mohamed Abdullahi Mohamed 119, 123, 131

Glélé, Maurice 56, 59, 66

Hegel, Georg Wilhelm Friedrich 56, 201, 205, 207, 214

Kant, Immanuel 205
Kapenguria Six 95, 98
Kariuki, J.M. 91 f.
Kenyatta, Jomo 13, 41, 77 f., 80–86, 88–100
Ki-Zerbo, Joseph 52, 56, 58, 68
Kihoro, Wanyiri 98
Kimathi, Dedan 96, 98
Kimmerer, Robin Wall 14, 211–213

Leopold II, King of Belgium 1

Maathai, Wangari 14, 208 f., 211

Mandela, Nelson 39 f.
Mazrui, Ali 52 f., 68, 97, 204, 209
M'Bow, Amadou-Mahtar 47 f., 61
Mboya, Tom 80, 88–90
Mengistu, Haile Mariam 116
Mohamud, Hassan Sheikh 122 f.
Moi, Daniel arap 13, 91–94, 96–100, 134, 209
Mutunga, Willy 98

Nkrumah, Kwame 5, 68
Njoya, Timothy 93

Ochwada, Hannington 51
Odinga, Oginga 83, 89 f., 93, 96
Ogot, Bethwell Allan 51 f., 60, 63

Pinaud, Pierre 178

Ranger, Terence 65 f.
Renan, Ernest 8, 13, 112
Rhodes, Cecil 1 f., 7–9, 84
Rodney, Walter 66
Rouby 180, 183 f.

Samatar, Mohamed Ali 122
Sartre, Jean-Paul 179
Sharmarke, Abdirashid Ali 115
Sisulu, Walter 40
Smith, Linda Tuhiwai 14, 210 f.
Soyinka, Wole 62, 67

Thiong'o, Ngũgĩ wa 12, 47, 50, 52, 60 f., 92, 202 f., 210
Trevor-Roper, Hugh 56, 201
Tubman, William VS 162

Vansina, Jan 27, 49, 56, 62

Wondji, Christophe 68

Index of places

Accra   5, 48, 149
Algeria   14, 169–188
Austin   195

Barcelona
– Modelo Prison   41
Basel   15
Beirut   117
Belgium   1
Benin   56
Berlin   15, 117
– Humboldt University   16
– Zentrum Moderner Orient   15
Bristol   1
Britain   69, 84, 131, 147, 170, 181
Buenos Aires
– Malvinas e Islas del Atlántico Sur   41
Bur'o   116

Cairo   57
Cape Town   1, 11f., 23, 29
– Pollsmoor Prison   23, 25f., 28f., 31–38, 40, 43
– Table Mountain   1
– University of Cape Town   1
– Valkenberg Psychiatric Hospital   23, 30
Charlottesville   11
Congo   87, 109

Dahomey   63
Dresden   117
Düsseldorf   15

Egypt   6, 57, 59
Ethiopia   1, 116f., 120, 122, 131
Exeter   147

France   5, 14, 69, 169–173, 175–184, 186–188

Gebiley   107f.
Germany   8, 15, 208

Ghana   5, 10, 13, 16, 63, 65, 149f.
– Elmina Castle   16
Glasgow   10
Grand Cape Mount   162, 164f.
Guadeloupe   11

Hannover   15
Harar   1
Hargeysa   107f., 116f., 119, 121–125, 127–133
Heidenheim   8f.

Kenya   12–14, 41, 51, 77–100, 122, 125, 129, 134, 181, 207–209
– Central Province   77, 81f.
– Happy Valley   181
– Rift Valley   77, 82

Lagos   147, 150, 153
Liberia   14, 143–146, 148, 159–163, 165f.
London   15, 63, 117, 122
– SOAS   15, 63

Madrid
– Dirección General de Seguridad   34
Marburg   15
Mogadishu   108, 114f., 120, 122–124, 126, 130f., 133f.
Monrovia   165
Morocco   178

Nairobi   80, 84–86, 91, 96, 122, 209
– Uhuru Park   209
New York   11, 14
New Zealand   210
Nigeria   14f., 52, 143–145, 147f., 150f., 153f., 157, 161, 163, 166

Oxford   1f., 16
– Oriel College   2
– St. Cross College   16

Index of places

Paris   176, 183
– Universal Exhibition   176
Polkton
– Brown Creek Correctional Institution   32
Port Hartcourt   147
Puntland   115, 122, 128

San Francisco
– Alcatraz Federal Prison   41
Senegal   16, 47
– Gorée island   16
Seoul
– Sŏdaemun Prison   41
Sierra Leone   119, 147
Somalia   13, 107–109, 111, 113–118, 120–125, 129–134
Somaliland   13, 78, 107–115, 117–119, 121–134
South Africa   1–4, 6f., 11f., 16, 23, 26, 29–31, 34, 36–44, 84, 115, 200

– Apartheid Museum   7
– Cape Peninsula   23
– Constitution Hill complex   7
– Freedom Park   7
– Luthuli Museum   7
– Ncome/Blood River Museum   7
– Nelson Mandela Heritage complex   7
– Robben Island   7, 12, 16, 41–43
Switzerland   15, 196–199, 214

Texas   195f., 214
Tunisia   178

United States   2, 32, 41, 69, 93, 108, 119f., 122f., 146, 159, 163, 197f., 208, 211

Zanzibar   16
– Slave Market Memorial   16

www.ingramcontent.com/pod-product-compliance
Lightning Source LLC
Chambersburg PA
CBHW071739150426
43191CB00010B/1637